WITHDRAWN BY THE
UNIVERSITY OF MICHIGAN

Solving Problems Without
Large Government

SOLVING PROBLEMS WITHOUT LARGE GOVERNMENT

Devolution, Fairness, and Equality

GEORGE W. LIEBMANN

PRAEGER

**Westport, Connecticut
London**

Library of Congress Cataloging-in-Publication Data

Liebmann, George W.
  Solving problems without large government : devolution, fairness, and equality / George W. Liebmann.
    p. cm.
  Includes bibliographical references and index.
  ISBN 0-275-96852-9 (alk. paper)
    1. Neighborhood government.   2. Citizens' associations.   3. Local government.
  4. Political participation.   I. Title.
  JS211 .L54 2000
  323'.042—dc21   99-054745

British Library Cataloguing in Publication Data is available.

Copyright © 2000 by George W. Liebmann

All rights reserved. No portion of this book may be reproduced, by any process or technique, without the express written consent of the publisher.

Library of Congress Catalog Card Number: 99-054745
ISBN: 0-275-96852-9

First published in 2000

Praeger Publishers, 88 Post Road West, Westport, CT 06881
An imprint of Greenwood Publishing Group, Inc.
www.praeger.com

Printed in the United States of America

∞™ The paper used in this book complies with the Permanent Paper Standard issued by the National Information Standards Organization (Z39.48-1984).

10 9 8 7 6 5 4 3 2 1

Copyright Acknowledgments

Excerpts from *Tax Policy in OECD Countries* by K. Messere (Amsterdam: IBFD Publications, 1993) are reprinted by permission of IBFD Publications BV. • Excerpts from *Decentralist Trends in Western Democracies* by L. Sharpe (London: Sage Publications, 1979) are reprinted by permission of Sage Publications, Inc. • Excerpts from *L'Ancien Régime* by A. de Tocqueville (Oxford: Blackwell Publishers, 1947) and *The Greek State* by V. Ehrenberg (Oxford: Blackwell Publishers, 1960) are reprinted by permission of Blackwell Publishers. • Excerpts from *Beyond Adversary Democracy* by J. Mansbridge (New York: Basic Books, 1980) are reprinted by permission of Basic Books. • Excerpts from *The Public Choice Approach to Politics* by Dennis C. Mueller (Cheltenham, UK: Edward Elgar Publishing Limited, 1993) are reprinted by permission of Edward Elgar Publishing Limited. • Excerpts from *The Calculus of Consent: Logical Foundations of Constitutional Democracy* by J. Buchanan and G. Tullock (Ann Arbor: University of Michigan Press, 1962) are reprinted by permission. © The University of Michigan Press.

Contents

Preface — vii

Introduction — ix

Chapter 1 The Future of Neighborhood — 1

Chapter 2 Enfranchising Citizens — 81

Chapter 3 Resolving Disputes — 111

Chapter 4 Funding Neighborhoods — 117

Chapter 5 Promoting Equality — 141

Chapter 6 Proliferating Initiative — 161

Conclusion — 169

Selected Bibliography — *171*

Name Index — *181*

Subject Index — *187*

Preface

This book is the third work I have written on sublocal institutions: *The Little Platoons: Sublocal Governments in Modern History* (1995) discusses the use made of such entities in seven major countries; *The Gallows in the Grove: Civil Society in American Law* (1997) discusses their legal setting in the United States; and this work discusses their potential uses and means of avoiding concerns that such groupings oppress minorities or aggravate economic inequalities.

This book was largely written during two visiting fellowships at Wolfson College, Cambridge; for these, I am indebted to President Gordon Johnson; Professor Charles Alan Wright, an Honorary Fellow of Wolfson; and the Fellows. Robert Ellickson, Walter Meyer Professor of Law at Yale Law School; William A. Fischel, Professor of Economics at Dartmouth College; and Mary Ann Glendon, Learned Hand Professor of Law at Harvard, read portions of the manuscript; its remaining defects are mine and not theirs

I am also indebted to my wife, Anne-Lise Liebmann, for her patience and forbearance, and my partner, Orbie R. Shively, and secretary, Jeanette I. Scott, without whose help I would not have had the time to devote to the preparation of it.

GEORGE W. LIEBMANN
Baltimore, Maryland
February 14, 2000

Introduction

Centralization imparts without difficulty an admirable regularity to the routine of business; provides skillfully for the details of social control; represses small disorders and petty misdemeanors; maintains society in a status quo alike secure from improvement and decline; and perpetuates a drowsy regularity in the conduct of affairs, which the heads of the administration are apt to call good order and public tranquillity; in short, it excels in prevention, but not in action. Its force deserts it when society is to be profoundly moved, or accelerated in its course; and if once the cooperation of private citizens is necessary to the furtherance of its measures, the secret of its impotence is disclosed. Sometimes the centralized power, in its despair, invokes the assistance of the citizens; it says to them: "You shall act just as I please, as much as I please, and in the direction which I please. You are to take charge of the details, without aspiring to guide the system; you are to work in darkness; and afterwards you may judge my work by its results." These are not the conditions on which the alliance of the human will is to be obtained; it must be free in its style, and responsible for its acts, or (such is the constitution of man) the citizen had rather remain a passive spectator, than a dependent actor, in schemes with which he is unacquainted . . .

Do you not see that religious belief is shaken, and the divine notion of right is declining?—that morality is debased, and the notion of moral right is fading away. Argument is substituted for faith, and calculation for the impulses of sentiment. If in the midst of this general disruption, you do not succeed in connecting the notion of right with that of private interest, which is the only immutable point in the human heart, what means will you have of governing the world except by fear?

—*Alexis De Tocqueville*[1]

Two conflicting developments have recently characterized civic life in the United States.

Courts, the press, and elective politicians have continued to engage in a thoughtless centralization of formal agencies of government. Tocqueville observed of the similar development set in train by the eighteenth-century French Economists, the Thatcherites of their time:

They were . . . very favorable to the free exchange of commodities, to laissez-faire and laissez-passer in commerce and industry; but as to political liberties properly so-called,they did not dream of them. . . . No grades in society, no classes distinct, no fixed ranks; a people composed of individuals almost alike and wholly equal, this confused mass recognized as the only legitimate sovereign, but carefully deprived of all the means which would enable it to direct or even to superintend its own government.[2]

This presaged the centralized tyranny produced by the French Revolution. Prince Kropotkin's criticism of fifteenth-century advocates has considerable relevance to the contemporary American bar, with its centralizing influence:

Lawyers versed in the study of Roman law, flocked into [cities]. . . . The very forms of the village community, unknown to their code, the very principles of federalism were repulsive to them as "barbarian" inheritances. Caesarism, supported by the fiction of popular consent and by the force of arms, was their ideal and they worked hard for those who promised to realize it.[3]

However, there has also developed, under the politicians' radar screen and in response to felt need, a whole new layer of sublocal institutions, public and private, "in the real estate field, outside the cognizance of the social sciences."[4] These include several hundred-thousand residential community and condominium associations established by private-deed covenants, governing about a quarter of the American population, with $100 billion in housing stock, $12.5 billion in expenditures, and $5 billion in reserves in 1987;[5] 1,000 property-owner-based business-improvement districts in nearly all major cities;[6] historic preservation and special districts in many towns, not all of them old; an increasing number of neighborhood improvement districts in large cities; some street and block associations; and a handful of self-governing public schools. In the view of this author, this hopeful development is just beginning; this book enumerates additional functions that are likely to be assumed by sublocal instrumentalities, and endeavors to lay to rest the principal fears about them raised by superficial critics: That they are inherently and inevitably oppressive, and inherently and inevitably disequalizing.

This book seeks to build on and expand the ideas in two earlier works. The first of these, *The Little Platoons: Sublocal Governments in Modern History* (1995), reviewed the use made of small units of social provision in seven major countries in their historical setting, and concluded with some general suggestions as to the utility of such units in the United States. The second book, *The Gallows in the Grove: Civil Society in American Law* (1997), discussed the obstacles that recent adventures in

American constitutional doctrine place in the way of a more constructive American politics by weakening the initiative and autonomy of local and state governments, unions, churches, neighborhoods, and families; it concluded with a discussion of a number of foreign institutions and practices that could usefully be imitated in the United States. This third work is concerned with the practical rather than legal obstacles in using small public units, and suggests means of dealing with concerns based upon possible oppression of minorities and upon possible adverse effects on economic equality if such units find greater use; it also discusses the uses of small units.

A student of economic development in underdeveloped countries has described the uses of village-sized communities in terms that have clear applicability to underdeveloped areas in Western cities:

Uniquely fitted to reinterpret custom in terms of modern needs, to mobilize leisure-time labor, to add new facilities to the ancient patrimony of communal resources, and generally to help its people take their place in a market economy and in a professionally serviced society . . . if its . . . self-management rather than its governmental character is stressed.[7]

One prerequisite to this happening is that concerns about economic inequalities that have fueled centralizing approaches be addressed. As Warren Magnusson has observed:

The most powerful argument for consolidationist reform is that it will equalize conditions of life as between town and country, slums and suburbs . . . bigger government is still believed to be necessary for equalization. . . . It is time to recognize that the old form of neighborhood democracy provides what is lacking in the new. It can enable people to govern themselves. As such, it can contribute to both equalization and social integration. The task for reformers is to show how it can be reconciled with the inescapable requirement for strong central government.[8]

A number of devices, familiar to students of public finance, are available to address concerns relating to equality as between small units; we shall explore methods such as tax sharing, revenue sharing, vouchers, grants in aid, and co-optation of members.

The emphasis of this work is neither theoretical nor utopian. A critic of one of the earlier works suggested that it was "under-theorized." To this charge, the author cheerfully pleads guilty. He shares the view of Justice Holmes that "the felt necessities of the time have more to do than the syllogism with the way men are governed"; he also believes that, in the Anglo-American system at least, the progress of the law should be empirical, and that concrete illustrations founded on institutions that have actually functioned are of as much value to the law as deductions from models based on partial views of human nature. Dennis Mueller, one of the wisest of public-choice theorists, has decried ". . . ever-more-refined model building on a narrow behavioral foundation rather than [a] shift out to the extensive margin where economics, rational politics, sociology and psychology come together."[9]

The critics on the left of public-choice theory frequently reach conclusions by different routes that confirm its insights as to the value of small political units. Thus we are told by Robyn Dawes and colleagues that "discussion promotes cooperation vis-à-vis the parochial group but not the group with which there was no contact";[10] by Jane Mansbridge that "arrangements that generate some self-interest return to unselfish behavior create an 'ecological niche' that helps sustain that unselfish behavior."[11]

The writer believes that many present social deficits can only be economically addressed through greater use of more local institutions, that bureaucratic institutions have reached their limit, and that in consequence the time is ripe for a partial reversal of the movement toward centralization that has dominated American politics from its inception:

The most likely functions for community control would appear to be functions where face-to-face service delivery by a labor-intensive bureaucracy is characteristic and where economies of scale are exhausted at a rather small size. Services such as police patrol, education, garbage removal, fire protection, and street maintenance would fit these criteria.[12]

Recent developments in many countries confirm this analysis. "Community policing" and probation are now-fashionable mantras in the United States, as they have always been in Japan; self-governing schools on the Swiss model have been introduced in Britain, Australia, and New Zealand; American residential community associations increasingly assume responsibility by "contracting out" for trash collection and local road-maintenance functions long performed by equally small French communes; the volunteer fire department continues to function in most parts of the United States.

One benefit of the proposed reversal of the tendency toward centralization is a greater amount of civic participation; but this book, unlike others, is not solely an exhortation to participation for participation's sake. Demands for participatory democracy on a national scale are almost certainly misplaced; but, as Jane Mansbridge has said, "with decentralization, a nation operating primarily as an adversary democracy need not condemn its citizens to selfishness or amorality."[13] In Mill's words, "[t]he spirit of a commercial people will be . . . essentially mean and selfish, wherever public spirit is not cultivated by an extensive participation of the people in the business of government in detail."[14]

Any appeal for local particularism runs athwart modern liberal ideologies. In a penetrating critique of Rawls's *Theory of Justice*, Dennis Mueller observes:

For the just society Rawls desires to become reality. . . . The strong bonds of identification that are established in a close-knit family must be extended to include, eventually, all of mankind. . . . [But i]f we are to learn more of those far away, we must inevitably neglect those close at hand.

Modern developments do enhance the individual's ability mentally to change place with others. . . . It may well be that once one has met one post-industrial man, one has met them all. This possibility raises . . . at least one disturbing paradox. The developments that produce the universal values are the same developments sociologists and psychologists list as causes of the identity crisis and anomie that supposedly characterize man in the modern society. One is left wondering whether the just society toward which we are heading is one of empathy and impartiality, or loneliness and indifference.[15]

In consequence, much has recently been written about the need for "community" and for "mediating structures." Little of that literature is concrete; that which is, tends to be utopian. Benjamin Barber, one of the more specific writers, offers "one integrated agenda—not a cafeteria menu from which items can be selected at whim but a dinner menu with a prix fixe that must be accepted in full."[16] This book, addressed as it is to decentralized democratic legislatures and those who elect them, by contrast offers a smorgasbord, accompanied by various condiments and hors d'oeuvres. The extent to which any of its suggestions will be found valuable is a function of time, place, and public opinion, not of a political agenda imposed by national political or judicial decree. Unlike others, I see no reason to deplore the fact that in the United States

[t]he role of government has been largely permissive and promotional rather than regulatory or directive.[17] Active participation should enhance each individual's willingness to comply voluntarily with the rules of society, because he feels that they are his rules, the legitimate expression of a decision process in which he has participated and consented.[18]

What is here offered is a repertory of techniques and safeguards that have been found useful at other times and other places and that may, if taken seriously and not impeded by the courts, provoke an unorganized "release of energy" similar to that instigated by a nonprescriptive nineteenth-century commercial legal development, the general incorporation law, which favored "dynamic rather than static property, property in motion or at risk rather than property secure and at rest."[19] What is promoted here is what Robert Nisbet has called "a new kind of laissez-faire, one directed at social groups rather than individuals."[20]

There is little doubt as to the practicability of these suggestions for radical devolution. As Dennis Mueller has observed:

Both police and fire protection can be supplied at neighborhood and town levels as supplements to their provision at higher levels of government. Trash collection can be provided either directly by smaller units of government or by these units contracting with private haulers. Most importantly, the local community could be responsible for educating its children. . . . That parents would not take an active part in a democratic assembly, if it had full authority for the local school's personnel and program, is inconceivable.[21]

A distinguished economist, Joseph Stiglitz, tells us that such small, government-facilitated mechanisms as oil unitization and land-readjustment associations save on transaction costs and avoid free-rider problems. . . . The provision of organizational services itself is a public good. Indeed, the government may be looked upon as precisely the mechanism individuals have set up to reduce the welfare losses from externalities.[22]

A role for government in assisting the organization of such associations has also been defined by Elinor Ostrom:

Individuals may be able to arrive at joint strategies to manage resources more efficiently. . . . They must have sufficient information to pose and solve the allocation problems they face. They must also have an arena where they can discuss joint strategies and perhaps implement monitoring and sanctioning.[23]

Michael Taylor has similarly noted the importance to cooperation of "assurance that others around one are altruistic or at least willing to cooperate—an assurance that one will not be let down if one tries unilaterally to cooperate."[24]

However, even if devolution is feasible and not productive of inequality, its critics urge that it may imperil individual liberty. The classic formulation of this concern is that of James Madison in *The Federalist*, No. 10:

[In a] pure democracy, by which I mean a society consisting of a small number of citizens, who assemble and administer the government in person . . . [a] common passion or interest will, in almost every case, be felt by a majority of the whole; a communication and concert results from the form of government itself; and there is nothing to check the inducements to sacrifice the weaker party or an obnoxious individual. Hence it is that such democracies have ever been spectacles of turbulence and contention; have ever been found incompatible with personal security or the rights of property; and have in general been as short in their lives as they have been violent in their deaths.

As a description of either classical antiquity or more modern Swiss communes and Vermont towns, this passage seems rather highly colored. For there are varied political devices that have been utilized to meet Madison's concerns, ranging from supermajority and unanimity requirements to schemes for rotation in office and supersession by higher governments. These devices, which have regulated institutions ranging from the towns of colonial Massachusetts to today's residential community associations, are discussed in the third section of this work.

Robert H. Nelson has suggested that

if [residential community associations] were to become the prevailing mode of social organization for the local community, this development could be as important as the adoption in the [nineteenth-century] United States of the private corporate form for business property.[25]

That private business development was preceded by an era in which municipal charters were made freely available under general law and were only in form "grants not contracts."[26] In the first half of the last century,

[m]unicipal corporations were the dominant type of corporation . . . the difficulties of obtaining private corporate charters prior to the general incorporation statutes . . . made municipalities the best outlets for the savings of strangers. Municipalities competed fiercely with one another for . . . development.[27]

Even smaller entities than municipalities have a role to play now, in providing or contracting out for labor-intensive social services that collectively may account for a large part of the gross national product in a service economy—police patrol, day-care, care of the elderly, elementary and much secondary education, local street maintenance and governance, neighborhood regulation of small shops and accessory apartments, and block associations to cooperatively remove urban blight.

It is now clear beyond doubt that "given the ability to exclude nonpurchasers, private producers can produce public goods efficiently."[28] This book is thus a call for re-creation of an earlier era of municipal and submunicipal creativity—a re-creation that can combat the dangers of centralization and the withering of civil society that Tocqueville warned against.

NOTES

1. A. de Tocqueville, *Democracy in America* (tr. F. Bowen). London: Longmans, 1863, 112–19.
2. A. de Tocqueville, *L'Ancien Régime* (tr. M. Patterson). Oxford: Blackwell, 1947, 169, 172.
3. P. Kropotkin, *Mutual Aid.* Harmondsworth, UK: Penguin, 1939, 175.
4. S. MacCallum, *The Art of Community.* Arlington, VA: Institute for Humane Studies, 1970, 1.
5. Community Associations Institute, *Community Associations Factbook.* Arlington, VA: CAI, 1988, 1–3.
6. D. Kennedy, "Restraining the Power of Business-Improvement Districts," *Yale Law and Policy Rev.*, 15 (1996), 283, 290.
7. W. Wickwar, *The Political Theory of Local Government.* Columbia: University of South Carolina Press, 1970, 96.
8. W. Magnusson, "The New Neighborhood Democracy: Anglo-American Experience in Historical Perspective," in ed. L. Sharpe, *Decentralist Trends in Western* (London: Sage, 1979), 142.
9. D. Mueller, *The Public Choice Approach to Politics.* Cheltenham, UK: Elgar, 1993, 513–14.
10. R. Dawes et al., "Cooperation for the Benefit of Us," in J. Mansbridge, *Beyond Self-Interest* (Chicago: University of Chicago Press, 1990), 106.
11. J. Mansbridge, "The Relation of Altruism and Self-Interest," in Mansbridge, supra, 137.
12. R. Bish and H. Nourse, *Urban Economics and Policy Analysis.* New York: McGraw-Hill, 1975, 207.
13. J. Mansbridge, *Beyond Adversary Democracy.* New York: Basic Books, 1980, 297.
14. J. Mill, "M. de Tocqueville on Democracy in America," in M. Cohen, *The Philosophy of John Stuart Mill* (1961), 141, quoted in M. Walzer, *Radical Principles* (New York: Basic Books, 1979), 106.
15. Mueller, supra, 64.
16. B. Barber, *Strong Democracy.* Berkeley: University of California Press, 1974, 265.
17. E. McKenzie, *Privatopia.* New Haven, CT: Yale University Press, 1994, 105.
18. Mueller, supra, 72–74.
19. J. Hurst, *Law and the Conditions of Freedom in the Nineteenth-Century United States.* Madison: University of Wisconsin Press, 1956, 24.
20. R. Nisbet, *The Making of Modern Society.* Brighton, UK: Wheatsheaf, 1986, 147.
21. D. Mueller, *Constitutional Democracy.* Oxford: Oxford University Press, 1996, 98.
22. J. Stiglitz, *Economics of the Public Sector*, 2d ed. New York: Norton, 1988, 219, 354.
23. E. Ostrom, "Covenants with and without a Sword: Self-Government Is Possible," *Amer. Pol. Sci. Rev.*, 86 (1992), 404.
24. M. Taylor, *The Possibility of Cooperation.* Cambridge: Cambridge University Press, 1987, 166–67, 170–71.
25. R. Nelson, "The Privatization of Local Government," in Advisory Commission on Intergovernmental Relations, *Residential Community Associations.* Washington, DC: ACIR, 1989, 51.
26. Wickwar, supra, 4.
27. W. Fischel, *Regulatory Takings* (Cambridge, MA: Harvard University Press, 1994), sec. 7.9, citing E. Monkkonen, *America Becomes Urban, 1780–1980* (1988).
28. H. Demsetz, "The Private Production of Public Goods," *J. Law and Econ.*, 13 (1970), 293; see also F. Foldvery, *Public Goods and Private Communities: The Market Provisions of Social* (Cheltenham, UK: Elgar, 1994).

Chapter 1

The Future of Neighborhood

PROPERTY-RELATED FUNCTIONS

The politics of homeownership in America has traditionally centered on three questions: crime, schools, and the level of property taxation. These are each perceived as matters within the control of local government, properly so-called. The first two at least are in process of being carelessly nationalized. Other means of allowing homeowners to influence and govern their immediate environment have been neglected, though street-level governance has aroused great interest in Western Europe. In recent years, however, condominiums and other organizations to promote the common interests of property owners have begun to proliferate in the United States. A discussion of the principal functions that may be discharged by such narrowly defined property-owners' associations may be instructive. We shall consider first, street governance; second, the renewal of city blocks; third, the rendition of trash collection and other property-related services; and fourth, the regulation of land use.

Street Governance

It has of course long been recognized that small entities cannot be entrusted with the maintenance of through roads. Parish roads in England were "unmaintained when little used" by local residents.[1] The French and Belgian communes prior to World War II were accorded varying degrees of exclusive control; in Belgium only over roads not serving groups of houses; in France only over footpaths and streets not connecting with railroad stations or other hamlets.[2] It is said that French communes with populations of between 1000 and 2000 characteristically employed "a municipal secretary, a clerk, and a charwoman and a road-worker."[3]

The *woonerf*, or residential street-government regime, is a Dutch innovation of the 1970s, although precursors of it can be found in laws in England and New York allowing the closing of playstreets. These earlier mechanisms involved transfer of street uses from traffic to people. The Dutch innovation rested instead on what Rodney Tolley has called the "startling and revolutionary notion that in residential areas traffic and people should not be segregated but instead should be integrated . . . admitted on the residents' terms . . . slowly and without superior rights."

Woonerven in The Netherlands began in 1976, when a law authorized elimination of curbs and the integration into one surface of sidewalk and road areas, giving the visual impression of a residential yard.

Pedestrians may use the full width of the road within an area defined as a woonerf; playing on the roadway is also permitted. Drivers within a woonerf may not drive faster than [about 8 to 12 m.p.h.]. They must make allowance for the possible presence of pedestrians, children at play, unmarked objects . . . traffic approaching from the right at whatever speed always has priority. Drivers may not impede pedestrians. Pedestrians may not unreasonably hinder the progress of drivers.

This innovation offers important benefits to the upbringing of children, to safety, and to the creation of a sense of community in both suburban and city areas.

Traffic in *woonerven* is controlled by ramps, speed bumps, narrowings, changes in axis, street furniture, planters, and trees. Parking is permitted only in specially designated spaces. *Woonerven* in The Netherlands may be petitioned for by a 60 percent vote at a meeting attended by a majority of neighborhood citizens. Because they result from local initiative, *woonerven* have proven highly popular. By 1983, 2700 *woonerven* had been created, leading to a 50 percent reduction in injuries within them. In Germany, there was a 20 percent reduction in accidents and a 50 percent reduction in severe accidents.

Advocates maintain that children and the elderly "should not have their links to the outside world severed by traffic flows past their doors." The creation of these zones has become a major environmental cause in Germany.

An Organization for European Community Development (OECD) study in 1986 stated as requisites to success the prevention of residential areas being used by through traffic, regulations and signage influencing driver behavior to follow planned routes at moderate speeds, and the use of physical measures in support of regulations. In Britain, where only physical measures in new developments have been used, the concept has been slow to take hold, due to the absence of legal provisions for the creation of traffic restraints on neighborhood initiative. Pending government proposals would empower parish councils to fund traffic calming works from their general revenues.[4]

The mechanism has been highly popular in Denmark. This may be due to the fact that many Danish streets in new developments are in private ownership. "Residents, if they wish [calming], must pay for it themselves," the cost approximating that of a new refrigerator. Similar private-street regimes exist in parts of St. Louis and in many of the newer American residential community associations, although as yet, aside from crude speed bumps and speed limit and stop signs, there has been little interest in the more sophisticated traffic calming devices.

The popularity of *woonerven* on particular streets has led to broader efforts to calm traffic in residential areas generally, through the use of 30 k.p.h. speed limits, numerous four-way stop signs, and street narrowings, speed bumps, and other speed reducers, popularized in the United States by Oscar Newman and others promoting concepts of "defensible space" to protect neighborhoods; The Department of Housing and Urban Development (HUD) has issued a pamphlet written by Secretary Cisneros sounding similar themes.

If *woonerven* are to be used and accepted in a country with the libertarian political traditions of the United States, they must be perceived as being an expansion of the legal rights of property owners. This result can be achieved through use of the Dutch mechanism for creation on neighborhood application, or by including their creation within the arsenal of powers of residential community associations as defined by their deed covenants, or by street privatization on the St. Louis model. In the short run, the Dutch mechanism is simplest, and has been found to result in "stronger social cohesiveness, much brought about by the involvement of the residents themselves in a sophisticated process of planning their own surroundings."

The developers of Seaside, Florida found that in order to avoid street width and curb regulations, it was necessary to characterize *woonerven* as "parking areas." In Germany, civil engineers resisted the encroachment of landscape architects into their field; it is now established that the former design the subsurface, and the latter the surface. Traffic calming, however, has some natural allies other than residents. According to Rodney Tolley,[5] in the most recent survey of the field: "The employment effects of traffic calming are labor intensive, with few machines being used and much planning and discussion required . . . employment effects are reported to be 4 or 5 times higher than the employment effects of conventional large-scale road construction. . . ."

There is a large literature on traffic calming, beginning with the pioneer work of the late Donald Appleyard, an American,[6] and including several books by Carmen Hass-Klau, Annette Moudon, and Rodney Tolley. Useful surveys have appeared.[7]

The paradox is that a form of privatization is needed for streets to fulfill the function of public property identified by Carol Rose:

In the absence of the socializing activities that take place on "inherently public property" the public is a shapeless mob, whose members neither trade nor converse nor play, but only fight, in a setting where life is, in Hobbes's all-too-famous phrase, solitary, poor, nasty, brutish, and short.

The general rule in the United States is that street closings require the assent of a majority of abutting owners, who may be assessed for the cost of works only to the extent of benefits conferred.[8] Cities like Laredo, Texas engaging in closings on a large scale accord owners the right to acquire the adjacent street beds.[9] The benefits from closings include "income from the sale, return of the property to the tax rolls; employment generated both by the construction and the occupants; elimination of the municipality's liability and reduction of public-maintenance responsibilities"[10] as well as "opportunities for additional parking [and] open space."

In St. Louis County, beds of streets were deeded to residents abutting them, subject to assessments enforceable by lien. The several-hundred resulting associations provide repairs, street lighting, traffic regulation, sweeping, and tree trimming; some provide a security patrol. Privatization is now permitted on petition of 95 percent of residents. "Provision by subdivisions allows for greater variation in service bundles among neighborhoods than provision by overlying municipalities."[11] It has been suggested that local governments stimulate the voluntary formation of additional such associations by offering one-time block grants or priority in allocation of municipal services as well as transfer of municipally owned real estate and relief from a portion of municipal taxes.[12] A British commentator has urged that street privatization and partial closing is complementary to the effectiveness of neighborhood security patrols.[13] Other commentators, reviewing the literature on "defensible space," have noted that

Territoriality does not apply to such a large scale as a neighborhood. Further, neighborhood populations, in contrast to street-block groupings, are not face-to-face groups. . . . The main practical implication is that, for now, crime-prevention efforts should focus on street blocks rather than on neighborhoods. Block-level theories have advanced substantially in recent years. Models describing both the resident-based and the offender-based processes linking design and crime have been specified and tested in several cases.[14]

A bolder suggestion is that

all property-owners along streets would be considered required members of amenity cooperatives . . . public subsidy could be granted depending on detailed correlation and determination of improvements provided by and perhaps required of the amenity cooperative. . . . Preferential treatment to capital expenditures for approved street development, if properly rewarded, could lead to far-flung private programs to improve street quality according to revised concepts.[15]

Some American jurisdictions, led by Montgomery County, Maryland have provided tax abatements to residents of community associations maintaining streets.[16] Scandinavian neighborhood councils in larger cities are accorded jurisdiction over street closings and the location of telephone boxes and bus stops.[17]

Thus far, residential traffic calming has made only limited progress in the United States, notwithstanding Lewis Mumford's observation of sixty years ago that "whatever traffic filters into a neighborhood must be that which directly subserves it, moving at a pace that respects the rights of a footwalker. Even country villages today often lack this element of safety and freedom from anxiety."[18] The institutions needed to popularize it are self-organized traffic calming or street-ownership associations at the block level, which require some form of state or local authorizing legislation. The internal governance of these associations should involve supermajorities to insure that neighborhood consensus exists. Financial assistance from government would appear to be not needed, since traffic-calming works are fundable by use of special-benefit assessments; the sums involved in any case are sufficiently modest so that small subsidies for poorer neighborhoods are within the limited redistributive capacity of municipal governments. The deeding without consideration of street-beds might be considered in many places, since its effect may be to relieve municipalities of maintenance expenses and restore property to the tax rolls. What is most needed is enabling legislation that expands the rights of abutting property-owners, together with publicity relating to the safety and social benefits and the less well-known techniques, such as narrowing of roadways, use of planters, creation of separated bicycle paths, and use of varying road surfaces.

Block Reorganization

A more far-reaching form of property-owners' association is an association for purposes of urban renewal.

Americans are prone to assume that only two methods exist for the assembly of land for purposes of urban renewal: The first of these is *eminent domain*, which involves the condemnation by public authority of large tracts of land, which are then generally sold off to private developers. While, since the postwar decision in *Berman v. Parker*, there are few restrictions on the use of this technique, it has many disadvantages. Because each property-owner has a right to jury trial as to valuation, there are long delays and unpredictable costs. While litigation proceeds, "planning blight" descends, and constructive endeavor in the area ceases. Dissenters must be evicted and coerced before construction begins, and few condemnees are enthusiastic about their fate, since juries are drawn from taxpayers and are frequently parsimonious. The public authority must pay for land as values are determined and hold it through the construction process, incurring substantial capital and carrying costs.

A second method is *private land acquisition*, such as that carried out by the Rouse Company preparatory to the creation of Columbia, Maryland. This, to be successful, requires great stealth and the use of dummies and intermediaries, and the last landowners to sell usually must be paid exorbitant prices. Once again, land-acquisition money must be fronted by the developer.[19] A variation on this was the device used to assemble land for a casino in Atlantic City: an above-market-value offer to owners, conditioned on there being no holdouts, resulting in "great pressures [being] put on the elderly holdouts by members of their own neighborhood."[20]

The combination of cost, coercion, and planning blight have discredited American urban renewal, and private land assembly is rarely attempted in large cities, where news of buyer interest travels fast. It is far less costly for private developers to acquire large tracts of exurban land rather than attempting urban redevelopment.

There is, however, a third method of urban land consolidation, popularly referred to as "Land Readjustment," that has been in active use in almost all major countries other than the United States and Britain for about a century, and has proven especially useful in reclaiming totally decayed slums and repairing war damage. At a time when many American inner cities literally resemble war zones, with vacant lots and vandalized buildings, use of this technique deserves exploration.

Land readjustment is a scheme whereby a specified supermajority of owners of contiguous land are permitted to establish a redevelopment area by petition approved by public authority. When its boundaries are established, dissenting owner-occupiers have the right to be excluded from the area on request. Other dissenters can insist that the petitioners immediately buy them out at an impartially appraised value, a remedy like that sometimes given dissenting shareholders in corporate reorganizations. The need for even this mild coercion of dissenters might be obviated by a mechanism that permitted landowners to bindingly commit themselves to a land-readjustment scheme that is conditional upon a specified percentage of landowners similarly committing themselves, a mechanism further considered in this book in the discussion of rights of exit. The remaining petitioners then have their properties impartially valued, and receive proportionate shares in the common enterprise. A committee is then elected to manage redevelopment, which either funds construction by borrowing against land values or enters into joint ventures with builders. When work is complete, each petitioner receives either a building representing his *pro rata* share of the new development, together with fractional cash payments, or a *pro rata* share as owner in common of it.

This scheme makes it possible to redevelop with reasonable speed, since the petitioners have a profit incentive to cooperate rather than hold out. It also makes possible redevelopment without the necessity of raising large sums of public or private funds for land acquisition and carrying costs. So long as the scheme is approved by public authority and provides adequate compensation for dissenters, it presents no constitutional difficulties in the American system. Similar mechanisms have sometimes been used in America to reconsolidate lots in failed developments of recreational land, and in connection with "unitization" of oil fields; the legal precedents developed in the latter context will be useful in sustaining the validity of land-readjustment schemes.

Land readjustment has two remote antecedents in American practice. The first of these was the use of the so-called "benefit-offset" principle in private eminent domain, which permitted railroads and utility companies to offset against the amounts of compensation due landowners the benefits to be received by them as a result of the contemplated improvement.[21] The second was the practice of excess condemnation in which condemning authorities sought to capture the value added by improvements by condemning portions of the land to be benefitted by them. More recently, there has been limited resort to the organization of special districts with the right to use tax-increment financing.

In Western nations, this land readjustment system received its earliest use in Germany. Because of the lack of primogeniture and resultant splintering of agricultural land, mechanisms were provided to consolidate it. The Burgomaster of Frankfurt, Franz Adickes, agitated for ten years for similar measures for urban land. Under the Lex Adickes (1902), upon institution of a scheme, prior owners received shares in the newly plotted land proportionate to their shares in land as originally plotted. Lots with buildings were restored to the owners with appropriate boundary modifications. Unavoidable differences in value were settled in money. An English writer[22] observed that: "The mere possession of the power to compel unwilling owners to come into the pool made its application unnecessary."

During the first ten years 14 areas with a total extent of 375 acres were pooled and redistributed, with the assent of the owners. Originally consisting of 643 lots belonging to 149 different owners, the land was reparceled into 198 lots after a deduction ranging from 25 to 40 percent for street purposes. Adoption of the plan was rejected in the British *Uthwatt Report on Compensation and Betterment*[23] on the basis of a misunderstanding: That the plan required redistribution in kind. In fact, as Professor Peter Hall pointed out, participants would get shares, which they could either redeem in kind or sell. The Adickes plan was extensively utilized in the reconstruction of postwar continental cities, including Kiel and Rotterdam, and variants of it accounted for more than half of reconstructed Japanese housing, in addition to much housing in Korea and Taiwan. Its possible application in America has been discussed,[24] and, prior to the creation of federal housing programs during the New Deal, several variant schemes were put forward, which have left some residue in the Illinois land trust system and the urban renewal laws of eight to ten states.[25] A summary of the principal foreign enactments follows; it is hoped that this summary will awaken quickened interest in the United States.

Germany

The first European land-readjustment law with applicability to urban areas is popularly thought to be the "Law Concerning Land Transfer of Frankfurt" of 1902, popularly called the Lex Adickes after Franz Adickes, the mayor who sponsored it in the Prussian diet over a period of ten years beginning in 1892 and who finally secured its enactment for Frankfurt only.[26] In fact, by 1902 similar legislation had been enacted in Hamburg (1892), Baden (1896), and Saxony (1900). In 1950, the principles of the law were extended to land containing structures; in 1960 a system of valuation boards was introduced.[27] The federal Land Procurement Law of 1953 provided for expropriation of vacant land, land with destroyed buildings, and land that was minimally used in relation to surrounding land, and allowed compensation to be provided in the form of substitute land; while fundamentally a condemnation law, the Law was significant in that it allowed expropriation proceedings to be begun by private entities as well as the state:

It was necessary to have made a good-faith effort to purchase the property at a fair price, and to demonstrate an ability to begin actual construction within one year . . . (two years in the case of a town). Property owners could defend themselves . . . by proving an ability and desire to build and then actually starting construction.[28]

Japan

The first formal land-readjustment enactment in Japan was the City Planning Act of 1919, though this was preceded by the Agricultural Land Consolidation Law of 1899. The 1919 Act extended the ALCL system to urban areas, and was rendered more appropriate to them by enactment of the Special City Planning Law of 1923 following the great earthquake of that year.[29] A special Town Planning Act, focusing on war reconstruction, was enacted in 1946, and was in turn supplanted by a comprehensive land-readjustment law in 1954.[30] A revision of the 1919 Act in 1969 classified land as "urban" or "urban reserve" for purposes of determining availability of land-readjustment procedures.[31] In 1975, a special law allowed towns to designate readjustment areas of at least five hectares in their town plans, and to intervene if private land adjustment does not get under way within two years.[32] In 1982 a provision was introduced allowing persons desiring to continue to farm to transfer their holdings to a designated part of the development area.[33]

Korea

Land readjustment on the Japanese pattern was introduced in Korea during the Japanese occupation of 1905-45, the critical enactment being the Korean Land Readjustment Act of 1934.[34] In 1966 a Land Readjustment Project Act was enacted, which, while permitting readjustment by private initiative, placed greater emphasis on readjustment initiated by local authorities.[35] Korea is unique in its effort to use land adjustment for the purpose of creating low-income housing by provisions in the 1980 Korean Master Plan for Public Housing Construction and National Urban Land Development.[36]

Taiwan

Agrarian land readjustment was begun on a trial basis in 1958 and extended to a national program in 1962,[37] which was continued until 1971. A second national consolidation program on somewhat different principles was carried out from 1977 to 1982. Article 143 of the 1949 Constitution expressly refers to land readjustment.[38]

It is now codified as Sections 6, 7, and 13 of the Town Planning and Development Act 1928–1979.[39]

France

Legislation in 1865 authorized formation of land-development syndicates.[40] This permitted involuntary inclusion of landowners by prefectoral resolution. The scheme was further developed by decree in 1927. In 1967, initiation of schemes by landowners was authorized.[41]

Australia

The Western Australia Town Planning and Development Act of 1928 authorized a system of land pooling under which land was transferred to local authorities and then retransferred to the original owners. The scheme has been extensively utilized in the Perth area since 1951 to consolidate lots on the outskirts of communities, and was recodified in 1996.[42]

India

Land readjustment on the Western Australian model was introduced in the 1915 Bombay Town Planning Act and continues in the successor states of Maharastra and Gujarat.[43]

Sweden

A Joint Development Act of 1 July 1987 authorized land readjustment in Sweden, though only after prior municipal authorization and without coercion of dissenting landowners.[44]

Land readjustment will be easier to organize in a period of rising prosperity: "The costs of organizing voluntary cooperative arrangements will not be so great in a dynamic situation as they will be in a static one." It will have little application in undeveloped exurban areas:

It will be to the advantage of the individual owner of a parcel of land to allow the whole subdivision to be developed as a single unit. . . . Only through unified development can a social "surplus" be created. Individual bargaining seems likely to be considerably less intense here . . . it may be quite rational for individuals in the older residential areas of a city to choose collective action . . . and at the same time it may be irrational for owners of undeveloped units to agree.[45]

A scheme similar to land readjustment has been proposed by Robert Nelson: Allowing established neighborhoods to sell entry rights by waiving zoning restrictions, and by selling all properties.

Such sales of whole neighborhoods would be most likely to occur near subway stops, highway interchanges, or in other circumstances where the neighborhood's land had a much higher value in an entirely new use. . . . Neighborhoods and municipalities have little current incentive to make room for development, as long as there is no financial gain to them. . . . The creation of private neighborhoods with saleable rights of entry would create such an institution.[46]

The principal necessary contribution of higher levels of government to land adjustment would be the provision of an appropriate mechanism for incorporation of associations, together with impartial tax assessment and mediation facilities and, in some circumstances, the deeding of streets. At a later stage, some consideration might be given to cooperative credit mechanisms for land-readjustment groups, such as the municipal bond banks or pools offered by some states to their smaller municipalities. The internal governance of the associations requires careful definition by statute of opt-out rights, and some provision for public review of the organization decision to guard against externalities and the oppression of dissenters. Much work was done on this subject in the early 1930s in the United States but was largely abated by the availability of large-scale federal financing for urban renewal.

Trash Collection

Many associations provide services to their residents that do not strictly involve maintenance of common areas or association property, but that are so closely linked to common interests of property-owners as to deserve consideration here. A survey by the Community Associations Institute disclosed that 72 percent of the 130,000 residential community and condominium associations (RCAs) extant in 1988 engaged in trash collection, an activity sometimes required by deed covenants and sometimes resulting from negotiations with municipal governments. Significant economy and convenience can result from this activity, including use of communal dumpsters and recycling bins in place of individual bundling of trash and the ability to use competing private contractors rather than a unionized municipal work force.[47] It is said that public waste collection is frequently 50 percent more expensive than waste collection by private contractors.[48] Houston and Kansas City have provided property tax rebates to residential community associations engaging in trash collection, and a recent New Jersey statute also includes snow and leaf removal and street lighting.[49]

An indication as to types of activity that can be transferred by municipalities to community associations or sublocal governments is supplied by a survey of privatization efforts by local governments in the Tampa-St. Petersburg, Florida area during 1982–87. Nearly all the privatized functions are amenable to transfer to community-level government, an indirect form of privatization. Among the functions privatized by more than 10 percent of the surveyed governments were buildings and grounds, child care, care of the elderly and handicapped, recreational and cultural facilities, solid-waste collection, street maintenance, street lights, and vehicle towing.[50] Community associations have an advantage in rendering such services because of their very smallness:

> RCAs operate in the local public economy as collective consumers who employ outside parties-either private firms or local government agencies-to produce and deliver services to them. Such pure provision units have possible advantages insofar as elected officers are free to focus on the representation of consumer interests rather than having to balance the interests of consumers against producers, as must happen when a local government directly employs a large public bureaucracy. Consumer interests may tend to be represented more accurately by pure provision units.[51]

Services that are more difficult to devolve or privatize are those where there are few bidders, long-term contracts, need for close supervision, uncertain cost, or vulnerability to corruption; services involving the ticketing and towing of automobiles have caused difficulty in the last respect,[52] and illustrate the dangers of devolving adjudicatory powers.

Clearly,

> there are several public goods and services that are often or could feasibly be provided at the level of a city neighborhood or by a rural village or town. These might include, in an urban neighborhood, schooling, parks, trash collection, and the like. In a small, isolated community police, fire protection and other similar services could also be efficiently provided by the local polity.[53]

The North Rhine-Westphalia reorganization of local government in 1974–75 provided for establishment of district councils within metropolitan areas, with responsibility for garbage services and some other functions.[54] The operation at a sublocal level of services of this type does not require a freestanding entity like a self-governing school or land-readjustment association, but can be carried on by a general purpose neighborhood government or residential community association, the activities being funded either by property taxes or assessments, user charges, or combinations of them.

The entity need not be a governmental entity, but can be created by deed covenants. The services it renders may be collective goods, but they are not necessarily public goods in the economic sense. As Fred Foldvery has trenchantly observed:

> It is not often recognized that territorial goods are a class of excludable goods, and that most civic goods are territorial. . . . For excludable goods, one can charge

admission into the domain of usage, so contractual provision is feasible. . . . Human beings are land animals, creatures that live in three-dimensional space on the surface of the earth, a fact that is obvious to everyone except an economist writing about public goods.[55]

Because effective rendition of services by community associations is capitalized into land value,"the potential for gains and losses constrains shirking" by members of the association.[56] In addition, effects on property values constrain associations from adopting oppressive rules, leading to the expectation that "the quality of the constitutions of contractual governments should increase over time."[57]

Building Repairs

In conventional American practice, building repairs are a matter for the homeowner himself, if he is fortunate enough to be such, or otherwise for a more or less remote landlord or housing authority. Only of late has there been self-conscious neighborhood organization addressing such needs with respect to both owned and rented property.

The American Residential Community Association has as its fundamental object building maintenance, as do the tenants' associations and associations of leaseholders extant in other countries, including those created in recent British legislation. In Britain, the 1985 Housing Act allows tenants' associations with 50 percent membership to petition for the right to manage public housing; the Housing Act of 1988 provides for votes of tenants to replace existing management with Housing Action Trusts;[58] the Local Government and Housing Act of 1989 allows three-fourths majorities of tenants with common-area repair obligations or owners of adjacent terrace housing to apply for repair grants. The recent British approach has been criticized for its emphasis on privatization of housing estates as distinct from devolution of management to tenant-approved entities in the fashion proposed by the pioneer housing reformer Octavia Hill at the turn of the century.[59] In France, a mechanism—the Operations Programmes d'Amelioration de l'Habitat—was created that allows owners to unite to receive grants for structural repairs.[60] The limits of "architectural determinism" have at last been perceived, and planned communities are now accompanied by the creation of organizations for their future governance.

Polish municipalities with more than 200,000 population have sub-municipal units, which function as electoral units, and have responsibilities for street lighting, lawn maintenance, housing inspection, and cultural activities.[61]

The customary mechanism for funding of such associations in public housing is allowance to them of a share of rents. Associations of private owners are appropriately funded by the same means as residential community associations: property taxes, special assessments, and user charges as appropriate. Where associations are organized with respect to already-developed property, the definition of opt-out rights becomes important; any forced membership should require not only a large supermajority but some public review.

Zoning Waivers

Legislation properly so-called is rarely thought of in the United States as a sublocal function, but recent years have seen an explosion, in response to felt need, of agencies such as historical preservation and business-improvement districts, empowered to impose aesthetic or behavioral regulations; such rules are also imposed by residential community and condominium associations created by deed covenants.

Regulations of this type are the most frequent cause of dissension in residential community associations and other small entities. Another consideration militates against them: "The chances of inadvertent and excusable error in the ascertainment of law are quite high."[62] Thus some commentators have urged associations to limit such restrictions.[63] On the other hand, many existing neighborhoods have organized historic-preservation districts precisely to gain the benefit of such restrictions, and Robert Nelson has urged that existing neighborhoods be given the right to choose to have the authority to impose aesthetic and behavioral restrictions.[64] Among common restrictions are those relating to cable access, satellite dishes, clotheslines, pets, and parking, as well as architectural-committee approval. Recent proposals would place durational limits on restrictions in large-scale developments other than those relating to the payment of assessments.[65] Here it is important that internal, supermajority protections be met in order for new restrictions to be adopted, with opt-out grandfather rights for those affected. The benefits of restrictions are so closely property related as to render the property tax or assessment the preferred financing mechanism.

Zoning and planning powers in the United States are generally reposed at a county or municipal rather than neighborhood level, and the municipalities are generally of far greater than neighborhood size. Little thought has been given to further devolution of zoning powers, sometimes because of fear of parochialism and external effects, but more generally because of simple inertia. The existing system, however, is almost universally regarded as both ineffective and corrupt. Devolution of some powers may make possible liberalization of outmoded restrictions on denser or mixed uses, and may provide a mechanism for the compensation of neighborhoods that would otherwise resist change.

The 1984 French decentralization measures gave the very small communes new powers over grant-of-planning permission. To be sure, the exercise of these powers requires the use of technical services, unavailable to the very smallest entities.[66]

Efforts at devolving some powers over zoning and planning to large neighborhood councils with populations of thirty to a hundred thousand have not been conspicuously successful. In Winnipeg, the councils were dominated by "citizen activists . . . talking about matters of little interest to the general population."[67] By contrast,

> One interesting feature of the British situation was that the [smaller] parish councils—which had been preserved in rural districts as minor administrative units—had begun to take on the role of neighborhood pressure groups, especially in districts which had been changed by urban settlement. They were particularly active in dealing with issues connected to physical planning and environmental management.[68]

For this purpose, community councils without administrative responsibilities were created in Scottish cities.[69] The Royal Commission on Local Government in England discovered that parish-sized neighborhoods were the areas with which people most identified, but assumed that these areas were too small to have their own governments.[70] Recently proposed British legislation would require parish councils to be informed and consulted with respect to a wide range of land-use issues.[71]

A number of writers have suggested that small-scale governments or RCAs be given the power to waive zoning restrictions. One proposal would require variances to be approved by all owners of adjacent property, and 90 percent of the rest of the owners in a zoning district, with purchased consents being permitted: "In this way adjacent owners and others would receive compensation for any external diseconomies that they might incur."[72]

Robert Nelson has made similar proposals, except that the funds for purchased consents would flow to a community association.[73] It has been objected that "the scheme's straightforward transfer of property rights from outvoted owners of undeveloped land to a majority of preexisting residents is what a regulatory takings doctrine most clearly seeks to prevent."[74] A more modest scheme, which would not entail direct wealth transfers, would allow communities acting in their own interest to waive higher-level zoning restrictions against convenience facilities such as shops, small offices, day-care and other social-service facilities, accessory apartments, and demand-response transportation facilities.[75] The Singapore government as a matter of policy relaxed restrictions on street hawkers within housing developments in order to organize a system of rotating markets, thus both relieving social dullness and "creat[ing] new jobs for some residents and . . . keep[ing] the problems of illegal street-hawking and unsanitary food-handling under control. Since families could eat out in these environments conveniently and quite cheaply, some women were freed from cooking chores and have begun working in the nearby light industries."[76] "A large covered market . . . [was] built in each neighborhood center, around a pedestrian concourse free from vehicular traffic."[77] It has been pointed out that RCAs themselves came into existence to assist in the "move away from big-lot development, in which each family had a large yard, to smaller individual lots supplemented by common areas for recreation and other activities."[78]

Because zoning waivers can affect neighboring properties unequally, it is important to provide opt-outs in the form of requirements of individual consent to owners immediately abutting the proposed use, thus giving them the power to bargain for compensation; supermajorities of other owners should be required. Funding is not an issue in this context, since the waivers will generate receipts. These should accrue to the association in the first instance, with power in the association to compensate specially affected owners by supermajority vote.

PUBLIC GOODS

We turn now to a group of basic services to association residents that do not relate to the protection and use of property but rather to the welfare of association members, but in which a sufficient common interest is thought to exist to warrant some measure of compulsory participation, if only through the payment of taxes. Such goods include law enforcement assistance, schools and youth groups, the provision of aid to newcomers and migrants, probation services, and the services of general-purpose sublocal governments.

Community Schools

Recent political dialogue about American education has involved a contest between those advocating ever-greater national government funding and control of the curriculum on the one hand, and those advocating vouchers and privatization on the other. Tocqueville supplied the short answer to the first faction: "The sole guarantee imagined by them against the abuse of power was public education. . . . It was this trifling literary gibberish which was intended by them to replace all political guarantees."[79] The last prescription for privatization is in part a counsel of despair, founded on the view that public schools are so beset by union rules, grievance procedures, federal interference with school discipline, busing orders, mandates relating to special and bilingual education, and legal restrictions on the hiring of competent teachers that they are beyond repair. Here also a case can be made for a measure short of or at least complementary to vouchers and privatization: radical decentralization of public school governance. In the United States, schools have traditionally been governed on a territorial basis by school district boards. These originally encompassed only one or two schools.[80] However, with the growth of population and the fashionable movement for consolidation of school districts, these political entities have become progressively larger and more bureaucratic; the impersonality of the systems, particularly since the Second World War, has fostered the organization of teachers' unions, which have generated problems of their own. The teachers' unions have induced the states to employ an array of techniques to force consolidation upon school districts, including fiscal incentives, countywide rather than district approval of consolidations, prohibition of incorporation of new districts, aid formulas discriminating against small districts, and direct mandating of consolidations.

The number of school districts decreased from 108,579 in 1942 to 34,678 in 1962,[81] to approximately 15,000 in 1996. There is some evidence that the size of districts is inversely related to student accomplishment.[82] At the same time, the governance of schools has increasingly become a professional monopoly. Teachers are required by state law to have taken large numbers of education courses, which characteristically involve indoctrination in professional ideology rather than deepening of knowledge about subject matter. Principals in many places are required to have doctorates from colleges of education.[83] Union contracts render it virtually impossible to remove or transfer inadequate teachers and require that replacements be hired from seniority lists rather than being "handpicked" in accordance with local needs. Typically, for example,

The employee with the least amount of seniority shall be identified for layoff. . . . Tenured teachers will be recalled first in reverse order of layoff. No teachers will be hired in areas where a layoff has occurred until the teachers laid off have been recalled. . . . Teachers shall not be required to perform . . . school cafeteria duty, . . . playground duty . . . detention duty . . . the duplication of teaching materials.[84]

In France, by contrast, there has been a more modest decline in the number of primary schools because of consolidations, rural depopulation, and a decline between 1960 and 1982 of about 10 percent in the numbers of children in the age group in question. However, the proportion of single-class schools to total primary schools has remained constant. Of the 74,268 primary schools in 1960, 19,010 were single-class schools, of the 43,778 primary schools in 1982, 10,778 were single-class schools "proof . . . of the realization by small rural communities that their future depends upon the retention of the local school and of their determination to resist its loss. Proof also of an understanding attitude on the part of the government and its officers."[85] "For two-room schools . . . an enrollment of 23 students has been required since the early 1980s to keep both classes open (before 1976, the number was 26)."[86]

All major European countries, in contrast to the United States, have in recent years significantly decentralized school governance and have sought to end the professional monopoly over it. Their varied efforts to extend the parental role in education are expressly referenced in Article 126 of the Maastricht Treaty, which calls for "cross-cultural cooperative research in the field of parents in education."

As a result of reforms enacted by the Giscard government in 1975, which had been partly implemented in 1968 following the student disturbances of that year,[87] each French college (12–15 year-old-age group) and lycée (15–18) was given a School Council presided over by the principal and including five teachers, five elected parents, five staff members, five community representatives, and two student (five for lycées). Primary and nursery schools had a teachers' and parents' council with five parent members; the maire had a right to attend but not to vote. . . . This committee votes the school budget and the various school rules, and a committee of it reviews disciplinary recommendations for expulsion, together with the school social worker and guidance counselor. The council also reviews the bursar's accounts and may comment on the teaching. The rules relate to such matters as safety, attendance, promptness, marking system, school records, transport, dress, smoking, permission to leave the premises, library rules, and rules relating to student activities and publications. "The Haby Reform ruled out any formal parental influence on instruction, the form or content of curriculum, grading, or homework. The classroom itself remained untouched by the parent committees."[88]

The councils were given control over 10 percent of each school's timetable and budget for matters of local choice, but as to the core of school operations the French system remains highly centralized. It has been said of the Catholic system, state-subsidized since 1959, that "one of its main attractions has been school autonomy: a Catholic head differs crucially from his state counterpart in being able to recruit his own staff and thus build up a team and a school ethos."[89] It is said that on disputed matters the staff representatives follow their principal, the teachers their union, and the parents the guidance furnished by competing national parents' organizations. The studies of the reform suggest that new local leaders sometimes arise through the parent committees, and that they operate to restrain rapid change by new teachers. The council must meet once a term, and extraordinary sessions may be called by the principal or half the members; an executive committee meets between sessions.[90] Participation rates in parent elections have declined somewhat, from 45 percent in 1968 to about 30 percent in 1989, but the school boards have been used to defuse some major controversies, as by allowing local option as to whether students may wear the Islamic veil.[91] Nonetheless, "a whole concept of the school as an almost closed professorial preserve has been swept away."[92] There are also class councils consisting of the principal and the teachers of each class, two parents, and two students. "The places on the class councils are allocated in proportion to the number of votes received by the nationally organized parents' associations. Individualism is thus not encouraged."[93] "There are several rival national organizations of parents of children in State schools, the two most influential being respectively secular left wing and Roman Catholic."

At age 15, "the school, together with the pupil and the parents and aided by a trained guidance counselor, decides on the future "orientation" of the pupil. The actual decision is taken by the appropriate *conseil de classe* but the parents can if they wish contest the decision."[94] There has also been substantial erosion of the uniformity once characteristic of French education, by the opening up of catchment areas for students at the college (11–15 year old) level, through special provisions for disadvantaged areas, and by giving colleges greater discretion in implementing national goals.[95] In practice, control over the controversial issue of sex education in schools is exercised by the participation councils.[96] The provision and maintenance of school buildings (but not the instruction in them) has been a traditional function of the small commune in France.[97]

German schools have elaborate provisions for parent participation: "These include class councils, school councils and provincial councils as well as officially recognized parents' associations at all levels, culminating in a federal parents organization."[98] In North Rhine-Westphalia, the School Participation Bill of 1977 provides for a School Conference, including, in secondary schools twelve teachers, six students, and six parents to advise on methods of instruction, school finances, and examinations.[99] Parental conferences were active in successfully organizing opposition to a diluted form of comprehensive education in 1978.[100]

More far-reaching powers are conferred on participation councils in Hamburg and Hessen. In Hamburg, an Act of 1920, a holdover from a revolutionary council in 1919, created elected parent councils, including nine parents and three teachers for each school, with the power to elect head teachers. The Act was replaced by the Nazi regime with a system of nominated parent councils limited to extracurricular activities. After the war, separate parent and teacher councils were established for each school, with only advisory functions. A School Administration Act in 1968 added student representatives. A School Constitution Act of 1973 gave the councils an enhanced but partial role in the selection of head teachers.

In Hessen, Article 56 of the postwar Land constitution declared that "parents and guardians have the right to participate in decisions on the general formation of educational policy." In 1958, the Hessian Supreme Court held that formation of educational policy was illegal without parent participation. A new Act of 5 November 1958 gave parent councils vetoes over "the adoption of school rules and organization within the framework of the general school regulations [and] for the overall planning of the curriculum of the school, if it is intended to depart experimentally from the general guidelines." A Land parents council was given power to pass on guidelines for promotions, and textbook selection. Deadlocks between parents and head teachers could be resolved only by express decision of the Land government. Litigation by parent councils delayed implementation of comprehensive schools for 12-to-14 year olds in 1972.[101]

Britain similarly vested control of its state-maintained schools in large Local Education Authorities. However, the existence of separate boards for each school continued since an act of 1870, and was carried forward by sections 17–22 of the Education Act of 1944. By the Education Act of 1902, parish councils were permitted to appoint one member to the boards of voluntary schools, a provision extended to all primary schools by the 1944 Act. Later, as a result of recommendations of the Taylor Committee in 1977,[102] a parent representative was added to each board. "The general principle tends to be that the L.E.A. settles 'the general educational character of the school and its place in the local system' while the governors have 'general direction of the conduct and curriculum of the school.'"[103]

More recently, the Education Act of 1980 provided for additional parent governors, and that of 1986 for equal numbers of local authority and parent governors and reports to parents.[104] Finally, the Education Reform Act, 1988, sec. 40 provided for drastic decentralization of the control of education. The boards of Local Authority schools are to be composed of specified portions of parents, teachers, local authority governors, and co-opted governors as provided in the Education (No.2) Act of 1986. The governors now receive an automatic budget share and authority "to spend any sum as they think fit for the purposes of the school," and to appoint and dismiss staff. They control some 87 percent of school budgets as well as, to a limited degree, admissions policy.[105] In addition, schools may elect to dispense with Local Authority control and receive direct grants from central government, in which case their boards must include five parents, one or two teachers, the head teacher, and co-opted governors outnumbering the others, at least two of whom must be parents. These changes, though prompted by central government-local authority conflict, are said to "have enfranchised parents and created a quarter million army of school governors."[106] It is said that "administrative and governmental arrangements have sought to promote consumer sovereignty by strengthening the mechanisms of parental influence over education. This may also serve to strengthen stratification and vocationalism."[107] Although popularly viewed as a product of the Thatcher government, a speech by a Labor Prime Minister, James Callaghan, in 1976[108] helped lay the groundwork for these changes, and their analogues in Australia and New Zealand were for the most part carried into operation by Labor governments.

Similar legislation has been adopted in New Zealand[109] and in all Australian states,[110] including Victoria, where

> every public school now has a school-site council of parents, teachers, and, for secondary schools, students. These . . . within a framework of state policies and priorities . . . set educational policy for the school, approve the budget, and evaluate the educational program. Principals are now appointed through a local selection process.[111]

Boards in the Australian Capital Territory exercise considerable control over the curriculum. The previous arrangements involving control of schools by special-purpose agencies are said to have "facilitated the influence of an increasingly autonomous teaching profession,"[112] as in the United States. The New Zealand boards of elected parents in poorer neighborhoods are said to be less successful than their British counterparts, due to the absence of the British provisions for co-opted governors and for training of governors.

In addition, Danish schools since 1970 have parent-elected boards, which include one member chosen by the local council, two teachers, and the principal without voting rights, together with seven parent representatives; this entity has authority to submit budget proposals, preparing short-lists of teacher and head-teacher candidates, and may be given authority over part of the budget, in addition to promulgating school rules, approving the timetable and teaching materials, deciding on referrals for special education, and making recommendations on the hiring of teachers and principals.[113] Five of the thirteen members of the district school board are elected by the school parent committees. The powers of the boards were enlarged in 1989.[114] It has been said of Denmark that

> the writings of the poet-clergyman, N.F.S. Grundtvig . . . provided ideological support for an essentially antibureaucratic conception of education. Grundtvig stressed the importance of voluntarism in education, the invidious pedagogic effects of formal examinations, the value of sustained personal interaction between learner and teacher, and the need for the school to be regarded as an extension of the home rather than of the state.[115]

Irish schools are generally sponsored by religious denominations, and receive state subsidies for all teachers' salaries plus 90 percent of building and equipment costs and 75 percent of maintenance costs. Under legislation enacted in 1976, each school has a Board of Management consisting of representatives of the sponsoring organization, teachers, and parents, with authority to govern the school, disburse funds, and appoint and remove teachers.[116]

Similar provisions creating school councils including various interest groups with managerial and assessment functions were enacted in Spain in 1985 and in Portugal in 1991; Portuguese schools have long had parent representation on class councils for discipline purposes.[117] There has traditionally been a parent representative on Dutch school boards; since 1982, participation councils of parents and teachers have been created in each school that the school boards must meet with at least twice annually under the Education Participation Act of 1992.[118]

Italy likewise, since Decree 416 of the President of the Republic of 31 May 1974, has boards for each school and class, elaborated as to primary schools by Law 148 of 1990. The school boards consist of six parents, six teachers, the principal, and one nonteacher and have authority to act on the budget, on acquisition of teaching equipment, and on supplemental, cultural, sporting, and welfare activities.[119] Upon the introduction of the system, 90 percent of teachers and 70 percent of parents participated in the initial elections.[120] It is now relatively easy for a school council to request experimental status; "the fact that such a request comes from a mainly elected body with parental representation gives it some legitimacy in coping with the bureaucracy."[121] While the percentage of parents voting has since greatly declined, especially in southern Italy, the councils are credited with local experiments and improvements.[122]

The Austrian School Law of 1986 accords parent councils limited powers relating to extracurricular excursions, school dress rules, and whether events are to be declared school-related, and may authorize two fund raising projects a year among the pupils, in addition to giving advice on the organization of extracurricular activities, school guidance, and health care.[123] In many of the Swiss cantons, control of primary schools is vested at the level of the commune, almost invariably an entity so small as to maintain only one primary school, or two or three small and scattered schools, which are essentially self governing.[124]

Swiss schools have traditionally been radically decentralized, certified teachers in many places being elected to their positions for short terms in a town meeting of the school commune.[125]

In Belgium the communes have wide powers over primary schools, although they traditionally contributed only one-third of the construction costs and none of the teaching costs.[126]

By contrast, schools in Stockholm have had purely advisory management committees since 1992. "Most parents (65 percent) feel they have little chance of influencing schools or the school environment. Perhaps the sense of powerlessness is due to these bodies being purely consultative, not policymaking."[127] There are also consultative boards for each school in Norway.[128]

In the United States and Canada, governors at the level of the individual state school are unheard of. In some large cities, subdistricts have been created, usually with populations in the tens or hundreds of thousands. "These regional school boards are dominated by politicians and school officials, not parents."[129] "Community control of schools . . . did not come into being on any wide scale. . . . It is quite widely agreed that the fears generated by the three years of violent and widely publicized conflict over political decentralization and community control issues in New York City destroyed them as viable solutions."[130]

One of the few mild movements in the direction of site-based parental governance was the enactment in Massachusetts of Chapter 188 of the Acts of 1985, that creates school-improvement committees for each school that are empowered to spend $15 per pupil (originally $10) of state aid. Even this timid initiative was amended in the course of enactment to reduce the per pupil amount from $50 to $10 and to provide school boards with a veto over improvement-committee decisions.

There had previously been state-mandated school-advisory councils in California, Florida, and South Carolina, and writings of educators urging enhanced parent participation.[131]

The only provincial legislation for participation councils in Canada is that created by Bill 27 of 1971 and Bill 71 of 1972 in Quebec, which creates purely advisory parent councils for each school consisting of 7 to 25 elected parent representatives, with the principal and a teacher representative attending in nonvoting capacities.[132] One writer on school-based management in Canada has observed of proposals to vest control of the school budget in parent-dominated governors: "No district in North America known to the author has experimented with this proposal." He also observes:

It seems to provide parents with a greater amount of liberty . . . if satisfaction is a product of control and involvement, then it should increase. . . . By proposing that public schools be reshaped in the model of private schools, the idea is not far from that of a voucher plan. The implementation of boards for each school, the reduction of the present roles of the district and state or province, the decentralization of collective negotiations are all significant departures from the ways in which districts are structured and operated now.[133]

The developments in Western Europe and Australasia (with the possible exception of those in England, the work of the Thatcher government) had their inception in the concerns for participatory democracy characteristic of the late-'60s student movements. This is true even though the French reforms were sponsored by the government of Charles de Gaulle; the disorders in Paris in 1968 were preceded, not followed, by his famous speech in March 1968 at Lyon declaring that the need for centralization in France had ended.[134] They had little influence in the United States where the student movement, one of "rebels without a program" in George Kennan's words, was concerned with an end to the Vietnam War, personal emancipation from social restraints, and centralization in the cause of civil rights.

Michael Walzer has observed that "the civil rights and antiwar agitations . . . turned out to be evanescent, leaving behind no organizational residue, no basis for an ongoing participatory politics."[135] In 1967 and 1968 he had presciently observed "the failure to involve them actively in university life, their failure to involve themselves: for all this, there will one day be, as the saying goes, hell to pay."[136] The legacy of the American civil rights and student movements, unlike their foreign counterparts, was a centralization of power in the national government and the federal courts. Even blacks now suffer from this; in Walzer's words, "political power must always be twice won. It must be won first with the help of the state or through the creation of parallel bureaucracies against established local or corporate elites. Then it must be won again by new popular forces against the state."[137]

In discussing the Western European tendency to create submunicipal governments in large cities, one commentator has observed: "Without operational functions and some powers of decision-making, it is argued they fail to evoke sufficient interest among the population.... Some form of functional decentralization, i.e., the creation of committees or citizens' councils for particular functions, would seem more effective."[138] The increasing use of school governors and elected parent committees confirms the force of this suggestion. Mechanisms for powerless advisory councils are almost inherently ineffective: "Their reports go not to the community at large but to those responsible for the service in the first place, so that the public may reasonably feel somewhat uneasy about their effectiveness."[139]

Jefferson's original design for ward government contemplated three years of free education in primary schools of forty students, each erected by taxation or compelled labor by a ward of 5 or 6 square miles with a population of about 500.[140] With the "school busing" controversies of the 1960s and 1970s, renewed attention was paid to the neighborhood school, busing being described by disinterested sociologists as "profound sociological folly"[141] and as "destroying activity in a realm (schooling) that is traditionally associated with vigorous neighborhood civic activity."[142] The Congress "declared it to be the policy of the United States that . . . the neighborhood is the appropriate basis for determining public school assignments,"[143] and later enacted a statute recognizing the role of secondary schools as community fora.[144] However, there is little provision for school-based governance except for limited experiments in New York City, in Hawaii, and in Kentucky, the latter much-vaunted experiment being limited by opposition from teachers unions to one school in each district.[145]

In some states, provision has been made for incorporation of a few new charter schools, which immediately become scapegoats for the unions, but no serious effort has been made to "charter" all public schools. A much-criticized court decision in Illinois invalidated elected boards of parents and teachers for each school as inconsistent with the Supreme Court's reapportionment decisions,[146] a result later modified, ignoring the caution of Robert Dahl that "it would be folly to think that a single mass-produced model stamped out according to eternal patterns can possibly fit all the kinds of associations we need in order to cope with our extraordinarily complex world."[147]

A comparative study of American public and parochial schools concluded that

One decision making area that showed a consistently large difference between public and Catholic schools ... was the hiring and firing of teachers.... Catholic teachers report that they spend fewer hours actually teaching in the classroom, but more hours doing other teaching related tasks, such as preparing lectures, grading, and tutoring students ... exercising more control over ... school-level policy and classroom practices . . . working in an environment that is more orderly and more personal for students . . . that promotes a greater sense of collegiality and community . . . higher levels of job satisfaction and a greater sense of professional efficacy [and] fewer teacher-related problems, specifically teacher absenteeism and lack of commitment, than public school[s].[148]

[T]he concept of the neighborhood . . . propounded in the Russell Sage survey of New York before World War I, developed by Patrick Geddes in Scotland, and adopted by Patrick Abercrombie in England during World War II . . . initially meant the catchment area of a primary school. . . . Here was a community of neighbors bound together by an interest in common services. Yet this physical and social reality found no expression in terms of Local government; for such a neighborhood was seldom a ward or precinct, let alone a local government unit; nor was it always even a census tract.[149]

Where local subdivisions control both zoning and the level of spending on education, the property tax becomes essentially a service fee based on demand for education.[150] This results in "sorting of the population" analogized by its defenders to the "American utopian tradition of people migrating to underdeveloped locales and setting up their own government."[151] Critics of this analysis urge that it "fails to acknowledge people's bonds to place . . . first and foremost, people must reside where they can get work . . . similarly, differences in housing costs and ethnic composition are obviously far more significant than variations in local government expenditures in determining residential movements."[152] "Some places do indeed end up with nicer packages than others, but these are for the most part nicer for anybody. The real differences between jurisdictions . . . are determined primarily by social class."[153]

The public-choice theorists do not deny that a sorting in schools based on social class takes place in a localized system; they merely maintain that more people's wants are satisfied at less cost than in systems that do not permit such sorting. Their critics note that "the Tiebout hypothesis requires that there be many competing communities. In most areas there are only a limited number of competing communities."[154] However, as to education, the creation of self-governing schools and the continued existence in many places of small districts invalidates this criticism.

Another criticism of confederal solutions is that the resulting entities will be too weak to carry out the reforms of centralized bureaucracies, including school bureaucracies, that are sought by supporters of public choice:

The coalitions of the technocrat have a solidarity not of a gang but of a guild, so that even when one member has been bought off or otherwise brought under control, the guild persists. This complicates the task of control. . . . The confederal polity is not up to this task. While it fragments the polity and the possibility of democratic control, the technocratic guilds, entrenched in the specialized services, will see that their conceptions of the public interest are promoted.[155]

In addition, it is said that because political conflicts in small organizations spill over into social relationships, consensus-seeking becomes the norm: "The small polity . . . hardly seems the right building block on which to found effective democratic control of the wide-ranging bureaucratic organizations of the modern state." These comments of Samuel Beer overlook the demonstrated capacity of small polities, from RCAs to self-governing schools to French communes to by-pass public bureaucracies, by contracting out to private providers. And as to schools at least, they underrate the intensity of parental interest and involvement possible when mechanisms of governance are provided. In Britain, governors receive some state regulation and assistance in the form of training classes, guidelines for procurement, and in some circumstances provisions for removal. They are, however, popularly and locally chosen and, despite the urgings of some,[156] are not properly characterized as "state volunteers."

Terry Nichols Clark has suggested that "education as it has existed in most of the West, has, at its higher levels, tended to disparage local, at least local community, concerns. The point at which the effects of education changed direction was very roughly the end of primary school in traditional European systems, and the beginning of college in the American system."[157] Even at lower levels, American education, as presently organized, "disparages community concerns." Richard Musgrave, a distinguished student of public finance, has observed that "ways . . . may be developed to secure increased competition within the public system, including reduction in the size of school districts and increased mobility."[158]

The funding mechanism for self-governing schools is a critical issue. In Britain, opt-out schools receive pro rata portions of the block education grant to local authorities, which in turn rests on an inverse-wealth formula, with some positive discrimination in favor of inner-city schools. In the United States, the funding mechanism used for Title I federal aid to public schools might be used; this ties aid to particular schools to the social composition of their student bodies rather than the average-wealth characteristics of the subdivision, and closely approaches a voucher system. The federal contribution to American primary and secondary education is sufficiently modest that it could be completely voucherized and made available to both public and private schools while still being earmarked for noninstructional expenses, thus avoiding any possible church-state problem. The use of vouchers allows aid to be focused on needy students rather than needy subdivisions, and is equivalent to an income transfer that can only be spent on public goods.

The internal constitution of self-governing schools would seem uncomplicated once boards have been chosen; election of board members by class or school rather than on a proportional representation system would seem desirable if involvement in local and national politics is to be avoided, and the self-governing schools should be independent of general-purpose local and sublocal governments to maximize parent interest and simplify political controversies. The competence of boards in poorer neighborhoods might be enhanced, as in England, by requiring the co-optation as well as election of governors, by additionally requiring the presence of governors with special skills in construction, accounting, and higher education, and by providing for state assistance in the recruitment and training of governors.

The benefits of local governance are manifold: The market discipline imposed on teachers and the greater vocational choice allowed them by the ability of schools to hire and fire freely; the ability of school principals to assemble compatible teams; greater parental and community support of public schools; the ability of schools, at least at the secondary level, to differentiate themselves and specialize and select students, thereby creating centers of excellence; defusing of controversies over social and moral issues that result when higher levels of government are the source of rules governing student behavior and discipline.

School-Care Committees

Aside from the use of boards for each school, several Western European countries also had an early and instructive history of using locally organized care committees to supplement schools' services to students.

The London School Care Committees functioned under the Inner London Educational Authority from 1907 at least into the 1970s. Their functions were essentially unaltered since the definition of their functions in 1907 as agencies "to prevent or alleviate physical and mental distress; to initiate schemes to promote the welfare of school children."

The committees were called into existence by the Education (Provision of Meals) Act of 1906 allowing local authorities to assist voluntary agencies in the provision of meals. The 1906 statute resembled several others of the same period in expressly providing for administration with the aid of voluntary associations. Another statute in the same year provided for the creation of Skilled Apprenticeship Committees to help school leavers. The Care Committees organized by the Charity Organization Society (C.O.S.) at the behest of the London County Council (L.C.C.), though promoted by the Provision of Meals statute, did not have meal provision as their primary aim; indeed the L.C.C. did not at first provide school meals. The C.O.S. considered that "personal work was needed in a far greater degree than the establishment of feeding centres under official control. . . . Careful, regular and sympathetic home visiting was necessary."[159] The system of home visitors initiated by the C.O.S. survived for more than sixty years.

In her study of Voluntary Work in the Welfare State in 1969, Mary Morris noted that the service was manned by 2,350 voluntary workers coordinated by a small professional staff, and that its members were regarded "as a friend of the family, and . . . not considered 'one of them.'" A care committee had been organized for each elementary school and insured that the benefits of programs for help with clothing, school journeys, and holidays were received by those needing them. "Many hard-pressed mothers are able to carry their heavy burdens because they can share them with regular and sympathetic listeners." In 1954 the system was extended to comprehensive and secondary grammar schools.[160] As late as 1966, care-committee members were asked to report on "the number of cases of acute poverty or financial hardship known to them, the main causes of poverty as they found them and the means they used to assist." The program strikingly departed from the bureaucratic and mechanical school breakfast and lunch programs of the United States.

The [Younghusband] Report on Social Workers in the Local Health and Welfare Services (1959), after alluding to the committees, rightfully noted "the cross-fertilization of statutory and voluntary effort typical of this country enriches each of these services and nourishes all; it has proved an example and an inspiration for many lands."[161] Integral to the voluntary effort was an emphasis on the C.O.S. principles of casework, self-respect, and the importance of the family.

In 1968, the Plowden Report (Central Advisory Committee on Education, Children and their Primary Schools),[162] though noting the work of the London care committees, which then had 2,500 volunteers and 80 paid organizers covering 1,237 schools, went on to observe that it was "not easy to recruit sufficient voluntary workers in all parts of the country, particularly in the areas where they are most needed. Moreover, scarce trained staff may become so burdened with the supervision of voluntary workers for whom few training opportunities exist, that their skills are not most efficiently used. . . ." Elsewhere, however, the report noted the usefulness of volunteers[163] and alluded to "a few London infant schools which have many children from problem families [which] have enlisted care committee workers to look after small groups of children with behavior difficulties for a day each week. This extra attention has had a valuable effect."

In the previous year, a report by the Social Research Unit of Bedford College on "The Social Welfare Services of the I.L.E.A." (the Jefferys report) had recommended a unified social-welfare service combining care-committee and truancy-enforcement functions. The Seebohm Report of the Committee on Local Authority and Allied Personal Social Services[164] recommended "that the voluntary effort devoted to the school care service of the authority must be maintained and increased." On October 1, 1970, the proposed unified educational welfare service was created: "area-based but school orientated (dealing with meals, clothing, journey and uniform grants, medical follow-up and attendance)."

The 1970 reorganization effectively subordinating the care committees to professional Education Welfare officers impaired much of the original ethos of the committees, and the change was not a wise or successful one. It is clear that there are functions that can be discharged by organized volunteers at which the state dismally fails, or which it can perform, if at all, only at far greater cost. Much of social casework may be one of those functions. Even staunch defenders of the welfare state have noted the distinctive role that can be played by volunteer organizations. Attlee in the third year of his premiership, on becoming president of a settlement house, declared: "Alongside everything done by the local authority and by the state there are people who want to do a bit more. . . . I believe that we shall always have alongside the great range of public services, the voluntary services which humanize our national life and bring it down from the general to the particular." Nearly fifty years later, a critic of the Thatcher government's privatization efforts, Maria Brenton, observed:

It should be no part of public policy to off-load functions and services which are best systematically organized and guaranteed within formal structures and with a paid labor force. It is in the areas of mutual aid, self help, neighborhood and community action, information and advice centres, etc.—that the voluntary sector comes into its own. Such functions belong uniquely to voluntary initiative, even when fostered within a statutory environment, and may variously serve as an alternative to, a complement to government . . . or at times as a bulwark against it.

French schools historically were supported by similar institutions to the school-care committees, the *caisses d'ecole*. These were called into existence to administer school-lunch programs. Their boards were elected by parents in each school in elaborately supervised elections; they also had *ex officio* members and sell honorary and life memberships. In addition to receiving state appropriations, they also had substantial private donations, administered concerts and entertainments; their members engaged in home-visiting and assisted in relieving temporary hardships and in referring to social services.[165]

In nineteenth-century Berlin and Vienna there were also local school boards at the *bezirke* [neighborhood] level with large memberships.[166]

Most American schools make informal use of volunteers; the creation of formal school-support organizations provides a method of enlisting and honoring volunteers from the professional and business communities as well.

In current American politics, concern about juvenile behavior usually manifests itself in demands for tougher sentencing of juveniles, or is an adjunct to controversies over welfare and abortion involving the design of state welfare programs and criminal laws. Here also, there is a neglected dimension of neighborhood organization and involvement.

The importance of organized youth activities, especially for young men, was more recognized at the turn of the century than it is today. At that time, the young Clement Attlee spent a half-dozen years leading the Haileybury Grays, a boys' club sponsored by his public school in London's East End. In her writings on the problem of nonsupport in 1907–8, collected in the anthology of her writings published as *The Long View* (1932), the great American social worker Mary Richmond observed:

On the side of prevention, it seems to me that all the alms wasted on sham families might be better expended in making more adequate provision for the disorganized period between the time when our boys and girls in large cities leave school and the time when they settle down in life. This critical period is quite unprovided for, and in it habits of idleness and irresponsibility are formed. The breaking down of the apprenticeship system, and our failure to develop the technical school as a substitute; the lack, so far, of any adequate number of boys' clubs; the absence of varied and absorbing occupations and amusements of a healthy sort—these conditions are more responsible for the married vagabond than the state of the labor market, or even the saloon. . . . To approach any relief question from the point of view of the child's welfare only and to consider nothing else, is a natural enough mistake to make, but its effect upon the child's life is disastrous. . . . We may hold the most approved views about family life, and still be actively engaged in breaking it up, when we fail to treat all questions of income and relief as the affair first of the head of the family, of the mother only secondarily, and of the children not at all.

Organizations of the type referred to by Ms. Richmond must of their nature be local. While voluntary organizations like the scouting movement (of which the all-but-forgotten First Lady Lou Henry Hoover was a leader in the United States) fill some of the gap for younger groups, little effort has been made to enlist voluntary or local support for young people in a transitional stage; volunteer services to runaways are inadequate and the Y.M.C.A. movement is beginning to atrophy, and state employment and training services focused on youth are nonexistent. Nor have efforts been made to strengthen the juvenile probation services with volunteers.

The Advisory Commission on Intergovernmental Relations suggested in 1967 that neighborhood units be allowed to impose fractional property taxes, or capitation taxes, for the purpose of funding "after-school programs for neighborhood children."[167] Winnipeg in Canada grants to its neighborhood councils 25¢ per capita to be allocated to community youth and cultural groups.[168] In Sweden, evening use of schools is coordinated by neighborhood councils.[169] These are all relatively noncontroversial activities lending themselves to administration by neighborhood councils; nothing precludes their funding by formula or inverse-wealth grants by higher levels of government.

The deterioration of American secondary education, which coincides in no small measure with the vitiation of effective local control, would have inspired somber reflections on the part of Tocqueville:

However rude a democratic people may be, the central power that rules them is never completely devoid of cultivation because it readily draws to its own uses what little cultivation is to be found in the country, and if necessary may seek assistance elsewhere. Hence among a nation which is ignorant as well as democratic an amazing difference cannot fail speedily to arise between the intellectual capacity of the ruler and that of each of his subjects. This completes the easy concentration of all power in his hands; the administrative function of the state is perpetually extended because the state alone is competent to administer the affairs of the country.[170]

One may add to this the concern we must feel arising from the declining importance of local government: Tocqueville told us "the American learns to know the laws by participating in the act of legislation, and he takes a lesson in the forms of government from governing."[171]

Advice Bureaux

Recent American concern with the position of migrants to large cities and immigrants to the United States is conventionally reflected in controversies over "affirmative action" and civil rights laws, in disputes over welfare, and in demands for restriction of immigration and "English only" legislation. There has been limited attention to means of assimilating migrants and immigrants, and the issues have been treated as matters for national rather than local politics.

Here too there are hopeful locally based approaches that can mitigate these divisive questions by promoting greater contact with and assistance to the groups perceived as being in or causing difficulty. Although the services in question are of benefit to their recipients, they can rarely be funded through user charges, and their benefit to the community justifies exactions in their support as public goods.

Citizens' Advice Bureaux (C.A.B.), another distinctive British social institution, were established at the outset of World War II by the National Council of Social Service, having been planned beforehand. Two hundred of these bodies began operations on the day war was declared; 1,000 existed by the end of the war. Their initial function was assisting the public in dealing with wartime call-up, evacuation, and rationing regulations. Although called into existence by the exigencies of total war, their close fit with the individualist, case work philosophy of the Charity Organization Society was attested by the fact that the C.O.S. itself operated 80 of the new offices when the war began.

At the end of the war, a National Standing Conference of Citizens' Advice Bureaux was established, and the functions of the bureaux redirected to assisting individuals with the regulations of the welfare state, including housing, hire purchase, and consumer-protection legislation. By 1969, according to Mary Morris,[172] the agencies had between 5,000 and 8,000 volunteers, 75 percent of them women, chiefly housewives and retired teachers, nurses, social workers, or professional men. Three-fourths of participants in bureaux were volunteers; the remainder were part-time employees. Some 500 bureaux existed, a modest increase over the 416 that survived in 1960, and a number close to the objective of 900—one for each population center of 30,000 or more persons. Each bureau has an average of 10 workers, each serving for at least one (an average of one and a half sessions per week, mostly during working hours on weekdays). Only five had full-time solicitors.

By 1994–95, there were 721 bureaux and 1,006 associated outlets. A study by the National Consumer Council revealed that 80 percent of the population had heard of C.A.B.s. The staff numbered 9,000. By 1982, there were 4.8 million inquiries; by 1986 the number had reached 6 million; and by 1994–95, 6.5 million, of which about 28 percent related to social security, about 15 percent to debt and consumer matters, and about 10 percent each related to family, housing, and employment matters. The last comprehensive government study of the system in 1984 disclosed 13,500 workers, only 1,000 of whom were paid; by 1995 there were 28,000 workers, about 90 percent of them unpaid, including 15,743 volunteer staff, 9,000 volunteer-management committee members, and 3,321 paid staff. Two-thirds of the bureaux functioned without paid help, and only nine had solicitors. However, in 160 offices, volunteer solicitors provided advice on a part-time basis.

In 1995, in a highly significant initiative, the Legal Aid Board made grants to 24 C.A.B.s to test the delivery of legal aid under franchise by lay advisers in the fields of debt management, housing, social security, immigration, and employment, and 70 specialist advisers were employed in these areas, in which "C.A.B.s have developed expertise and which have traditionally been neglected by solicitors."

In their emphasis on case-work and in their rendering of advice divorced from material aid, as well as in their rendition of services without a means test, the Bureaux represent a survival of the Charity Organization Society philosophy.[173] Far from being adjuncts of the state, the bureaux have been described by Geoffrey Finlayson as "a watch-dog in keeping the statutory services up to the mark." A board member, Sir Wyndham Deedes, observed in 1978: "If all the knowledge which resides in a movement of this kind were made available for the use of men who make legislation, we should have a force for the welfare and well-being of mankind second to none. . . ."[174]

In recent years, the national C.A.B. has increasingly spoken out on defects of administration. In January 1984 it criticized the administration of housing benefit schemes;[175] in June 1987 it threatened to sue the Department of Social Services over delayed processing of supplemental benefit claims;[176] in April 1991 it noted the dire effects on some persons of increases in water charges;[177] in June 1992 it issued a report on worthless loan-protection insurance offered consumers.[178] It issues periodic "evidence reports" summarizing reports from local affiliates on defects in national programs.

The financing of the C.A.B. has always been precarious. Grants from central government ended in 1950 and were not renewed for 10 years. In 1963, pursuant to recommendations of the Molony Committee, the C.A.B. received a grant from the Board of Trade to assist in consumer education and advice, and relatively nominal annual grants from a number of central government agencies. Later, in 1973–74 the C.A.B. received a development grant of £2 million over five years.[179] From 1974 to 1977 a total of £4.4 million in grants to local authorities to create Consumer Advice Centres (C.A.C.s) were made available, 120 such centres being created by 1979. In that year, grants to C.A.C.s were merged with the grant to N.A.C.A.B., which was increased from £1.85 million in 1879 to £4 million in the following year, gradually increasing to £6.04 million in 1983–84 and to £12.2 million in 1993–94, where it was frozen for the following year; local authority grants to centres approximating £10 million in 1983–84 and £40 million in 1994–95. In that year, about one-fourth of the national grant was passed through to local bureaux.

In March 1983, after the advent of the Thatcher Government, a major crisis arose when the responsible minister, Gerald Vaughans, shortened to six months the annual central-government allocation to the C.A.B. based on displeasure with the activities of some prominent members, including one who was active in the Campaign for Nuclear Disarmament. A backbench revolt led to the restoration of the cuts, the replacement of the minister in the cabinet reshuffle following the June elections, and his permanent departure to the backbenches, and the appointment of an investigatory panel, universally regarded as a face-saving measure for the government. The C.A.B.s received vehement support from prominent Conservative M.P.s, with Mark Carlisle declaring "I have never heard of any suggestion of political bias," Brian Mawhinney describing their performance as "excellent," and Peter Bottomley declaring that "there is unanimous support in this House" for the C.A.B.s. Another Conservative member declared: "Among those who are at the forefront of the C.A.B.s in my constituency, there are relatively few . . . who are either members of the Labour party or supporters of C.N.D." The value of the services rendered by volunteers was estimated at £64 million, which on a American scale would translate to $500 million, in that year, the number of volunteers having since doubled.

The ensuing Lovelock Review[180] of the National Association of Citizens' Advice Bureaux found that the C.A.B. "provides exceptionally good value for money."[181] The report felt that C.A.B. activities involving debt counseling and representation before tribunals should be given second place, and defined its publicity function as alerting authorities to facts, as distinct from arousing public opinion a distinction not always easy to observe. It defined the principles of the C.A.B. as impartiality, confidentiality, independence, freedom from charges, and provision of a generalist service, and noted that its reference and training materials—800 items in a four-drawer filing cabinet, supplemented monthly, received universal praise.

The greater conservatism of the local affiliates was attested by their resistance to proposals for addition of a legal-advice function. This proposal was rejected in 1986[182] before finally being accepted in 1993.[183] In 1994 the C.A.B. began to recruit debt advisers.[184]

The extensive training programs for volunteers are described in the 1969 Aves report on Volunteer Workers in the Social Services.[185] Active and successful efforts have been made to recruit volunteers from racial minorities.[186] Sixty percent of persons seeking advice are not working, 11 percent are single parents, 27 percent are black, and 90 percent have below-average income.[187] Three point four percent of volunteers are from ethnic minorities, which make up 5.1 percent of the population, 2.7 percent are disabled persons, and 54 percent are over the age of 55.[188] Approximately 4,000 volunteers are trained each year.

Margaret Wynn, in her 1964 study, "Fatherless Families,"[189] noted another aspect of the advice bureaux that resembles the original C.O.S. design: "[W]e have to act as a family service. Of course we give factual information as well but that's only half the job. Sometimes we are in close touch with mothers—and fathers—for years on end and we fight like tigers to keep children from going into care." Unlike bureaucratic agencies, the advice bureaux are said to offer their clients "the luxury of time to talk," and volunteers are expected to present all options and abstain from revealing their political complexion.

Margaret Brasnett has noted that the advice bureaux have been successfully imitated in many countries. A significant number of bureaux have been established in Ghana and Israel, and the concept has found more limited use in South Africa, Zimbabwe, India, and Guyana. Councils of Social Service in a number of Australian states have also imitated the service.[190] However, the proposals in Alfred J. Kahn's 1966 study of American neighborhood information centers sponsored by the Columbia School of Social Work were stillborn. The American "War on Poverty" was explicit in its favoring of class advocacy over individual casework, and its neighborhood offices were manned by professionals, not volunteers, and devoted themselves to efforts to overthrow rather than to produce conformity with existing social institutions. The prevailing ideology in American programs has stressed legal services rather than social work, and has fostered a culture of complaint rather than constructive endeavor.

The comment of Charles Loch Mowat on the advice bureaux is a just one: "As long as social work is done in the manner of the C.O.S., by casework, and in the spirit of the C.O.S., concern for the individual and the family, the Welfare State will be drawing on the legacy of the Victorians who made the C.O.S. and devoted themselves to its work nearly a century ago."[191]

From the experience of these organizations it is clear that there are functions that can be discharged by organized volunteers at which the state dismally fails, or which it can perform, if at all, only at far greater cost. Much of social casework may be one of those functions. Even staunch defenders of the welfare state have noted the distinctive role that can be played by volunteer organizations.

The institutions we have considered well illustrate this proposition, yet they have no counterparts in the United States. The perverse effects of the American welfare system, unmatched in the world, is in large measure due to the virtual disappearance of casework in its administration. The restoration of the casework tradition that was the C.O.S. ideal, and originally that of the social-work profession that grew out of the C.O.S., is a national imperative, reflected in the recent 1996 welfare-reform legislation requiring an end to "welfare rights, and a return to individualized but disciplined administration."

Professor William H. Simon has noted that "The [welfare] system is now staffed by people who lack both the power and the aspiration to assist claimants . . . the old ideal of frontline administration by professional social workers has been discarded and the small but influential number of social workers in the system at the time of Goldberg have been expelled." The creation or recreation of a casework system will not be easy. As George F. Kennan has observed: "One of the unique features of American government is, in comparison with other modern systems, its neglect of intelligent and discriminating administration."

In the provision of that administration, the organized volunteer has a much larger role than he has been accorded in the recent history of the United States. If Americans are to be summoned to national service, that service is appropriately rendered by true volunteers, not disguised conscripts; in local communities rather than in ideologized national institutions; by adults, not adolescents; and with something approaching what Adlai Stevenson called "the serene commitment of a lifetime," not merely for a season or a year. A corollary of the new approach should be federal, state, or charitable funding of American variants of the C.A.B. designed to provide lay advice in depressed or troubled communities. The financial demands of such institutions are modest, and the need to maintain enthusiasm and consensus among volunteers should operate to limit abuses of the groups by transient majorities. That, at least, has been the experience in Britain.

Law Enforcement

We have come by gentle stages to the ultimate public goods: Those concerned with security and law enforcement. American discussions of law enforcement generally resolve themselves into a dialogue in which one faction urges national-government social programs to combat the alleged causes of crime, while the other seeks more police and harsher laws and sentences. There is, however, a third tradition, seeking to revive past localized institutions, that complements if it does not supplant the other two.

Parochial law enforcement survived in England until the middle of the nineteenth century without the aid of professional police. It should not be forgotten that what enabled it to do so was the fact that "the powers of the vestry over locally administered poor relief and the tendency of local employers to dominate parish office-holding gave the parish sanctions over offenders . . . diminished their dependence upon formal judicial committals."[192] Even then, a critic of the new police legislation could protest that "the only police system that can ever really be efficient, morally and truly, instead of physically and superficially, must be one which is founded on mutual confidence and immediate local responsibility."[193] There is no reason to doubt Disraeli's conclusion: "[The] parochial constitution had already been shaken to its centre by the New Poor Law,"[194] with its elimination of locally dominated parish poor relief.

The Rural Police Act of 1839 made creation of county police optional. By 1853 Edwin Chadwick, originally the greatest advocate of centralization, urged local supervision:

The consultation of local feeling was necessary for the efficient operation of local forces. The County and Borough Police Act of 1856, while compelling all local authorities to set up police forces, vested authority in the petty sessional division, the lowest possible level. County control was not established until the Local Government (County Councils) Act of 1888.[195]

In Massachusetts from the earliest time, constables were elected for terms of one year, and hired substitutes if they could: "They were powerful only insofar as they did what the community wished; they could command compliance only when almost everyone was prepared to give it anyway and so would assist them against any who proved recalcitrant."[196] The basic premise was one of initial private policing: "He that knows the Offence, first of all goes himself to the Offender, and seriously endeavors to bring him to repentance."[197] When law enforcement could only be carried out by the people at large, it could be employed only to enforce rules that enjoyed widespread agreement:[198]

Town discipline in the Revolution resembled nothing so much as church discipline throughout the provincial era. Reform rather than retribution was its primary purpose, because punishment could, at best, purge the community whereas repentance restored its moral integration. . . . Physical force simply could not compare with social sanctions.[199]

The institutions that provided the basis of English and American law enforcement for 600 years, from the Statute of Winchester (1285)[200] until the statute of 1856 requiring all English counties to maintain professional police forces were four: The local constable, appointed in England, elected from small precincts in the United States; the night watch, later supplemented by a day watch, on which in theory all adult males were bound to periodically serve; the neighborhood hue and cry; and the *posse commitatus*, consisting of all males over the age of 15, a variant of the citizen militia established by the Assize of Arms (1181),[201] the antecedent of the "well-regulated militia" of the Second Amendment. As functioning civic institutions, all four of these have fallen into desuetude.

Their replacement by the professional police, initially created by Sir Robert Peel's police act for London in 1829,[202] has recently been ably recounted.[203] These institutions were each and all institutions of direct democracy, nonbureaucratic in nature, and these were the law-enforcement institutions taken for granted at the time of the enactment of the American Constitution and the Bill of Rights. The then best-known alternative to them was the "thorough" dictatorship of the Earl of Stafford, with its standing army quartered on the people; the Constitution and Bill of Rights constituted as much as anything else a series of prohibitions against creation of such an institution on American soil, hence the restrictions on duration of military appropriations and suspension of habeas corpus in the Constitution, the militia clauses of the Constitution and Bill of Rights, and the reservation of powers (including law-enforcement powers) to the states in the Tenth Amendment.[204]

The development of fast means of transportation and communication, the massive migration from rural areas into large cities, and large-scale immigration rendered the old system inadequate, both in the United States and England. The older institutions had as their premise private prosecution; the protections they afforded thus varied sharply with the means of the victim. Hence the rise of the professional police, who we take for granted as instruments of law enforcement, notwithstanding that they were "the kind of hireling body considered dangerous by conventional political theory." There was a felt need for what James Bryce referred to as "a force strong enough to suppress tumults in their first stage" having regard to the fact that "democracy does not secure the good behavior of its worse and newest citizens."[205]

Recent years, however, have seen not merely the dominance of the professional police but early signs of the spontaneous recreation of the earlier institutions. Today nearly 30 percent of the American population lives in residential-community associations with elected officers, a large percentage of which have assumed some security functions.[206] The systematic publicizing of crimes and wanted persons, once confined to the halfhearted posting of wanted posters in post offices, now extends to popular television programs, the sides of shopping bags, and the regular publication of police blotters in neighborhood and metropolitan newspapers.

"Neighborhood watch" groups have appeared in many communities. The ever-more widespread private ownership of firearms for purposes of individual self-defense revives a militia, albeit not a "well regulated" one. Law enforcement might benefit, without peril to liberty, from a more self-conscious organization and exploitation of these tendencies. The four institutions will be discussed in turn.

The Constable

The English constable was an appointed feudal remnant whose archetype in literature was Shakespeare's Constable Dogberry.[207] In his American manifestation he was an elected official, generally selected from a very small district akin to an election precinct. With the rise of professional police he, and his county equivalent, the elected sheriff, have increasingly either been abolished or had their functions restricted to service of civil process. Jefferson's vision of ward government in which an elected constable would be the principal agent of law enforcement in an area of six square miles with a population of 500 has never been realized.

The constable, in his original setting, had his virtues. These were extolled by the English opponents of the legislation of 1829 and 1856 establishing and generalizing the police. Professionals, it was said, make "no appeal to the sympathies of neighborhoods. [They] introduce brute force where moral persuasion ought to prevail. A box on the ear or a stroke or two with an ash plant might be as good as punishment for shaking an apple tree as a regular justicing under Peel's act."[208] In their inception, at least in the United States, the ward police departments were quite decentralized, adjuncts of the ward organization.[209] The recent interest in community policing may belie the prediction in 1977 that there is "little chance that the authorities will reopen the old precincts and restore their former boundaries." These proposals, however, contemplate decentralization of the police bureaucracy rather than recourse to popular institutions.[210] However, the increasing involvement in security matters of the hundreds of thousands of residential-community associations created by the developers of residential subdivisions since the early 1960s has given rise to a new sort of constable—the neighborhood watch or security committee chairman.[211] He too is elected by a local community and is not part of a police bureaucracy. The function of these new institutions is generally preventative in nature; the surveying of street lighting, locks, bars and alarms; the reporting of crimes to the police and to neighbors; and the mounting of watches whose purpose is to deter rather than to apprehend.[212] The instinctive reaction of many to these new developments is to reproach them as a new vigilantism or a recrudescence to the medieval walled town[213] or to express fear that the result will be a withdrawal of support from existing police institutions, or that they represent "a vigilantism of the elite ('haves') against the non-elite ('have nots') . . . the regulation of 'problem' population' by 'stable' ones."

While these warnings are appropriate, so long as the functioning of the residents' patrols is limited to radio-telephone communication with the police, there is an adequate "degree of public regulation of self-policing."[214] It is fair to suggest, on the contrary, that the appropriate reaction should involve an effort to extend these new institutions to established blocks, streets, and housing projects where crime problems are greater, by enactment of state laws authorizing and assisting small street and block associations, giving them powers to assess limited dues and imposts to support their activities.[215] These activities may include street regulation, as with the *woonerf* street associations of The Netherlands and the private street associations of St. Louis, and cooperation in law enforcement.[216] As Robert Dahl has observed: "Personal and political demoralization, apathy, cynicism, alienation are not going to be erased overnight by neighborhood governments or anything else. Yet it would be wrong . . . to deprecate the importance of developing governments more accessible and responsive to the politically weak simply because their initial participation would, foreseeably, be low . . . if we were to abolish democracy wherever substantial segments of the population failed to use their opportunities to participate, there might not be much in the way of rule by the people left standing anywhere in the world."[217]

The Night Watch

The night watch as originally conceived was an uncompensated body drawn by lot from among all adult males. Its desuetude began when the hiring of substitutes was permitted, leading it to be described in its American setting as "a decrepit force of unemployables." With the rise of professional police, any effort to enlist or enforce public participation in law enforcement was abandoned. An "enlightened" *Yale Law Journal* article in 1992 reproached the ten or twelve states that continue to maintain statutes allowing police officers to commandeer the assistance of bystanders.[218]

Yet the inevitability of this decline is far from obvious. "Until well into the nineteenth century volunteer watchmen, not policemen, patrolled their communities to keep order. . . . Their presence deterred disorder or alerted the community to disorder that could not be deterred."[219] The volunteer fire department continues to survive as a social instrumentality in many parts of the country,[220] and its decline in large cities was initially due not to the present need for special training but to the desire for political patronage and the interest of insurance companies (many of which started as fire companies) in being relieved of the costs of upkeep of the volunteer forces. It is said of it that "here the actual physical or social contact with one's neighbors may create or reinforce feelings of empathy. The uniform uncertainty over whose house may catch on fire next guarantees that each will do 'his fair share' with respect to not only fire fighting but possibly other community activities as well."[221]

The Neighborhood Hue and Cry

The recent decline in the perceived effectiveness of law enforcement has given rise to the organization of "neighborhood watch" activities by many of the mostly suburban residential-community associations, and proposals have been made to strengthen such activities through better definition of the power of citizen's arrest and statutory expansion of immunities from suit.[222] To these familiar suggestions one may add others: 1) that contributions or dues to neighborhood associations performing such functions be accorded the same tax deductibility as taxes paid to public bodies; 2) that organization of block and street associations in established neighborhoods and housing projects be facilitated; 3) that individuals participating in such watch functions receive, as did nineteenth-century and some contemporary volunteer firemen, recognition for their service in the form of exemption from other public obligations, such as jury duty;[223] and 4) that functions such as parking enforcement and the provision of school crossing guards be transferred to such bodies where appropriate.[224]

The utility of these watch organizations is primarily deterrent in nature, derived from improved security measures and reporting of crimes and crime suspects, particularly in metropolitan areas where the police are an alien force.[225] The programs have their limits: "[W]e cannot rely too much on voluntary citizen 'self-help,' given the difficulty of controlling citizen use of force and the virtual absence of residents from many neighborhoods during working hours."[226] Moreover, "voluntary association cannot easily be initiated or sustained in poorer, high-crime areas."[227] The increased emphasis on the social organization of housing projects, on concierge systems and concepts of "defensible space"[228] indicates that the relevance of this concept is not confined to the twelfth century.[229]

In its initial form, the hue and cry had as its object the organization of what Jane Austen called "a neighborhood of voluntary spies"[230] and involved shouting, the blowing of horns, and the ringing of church bells. With the advent of the press, these primitive mechanisms for organizing the general chase of an offender were replaced by printed warning and reward notices and directories of wanted criminals of the type outlined in Sir John Fielding's General Prevention Plan of 1772–73. The best-known publications were John Fielding's own broadsheet, the *Hue and Cry*, and Henry Fielding's *Covent Garden Journal*. Lord Mansfield declared in 1783: "How are felons in general taken up? From descriptions of them circulated in handbills."[231]

One of the critics of Peel's police bill observed in 1829, in terms that have continuing resonance: "Complete and speedy publicity of all acts of delinquency would effect far more good without a police than a police could effect without publicity."[232] It has been observed that "during the second half of the nineteenth century, the circulation of information about criminal offenders and offences increasingly became internalized within the police—narrow-casting to an audience of officials." Professional bureaucratic policing as it developed in England was not reconciled with a continuation of the kind of public participation that had underpinned the success of the eighteenth-century crime advertisement. The willingness of victims of property offenses to rely upon the new police and the tendency of the new police themselves to monopolize law enforcement played important roles here. So too, perhaps, did technological developments such as the telegraph, which was more suited to channeling criminal information through a police bureaucracy than to public broadcasting. It has been suggested that the police have used the new technologies of the telegraph, radio, and computer in pursuit of the mirage of instant apprehension of criminals, and at the expense of information-based activities directed at prevention of crime or delayed apprehension.

A great deal has changed since Tocqueville's observation that

> the criminal police of the United States cannot be compared with those of France; the magistrates and public agents are not numerous. Yet . . . in no country does crime more rarely elude punishment. The reason is that everyone conceives himself to be interested in furnishing evidence of the crime and in seizing the delinquent . . . in America he is looked upon as an enemy of the human race, and the whole of mankind is against him.[233]

The advent of new means of information transmission such as the television set and the fax machine has not given rise to significant expansion of use of wanted posters and publications by the police. Yet the public hunger for this sort of information is attested by the fact that virtually all neighborhood newspapers now publish discouragingly long lists of offenses, unaccompanied by any information that would assist in solving them. The publication on shopping bags of pictures of missing children and the advent of television programs depicting wanted criminals are entirely a product of private enterprise. "Privately funded reward policing is probably stronger now than it has been since the nineteenth century."[234] Critics of these programs allege that they constitute private distortion of fears about crime,[235] but this comes about by reason of the failure of public authorities to systematize similar measures.

It is hard to escape the conclusion that a revival of Fielding's *Hue and Cry* would be a useful and beneficial contribution to law enforcement, particularly in the inner-city areas where clearance rates are lowest, the crime problem is greatest, and policing cannot succeed without public participation. Indeed, the mere existence of such a newspaper-type collection of wanted notices might have a significant deterrent effect.[236]

The Posse Commitatus

Unlike the other institutions mentioned, the history of the militia and the origins and scope of the Second Amendment to the Constitution have not been neglected subjects in recent years. The controversy over gun control, however, has generated considerably more heat than light. It is clear, however, that private firearms ownership is now so widespread that any legislation curtailing it, if enforced by means consistent with the Fourth and Fifth Amendments, would have only limited significance in the short term. The fact is that private firearms ownership stems from a loss of confidence in public law enforcement, and that its suppression or curtailment will therefore be difficult.

There would also seem little basis to doubt that in some circumstances the public possession of arms may have political significance. It has been alleged that this was the case with respect to the defense by the anti-federalists of Jefferson's first election victory, and it may be that similar situations could arise under modern conditions. In the language of Madison in the *Federalist* (No. 46):

Besides the advantage of being armed, which the Americans possess over the people of almost every other nation, the existence of subordinate governments, to which the people are attached, and by which the militia officers are appointed, forms a barrier against the enterprises of ambition, more insurmountable than any which a simple government of any form can admit of.

Tocqueville observed: "When the Revolution arrived, it would have been hopeless to seek in the greater part of France for any ten men who were in the habit of acting together in any regular manner and of providing for their own defence."[237]

The evils that flow from widespread gun ownership are twofold: The possession and use of guns by those bent on crime, and numerous accidental homicides or deaths in the course of family quarrels. These sordid events seem far removed from the original political concerns; however, the widespread ownership of firearms undoubtedly operates as a deterrent to store robberies, nighttime burglaries, and other property crimes.

The original American militia law[238] required all males of military age to possess a rifle or musket (or pistol or sword if a member of a cavalry or artillery unit). The concept of a "well-regulated militia" embodied in the Bill of Rights in 1791 reflected George Washington's view that "a free people ought not only to be armed but disciplined."[239] The conception here resembled that of the Swiss militia system in which the universal ownership of military firearms has been found to be not inconsistent with a low homicide rate.[240] By the time of Story's *Commentaries on the Constitution*, there was a "growing indifference to any system of militia discipline."[241] Hamilton in the *Federalist* (No. 29) observed: "Little more can reasonably be aimed at, with respect to the people at large, then to have them properly armed and equipped, and in order to see that this not be neglected, it will be necessary to assemble them once or twice in the course of a year." Even if an expansive view is taken of the Second Amendment, the validity of state regulation of gun owners, if not of gun ownership, would seem unassailable.

Licensing of gun owners is both politically controversial and constitutionally assailable, at least as applied to military rifles, except with respect to felons and others not possessing civil rights. It is possible, however, to conceive of milder measures that would deny the right of ownership to those not subjecting themselves to a training course, with periodic reviews, in firearms safety, in self-defense (including alternatives to firearms use),[242] and in first aid and emergency response. This would be consonant with the original purpose of the Second Amendment and consistent with both its political and self-defense objects. Under this scheme, the acquisition, possession, or use of a firearm by a person who had not completed such a course would be subject to penalties, and those who had completed it would be deemed part of the organized militia, subject to being called to respond to public emergencies. This would recall the ideal of Jefferson's Second Inaugural, with its description of a society "where every man at the call of the law, would fly to the standard of the law and would meet invasions of the public order as his own personal concern." Some experimentation along these lines has been undertaken in which the incentive to participation was not criminal sanctions but the award to participants of decals and certificates the display of which was found to operate as a deterrent to crime.[243] Mention may also be made of the unarmed auxiliary police of New York and other jurisdictions[244] and the Special Constables now called to the aid of the police by the British 1964 Police

Act,[245] which now routinely supplement the force rather than serving as a reserve for emergencies. It is, of course, imperative that "auxiliary policemen should be screened carefully and trained, and the powers permitted them, particularly in the use of weapons, should be limited."[246] A still milder approach, not resembling licensing, would enact a presumption of lack of due care with respect to any suit or prosecution where injury results from firearms use by a person not participating in the training program. While this program would not enlist the support of an existing criminal element, it almost certainly would reduce the incidence of accidental and intrafamily homicides resulting from firearms as well as fostering social solidarity in high-crime neighborhoods and intelligent cooperation with the police. Given the political and legal constraints on firearms regulation, such an effort to discipline, discourage, and partially co-opt those claiming the right to possess firearms has greater promise than the present cosmetic restraints on ownership and sale and may yield a political consensus; the effort may, in time, alter the culture surrounding individual ownership of firearms.

The present political dialogue on law enforcement postulates its problems as involving a balancing of the rights and needs of the isolated individual and the commands and requirements of society, conceived as a bureaucratic state. This suggests the need for reference to a third tradition, one which recognizes that there is "no security except in association and no freedom that did not recognize the obligation of a corporate life"[247] and that calls for continued rediscovery of "the contribution an actively participating public can make to the detection and prevention of criminal offenses."[248]

Totalitarian states have, of course, misused sublocal institutions for law-enforcement purposes, the institutions being controlled and directed from the top down. A partial variant on these systems is the locally elected Ottoman submunicipal unit known as the *mukhtar*, created in 1863, which survives in Turkey, Lebanon, and other Middle Eastern countries, and that has as its function the issuing of vital statistics certificates, the notifying of military conscripts, the aiding of building inspections, the preparing of lists of children of primary school age, identification of diseases, and the informing of police of suspect persons. The *mukhtar* is subject to provincial governments and has no connection with the municipality.[249]

The Paris *arrondisement* system, though now democratized, traditionally involved administration by a maire and three adjuncts who were designees of the central government, and whose functions included vital statistics, election registration, the performance of civil marriages, and registration for the military draft, as well as administration of the former poor laws.[250] The mairies also administered licenses, sold government bonds, and contained branch public libraries, labor exchanges, and branches of the municipal savings-bank system.[251] The police force is also organized on an *arrondisement* basis[252] and "identifies the individual policeman more permanently and closely with a particular neighborhood than is customary in any American city."[253] The vice squads, the usual controller of corruption, "is entirely distinct, in its organization and work, from the patrol system." This system conforms to the ideal voiced in an earlier time by Joshua Toulmin Smith: "No stranger ought to be allowed, except for very special reasons, to be employed as peace-keeper in any districts."[254]

It has been urged that with respect to police patrol activities,

small jurisdictions may well be able to supply superior services (in terms of citizen satisfaction) than large jurisdictions . . . in those areas of police services where economies of scale are more likely (police training and crime laboratories) only the large central-city departments operate their own facilities . . . subfunctions of a public service can most efficiently be provided by different-sized organizations.[255]

This premise informs the French legislation of January 1983 that allows the 25,000 French communes, which typically have populations of barely a thousand, to establish their own police. These have primarily a crime-prevention function, but are trained and uniformed and have some arrest powers.[256]

Any devolution of law-enforcement related activities to a sublocal level requires careful regulation to ensure that the ability to adjudicate and punish remains in the hands of more detached and neutral officers. This should also apply in most situations involving arrest powers and the use of deadly force. Assumption of security functions by an RCA or neighborhood association should not be undertaken except with a large consensus. These limitations, however, do not vitiate the need for and utility of sublocal activity in target-hardening, discouraging and reporting crime, monitoring higher-level law enforcement, and assisting in reintegrating offenders into the community. Because of the benefit to property and property values of these activities, they are appropriately funded by property assessments, aided in poorer neighborhoods by inverse-wealth grants from higher levels of government.

Probation

In today's America, supervision of probationers and parolees is carried out by harried bureaucrats, employees of a state or national government.

Yet in underdeveloped countries, probation services have sometimes placed offenders under the care of traditional elders or village leaders.[257]

In developed countries, extensive use has at times been made of citizen volunteers as probation officers, who in earlier times were frequently clergymen. In Britain, probation was originally provided for by the Probation of First Offenders Act of 1887, enacted at the instance of police-court missionaries. Although employment of some full-time workers was provided for by the Probation of Offenders Act of 1907, that statute was worked almost entirely by volunteers. By 1922, there were 784 volunteer workers. A departmental committee reporting in that year[258] recommended that they be superseded by a professional service, which was accomplished by the Criminal Justice Act of 1925. Later, a reaction set in against complete bureaucratization of the service. In 1957, one of the early evangelical volunteers recalled that "the volunteer probation officer of the old days was a private citizen, who interviewed his cases in a private house or a church vestry. The delinquent did not feel on such premises the restraint that inhibits him when he makes his fortnightly visit to a room in the court building, or to an office that looks like a department of a public organization.[259] The reintroduction of volunteers followed the Reading Report in 1967.[260] By 1978, volunteers were being more widely used;[261] their expanded use was promoted by the Home Office in 1984 and 1991.[262] As of 1980, volunteers were being used in all regions of the British probation service and numbered more than 5,000. In 1985 a survey indicated that there was approximately one volunteer for each probation officer in the British service. About 56 percent of volunteers were women. More recently, the Conservative government, instead of pursuing the devolution of probation to church and community groups and parish councils, has entertained proposals for the "contracting out" of probation to private-sector managers.[263]

The British and American[264] use of probation volunteers is limited compared to that in other countries, including Denmark (194 officers, 1,000 volunteers, supervising 45 percent of the caseload),[265] Austria (189 officers, 579 volunteers, supervising 25 percent of the caseload),[266] Sweden, and Japan. In Sweden, for example, Becker and Hjellemo (1976) reported an average of 92 clients and 48 volunteers for each probation officer[267] [another study indicates that 9,000 volunteers handle 75 percent of the caseload];[268] and Hess (1970)[269] described the Japanese system where the average field officer's main responsibilities surrounded coordinating the work of approximately 65 volunteers each working with about four clients,[270] there being in all more than 56,000 volunteers. In France, there is less use of volunteers (476 officers and 770 volunteers), but institutions may serve as volunteers, and use is made of chapters of the Croix Bleue (anti-alcohol league), the Red Cross, the Secours Catholique, and the Emmaus Community.[271]

At least in the former Soviet Union it was common to parole offenders to work units, such as factories or collective farms.[272] In the juvenile probation area, the only area in which probation volunteers (in so-called "Big Brother" programs) have been extensively used in the United States, suggestions have been made for parole of juvenile offenders to inner-city church and community groups.[273] Assumption of such responsibilities by community organizations should require a large supermajority, and their powers as probation officers should be supervised either by a public probation officer, a court, or both. The association might be given the power to petition a court to revoke probation or to request a public officer to do so. Because of the external benefits and the concentration of the need in poorer neighborhoods, funding should probably take the form of either a voucher for each probationer or project grants from higher levels of government (the state, in the U.S. context).

Neighborhood Councils

Recent years have seen the creation of few new general-purpose local governments in America. Reformers are generally consolidationists: there is much "educated" clamor for metropolitan government, and little for neighborhood government. A different tendency obtains in Western Europe, where the limitations of bureaucracy are now more keenly appreciated by the political class, including that in the left-wing parties. Recently, however, in response to felt need, new business-improvement districts and neighborhood-improvement districts have been given significant authority, though nothing approaching complete home rule.

The politics of a multipurpose organization such as a parish or neighborhood council are apt to be more complex than those of a single-purpose organization such as a self-governing school: "If there are a variety of dimensions—some individuals are liberal on some issues and conservative on others—then the median voter is not well defined and there may be no equilibrium to the political process."[274] The Tiebout hypothesis about selection of preferred levels of public services through mobility operates best when "relative to the size of the population, (1) the number of public goods is small and/or (2) the number of distinct preferences for combinations of public goods is small."[275]

An Italian law of 1976 provides for local councils in cities with more than 40,000 persons.[276] In Germany, 60 of 71 municipalities with more than 95,000 persons have directly elected neighborhood councils.[277] Twenty Swedish municipalities have such neighborhood councils pursuant to a 1980 act.[278] The Dutch Municipal Law of 1964 provides for neighborhood councils whose members are selected by the city council from party lists, as does recent Norwegian legislation.[279]

The competing factors militating for and against the creation of sublocal governments have been summarized:

> On the one hand, there is the administrative perspective with an emphasis on efficient production of collective goods, internalization of externalities and economies of scale, all of which prescribe the largest possible political units. On the other hand, there is the classic political perspective on public activity which emphasizes a different notion of efficiency: effective allocation of goods to local constituents, sensitivity to differing preferences among constituent groups, awareness of the discrepancy between theoretic and actual access to public goods, and appreciation of the political payoff of decentralization as a response to inequities in the spatial distribution of public goods.[280] Formal explicit agreements to bring about cooperative behavior are required only for groups that are large, diverse and mobile.[281]

The importance of multiplying elective offices was stressed by Tocqueville:

> The circumstance which most contributed to secure the independence of private persons in aristocratic ages was that the supreme power did not affect to take upon itself alone the government and administration of the community. Those functions were necessarily partly left to the members of the aristocracy; so that, as the supreme power was always divided, it never weighed with its whole weight and in the same manner on each individual. . . . At a period of equality like our own, it would be unjust and unreasonable to institute hereditary officers, but there is nothing to prevent us from substituting elective public officers to a certain extent. Election is a democratic expedient, which ensures the independence of the public officer in relation to the government as much as hereditary rank can secure it among aristocratic nations, perhaps even more so.[282] Thus "a nation may establish a free government, but without municipal institutions it cannot have the spirit of liberty."[283]

One piece of data supporting all forms of devolution is a striking one:

> Among industrialized countries, federal countries tend to have the lowest total tax ratios (Australia, Switzerland, the United States) and they tend to increase the least (Germany, the United States). Of the ten countries that currently have the highest total tax ratios, only Austria in eighth place has a federal form of government.[284]

Dennis Mueller has noted the further benefits of direct as opposed to representative forms of democracy at lower levels of government:

The use of a representative form of government changes the nature of the political outcomes substantially, making government considerably larger than it would be if citizens directly determined outcomes. Moreover, in those Swiss municipalities in which representative democracy exists, the size of government is smaller if the citizens have the right to call a referendum and thereby reverse a government decision.[285]

In the late 1960s, American proponents of neighborhood government sought to have it both ways in that they were at one with their critics in resisting a parochial scale of organization. Although they talked of neighborhood autonomy, what they meant was that cities should be divided into boroughs like those in Greater London or Metropolitan Toronto. The advocates of double-tiered government wanted to show that it was consistent with large-scale administration, so by opting for big units they were able to avoid what they saw as the key criticism against creating a second level of local government.[286]

But it has been questioned whether there are any economies at all in large-scale municipalities. One of the most eminent of American political scientists, Robert Dahl, has observed:

In post-industrial society, the giant city becomes an obsolescent, unnecessary, and crippling habitat that persists less because of need than from inertia, sunk costs, a failure of imagination, and a lack of audacity.[287] Studies have failed to turn up any significant economies in city government attributable to larger size. The few items on which increasing size does lead to lower unit costs, such as water and sewerage, are too small a proportion of total city outlays to lead to significant economies. Even these are probably offset by rising costs for other services, such as police protection.[288]

In Massachusetts, "for a variety of jurisdictions ranging from those of fence-viewers . . . to those of the militia companies, towns were divided into districts so that men might serve only close to home, where they might derive benefit directly while they did their duty."[289]

Michael Hechter has defined from a sociologist's perspective the control mechanisms most productive of group solidarity. Some of these, such as limits on privacy and rewards for informants, most democrats will find repellent. Most of the other devices commonly employed to reinforce group solidarity arise almost automatically in small, residentially defined constituencies. These include architectural proximity, public rituals, specific obligations, consensual decision-making, effective positive sanctions such as public praise, group rewards arising from common-property interests, gossip, transparency arising from homogeneity of the group, utility of symbolic and public sanctions, and significant exit costs.[290]

Robert Axelrod has similarly urged: "Here is the argument in a nutshell. The evolution of cooperation requires that individuals have a sufficiently large chance to meet again so that they have a stake in their future interaction."[291]

When local government districts are used as units of provision, there is a strong case for small and homogeneous districts. It has been said of Northern Ireland that the districts created in 1973 are too large and religiously too heterogeneous to avoid the cleavages found in Northern Ireland as a whole if their councils were to be given responsibilities of any import. . . . A democratic local-government system with significant powers and based upon small, religiously homogeneous districts would not have solved all of Ulster's problems. But, even if only in a small way, it could have been a start.[292] Dennis Mueller, a public-choice writer, has similarly urged "drawing Federalist political boundaries to separate the cultural groups that feel hostility toward one another."[293] This is what was purposefully not done in Yugoslavia, with sanguinary results. "The more heterogeneous a nation, the more it [should] be expected to define a loose decentralized set of political institutions."[294]

This insight is lost on American supporters of metropolitan government, who indulge the illusion that race relations will be improved by the creation of large heterogeneous districts in which inner cities will seek redistribution of local resources from more prosperous areas. Under modern economic conditions, with high mobility of industry, to be effective, redistribution must be carried out at a level of government higher than a metropolitan area.

There are more abstract reasons for believing that political performance may be superior in very small units: information and voting costs are less and the returns from acquiring them greater than in large units. Anthony Downs has observed, in explanation of low voting turnouts:

Political information is valuable because it helps citizens make the best possible decisions. . . . However, every rational citizen discounts . . . when deciding what data to acquire because his voice [in large units] is only one among the many that make the decision . . . returns must be drastically reduced to accord with the infinitesimal role which each citizen's vote plays in deciding the election. As a result, the returns are so low that many rational voters refrain from purchasing any political information per se. Instead they rely upon free data acquired accidentally. . . .[295]

The consolidation of communes carried out in Sweden during 1969–74 reduced the number of communal representatives by 100,000. This gave rise to efforts to compensate for this loss by allowing the communes to arrange advisory referenda and by considering "further extension of the system of boards to include such smaller communal administrative units as individual schools, old age homes, and hospitals."[296]

Self-administered institutions are not fully satisfactory as substitutes for neighborhood-based general-purpose government. There are limits to the public attention that can be generated for a multitude of separate elections,[297] except those for schools, which have their own easily defined constituency and whose funding requirements sharply differ from those of property-maintaining governments. The observations of Gomme a century ago are still pertinent:

> The area formed by the common interests of a community for centuries back in the past is the true locality within which common benefit from new functions of local government will best operate. They will weld with the functions already in existence for the common benefit, and produce further cement for the binding together of the community.[298]

The scale of most of the Western European sublocal governments within large cities would appear excessive; parish-level institutions with 500 to 3,000 persons, such as the American RCA or French commune may furnish a better model. These can concern themselves with all the matters listed above with the exception of schools and land readjustment, with funding through a devolved share of the property tax, supplemented by user charges and inverse-wealth formula grants from higher levels of government, and checks provided by an appropriate combination of the political devices discussed below. A student of the contemporary French commune has noted:

> The extraordinary vitality of the rural communes, even the smallest ones. Three-quarters of France's 36,000 communes have fewer than 1,000 inhabitants, and their budgets are scarcely enough to pay the salary of one local worker. . . . However, even the smallest communes can partially overcome the problems relating to their size by forming themselves into syndicates with other similar communes, which ensure basic municipal services, such as waste disposal and provision of water. Moreover, communes have at least one major trump card in their dealings with outside authorities, or private sector interests . . . planning permission for public- or private-sector developments. . . . The vitality of local government and of civic participation at the microlevel of public affairs is one of the salient features of contemporary France. The importance of such microparticipation can be seen in all areas of French life. It can be compared with the disillusionment felt by many French people toward France's great national institutions. It can also be contrasted with the decline in activism in virtually all other areas of public and civic life. The great social movements which emerged after

May 1968, such as feminism, the ecological movement, and regionalism have all declined in importance, almost to the point of extinction. Fewer and fewer French people identify with the great national institutions of the past, or with the social movements inspired by May 1968. They identify far more with their localities, and are more willing to participate in local public affairs than ever before. Surveys show that there is no contradiction between local activism and participation or interest in national politics. On the contrary, whatever their social and professional category, those who are involved in local affairs tend to be more interested in local politics than those who are not. The renewed vitality of local life is a fundamental feature of the new French society.[299]

Swiss communes successfully retain even more extensive powers, encompassing conduct of elections, law enforcement, primary schooling, social and welfare services, local planning, and public transport.[300]

Even where small local entities deliver services themselves rather than hiring contractors who compete in the private market, significant competitive advantages are reaped. In the words of Joseph Stiglitz:

Local communities can respond to local variability more effectively than centralized control. . . . The opportunities for political participation and choice (voice and exit) provided by local communities are of value themselves in a democratic society. Even if voters have limited incentives for insuring that the public good is pursued, local administrations have incentives for demonstrating innovativeness and efficiency. (These incentives are still only loosely related to the preferences of their constituents, but similar arguments apply to firm managers.)[301]

PRIVATE GOODS

We now discuss types of good that individuals and families can provide for themselves at their own cost, without "free-rider" problems, but as to which there are great benefits to be derived from neighborhood cooperation: services to the very young, the very old, and their caretakers. As the Secretary of the British National Association of Parish Councils observed:

Our towns are declining into a characterless jumble of compromises with the traffic. Children still play on the pavements while their mothers go to work. Old people still live in lonely resignation. This multiplicity of problems of happiness is terribly important. Only voluntary and religious effort has hitherto done much about it. Now the local councils may be able to come in too. Is this a negligible or light thing?[302]

Old Age Clubs

When the elderly are discussed in current American politics, it is as passive recipients of government bounty in the form of social security, ERISA benefits, medicare, and medicaid. The "progressive" position is entirely defensive in character: variations on the theme "don't let them take it away." The rising proportion of the old in the population produces an assumption that the politics of aging involve only discussion of the nature and degree of retrenchment.

But it is possible to do better than this, as other countries have recognized. New neighborhood institutions hold the promise of less impersonal as well as more economical services, and a renewed concern with fraternity as well as equality with respect to a sector of the population conspicuous in the United States for its social isolation. The present writer has suggested elsewhere that it is no longer appropriate, if it ever was, to have land-use regulations that zone the elderly into the next county, and that the promotion of accessory apartments and "granny flats" may give the forgotten "babushka" a new social function. It is here also worth emphasizing that the old should have a role, not only in care of the young, but in care of one another.

The elderly tend to be persons of limited mobility. This is particularly true of the portion of the elderly most in need of care. Because most old or infirm people are ill or immobile only a portion of the time and are in need of constructive activity, considerable scope exists for organizing the delivery of many types of social services by the use of mutual-aid groups. Among services that can be thus organized are meals on wheels, domestic cleaning and local transportation, and services designed to periodically check on the health and welfare of the infirm and to provide companionship. These can provide a means of avoiding, or at least drastically postponing, the need for highly expensive institutionalization. One of the stronger critics of "public-choice" proposals, Peter Self, has conceded that "voluntary bodies in particular have a distinctive contribution to make in the care of the sick, old, and handicapped provided too much is not expected from their efforts."[303] Such services, which vary among individual recipients, are plainly not public goods in the economic sense. Even though the geographic immobility of the client population could be deemed as causing them to be excludable goods, literal exclusion of other providers of services to the elderly would scarcely be deemed consistent with civil liberty. Rather, such services are ordinary private goods in the organization and rendition of which neighborhood associations possess some important competitive advantages.

The Japanese have carried this approach further than any other country. These changes were a response to felt need: an unusual graying of the population resulting from Japan's low wartime and postwar birth rate. At its peak (in 2020), the old age population of Japan is estimated to reach 18.8 percent. The peak old-age populations then projected for Western countries was much lower: 14.1 percent in Britain (in 1980), 16.1 percent in Sweden (in 1990), and 13.7 percent in France (in 2000).[304] Subsequent improvements in life expectancy have caused some to estimate that the proportion of aged in Japan may go as high as 24 percent by 2025. The population over 65 is estimated to increase from ten million in 1979 to 26 million in 2020. The ratio of productive age population (15 to 64) to the elderly is projected to decline from 7.5:1 in 1980 to 3.3:1 in 2020. At the same time, Japan has been beset by many of the same disintegrating influences on family structure as the West, including greater mobility, a rising divorce rate, and the large-scale entry of women into the labor force.

The Japanese system was formalized by a Law Governing Volunteer Workers in Welfare Services in the early 1970s and by related policy changes throughout the 1980s, and has had two major components: Use of volunteer workers organized on a neighborhood basis, and the organization of Old Age Clubs for mutual assistance. Government response to the projected problem also has included curtailments in health-care expenditures designed to increase the already high savings rate and efforts to affirmatively promote the extended family and neighborhood institutions. The elderly must now bear a portion of the cost of hospitalization. Tax credits are allowed to family members caring for the elderly. The government actively promotes "a land policy aimed at pressing for three family generations to live in the same place or for family members to live within easy reach," and provides government loans for home remodeling in order that an elderly person may join the household.[305] Similar policies have been pursued in the allocation of public housing in Singapore, which gives "priority for nearby flats for members of the same family, to preserve the extended family structure, thereby ensuring care for the elderly."[306]

The basic premise of Japanese policy toward the elderly is that they "are expected to provide for themselves," with the aid of family members. Government administrators have built upon two preexisting institutions: The voluntary welfare worker, or *minsei-iin*, who numbered about 15,000 by 1930, and old age clubs, a development of the 1950s.[307]

As late as 1988, a five-country study revealed that while only 3 percent of Americans over the age of 60 wanted to live with their children, 58 percent of the Japanese expected to do so. For this reason, nursing-home care, except for very short stays in acute cases for people without relatives, is little developed in Japan, and recent government spending has focused on day-care centers and home-health services. As of 1980, 70 percent of persons over the age of 60 lived with children, as against 28 percent in the United States and 42 percent in Britain.[308]

Under the Law Governing Volunteer Workers, *minsei-iin* are appointed for three-year terms and are assigned to separate districts, where their task is to identify those in need of welfare services and to promote and foster community organizations. In a representative Japanese city of 244,000, there are said to be 344 *minsei-iin*, collectively carrying out work that would require 140 paid officials. Each was recruited by recommendations from neighborhood associations, though formally appointed by the prefectural governor. (This sort of Japanese practice, ironically, was an import from the Elberfeld system in Germany, current when Albert Mosse did his consulting work for the Meiji government in the 1880s.[309]) The volunteers typically call on elderly people and inquire of neighborhood organizations and storekeepers to identify those who have problems, and remind the elderly of the availability of free annual medical examinations and x-rays. They arrange for attendance at day centers and for home-health care and other benefits. These neighborhood leaders do not supply the sole route to local services, and do not function as political bosses.[310]

Old age clubs are organized by the *minsei-iin* to create networks of friends who can visit one another other when someone is sick, call a doctor in time of need, and run errands. The involvement of the elderly in club activities also provides respites for younger caretakers. The *minsei-iin* attend meetings once a month called by the district Council to explain regulations and programs and receive suggestions and complaints, including complaints about particular cases. *Minsei-iin* receive no compensation other than reimbursement of expenses, but they are regarded as civic dignitaries and treated as such. Typically they are women in their fifties.

The old age clubs, or *roojinkai*, have been fostered as a matter of government policy. The percentage of persons over the age of 60 participating in them is said to have increased from 12.8 percent in 1962 to 47.2 percent in 1973. Among their functions are the organization of trips, social events, and hobby clubs, the maintenance of community rooms, lobbying for local improvements such as changes in bus routes, and organizing the receipt of certain city health services, such as free medical massages, quarterly health classes at which the elderly are instructed in diet and exercise and taught to measure blood pressure, and above all mutual aid, particularly to those who are ill. A similar organization of mutual aid groups at block level using social workers was carried out as a matter of government policy in Hong Kong, the number of mutual-aid committees increasing from 1,214 to 3,132 between 1973 and 1980.[311]

Because the *minsei-iin* are volunteers and there are few professional social workers and because the old age clubs are not precluded from engaging in neighborhood advocacy, the system is not one involving rigid top-down government control. Old age clubs receive approximately 60 percent of their financial support from membership dues and contributions, roughly 20 percent from neighborhood associations, and roughly 20 percent from the city, administering funds provided by the Ministry of Health and Welfare. Since annual dues approximate ¥2,500 per year ($25), the amounts provided by government are exceedingly modest, perhaps $10 per member. Yet the availability of this modest subsidy was a large inducement to the expansion of old age clubs in the 1960s and 1970s. The quid pro quo for the subsidies was the conversion of the clubs from purely recreational entities to organizations providing health and education classes.

The lessons for American policy are obvious. Yet the emphasis of American lobbies for the elderly such as the American Association of Retired Persons (A.A.R.P.) has been on the defense of national government benefits rather than the creation of local institutions to take up the slack as demographic pressures cause those benefits to contract.

It would be difficult, given present Western rates of female labor-force participation, to recruit a comparable cadre of volunteers or to give them meaningful authority and honorific positions where they are being supervised by a large social-work profession. However, it could and should be government policy to recruit part-time assistants through the use of modest stipends, and to foster the self-organization of old age clubs. This might be fostered in two ways: 1) by widespread distribution, to millions of elderly, of guides to establishing such organizations, including samples of bylaws, lists of possible activities, and listings of government and private organizations in positions to provide further resources to interested clubs, particularly those relating to health maintenance and home care; and 2) by providing a very small tax deduction or credit for the first $50 or $100 in dues paid to such organizations. The cost of this would be extremely modest. Assuming 30 million elderly, 12 million of whom participated in clubs, a $50 deduction in the United States would cost about $240 million, but would do much to foster organizations of great social value.

Other countries have recognized the appropriateness of delivering some forms of care to the elderly through very local entities. Primary health care in Sweden is partly delivered by neighborhood councils, some of which have budgets in seven figures.[312] Sweden also has made extensive use of "institution boards" attached to day-care and recreational centers and old age homes that provide representation for clients and consumers.[313] There have been experiments with "parish wardens" for the elderly in Britain.[314] It has been said of Western countries in general that in the organization of health services, "only preventive medicine has normally depended on local government."[315] In France, the nineteenth-century system of poor relief relied heavily on neighborhood volunteer visitors organized at the *arrondisement* level in Paris and at the level of the commune in rural France.[316] Similar arrangements obtained at the *bezirke* level in Berlin, and other German cities; in Berlin service of designated persons on a relief committee was compulsory, with refusal of this civic distinction resulting in increased taxes and possible loss of civil rights.[317]

These groupings of the elderly raise neither the problem of majority oppression nor that of unequal finance. They are logically funded, as in Japan, by a modest central government tax credit, which could be a refundable credit or voucher for those below tax thresholds. The subject matter of the committees' work is nonadversarial and little attention therefore needs to be given to their internal voting regimes.

Playgroups

Observers of a series of carefully orchestrated White House conferences will have gained the impression that the only road to progress for preschool children is found in central or state-government provision of institutional day-care, a cause that has its partisans among feminists and public-employee unions. Both these interest groups contemplate with equanimity a condition in which 55 percent of mothers—as against 31 percent in 1970—enter the workforce while their children are still under a year old. American political rhetoric on this issue has been dominated by demands for emulation of the French or Swedish systems of crèches and day-care, although Professor Barbara Babcock, a promoter of the Swedish system, has conceded that its costs are such that the resulting taxation gives mothers no choice but to follow the feminist agenda by entering the workforce: They must be "forced to be free." Although promoters of this agenda express concern for the quality of care of children of the poor, it is noteworthy that the percentage of female labor-force participation is highest among the professional classes. A reaction against their demands has set in, manifesting itself in the 1990 legislation providing tax credits for caretakers of small children and the more recent family tax credit.

Here also there is a middle way through neighborhood organization between those demanding expanded government programs and those trusting to undisturbed private ordering. Preschool children are another local and immobile group. The use of small, highly local entities to deliver services to them is feasible. In Britain, preschool playgroups, voluntary agencies receiving small amounts of central government or local assistance, provide services to about 40 percent of 3 and 4 year olds. Although advocates of public provision of such services speak glibly of "market failure," in fact, day-care is not a public good, since it varies as between individual recipients. As with care of the elderly, any attempt to exclude others, particularly parents, from its rendition runs athwart of important civil liberties. Once again, we are confronted with an ordinary market good in the rendition of which neighborhood associations may have some competitive advantages: Preexisting means of communication among neighbors (newsletters, mailing lists), control of physical facilities that are possible meeting places, knowledge of their personnel, and confidence in their mode of governance. The alleged lack of supply of such goods exists only because of an exceptionally rapid change in demand, fueled by changing demography and mores, including an explosion of single-parent families and new vocational expectations on the part of women. The removal of regulatory and information barriers to cooperative forms of provision is a more appropriate role for government than efforts to provide monopoly or near-monopoly state services either by alteration of the compulsory education age or through increased taxation to supply private day care for two-earner families.

In 1961, the British National Association of Pre-School Playgroups (P.P.A.) (now the Pre-School Learning Alliance) was formed by private initiative—a letter from an affected mother, Belle Tutaev, to the *Manchester Guardian* soliciting the cooperation of others similarly situated. By 1968, 3,000 such groups existed, providing services to children from 2¹/₂ to 5 years old, usually for one day per week. These groups function with supervisors, three-quarters of whom are paid, and with unpaid volunteer helpers selected from parents with children in the classes on a rotation system. By 1987 all but 30 percent of the groups had at least one paid worker, with the average number employed being 2.8; approximately 45,000 paid workers were employed in all, most of them on a part-time basis at an average wage per session of £4.64, or about £1.85 per hour. Rates in London are about 50 percent higher.[318]

The playgroups conduct their own fundraising, liaison with local authorities, parents' meetings, and training courses. Many groups are said to include some children who cannot afford fees. A book published by the P.P.A. urges organizers to meet with a playgroup leader, the local representative of the P.P.A., the headmistress of the local elementary school, the Social Services Area Officer, the local health visitor, the landlord, and a general-practitioner physician.[319] Local health inspections are said to focus on space, lavatory and washing facilities, and the safety of stairs, steps, and heating. Operators must meet the legal requirements for childminders if the playgroup is located in a home and those for nurseries if it is located elsewhere.[320] Most children attend playgroups for two or three half-day sessions a week, though there are now about 1,336 (1992–93) playgroups offering extended hours for working mothers.[321]

Since enactment of the Childrens and Young Persons' Act of 1963, local authorities have been empowered to make direct grants to voluntary agencies. Impetus was given to the expansion of nursery education by the Plowden Report: Children and Their Primary Schools in 1968. This recommended replacement of the policy discouraging nursery education that had prevailed since 1933 except in wartime, with a policy favoring the establishment of half-day nursery groups: "Our evidence is that it is generally undesirable, except to prevent a greater evil, to separate mother and child for a whole day in the nursery." Under this principle not more than 15 percent of nursery places would be full time in nature, and in their allocation "mothers who cannot satisfy the authority that they have exceptionally good reasons for working should have low priority." Charges for nurseries were recommended by an eight-member minority, including the chairman, to prevent "injustices between parents who do not choose to make use of nursery schools and those who do." The Report recommended that playgroups be assisted as an interim measure and that the Department of Education inspect them and approve their staff training. Lady Plowden was president of the P.P.A. in 1972, declaring: "It is time for those who are planning . . . nursery expansion to look at the achievements of the playgroup movement."

A lone dissent by Mrs. M. Bannister recommended the policy that was ultimately adopted for reasons of cost. She criticized nursery education as "disrupting the mother, child, and sibling relationship" and urged that playgroups rather than nurseries be encouraged except in "educational priority areas." The provision of large numbers of nursery teachers would divert talent from the nursing and teaching professions at a time when the pool of available single women was declining. Concluding, she declared that nursery education "does little to enable mothers to participate in the early school experiences of their children. The mothers' loneliness and boredom are also major social problems which play centers and groups might help to solve."[322]

The Conservative government of the early 1990s was "committed to the continuation of a range of provision that will meet a variety of needs, in both the public and private sectors."[323] The Labour successor government is more sympathetic to government grants rather than vouchers as a means of delivering services, but it is not hostile to the maintenance of playgroups. The Seebohm report (Report of the Committee on Local Authority and Allied Personal Services [1968][324] recommended that the power to subsidize and inspect playgroups be vested in social service rather than education departments.

By 1994 there were more than 19,000 playgroups, including at least 4,828 mother-and-toddler groups. Two-thirds of the groups were organized under church or community auspices; 29 percent were private, some profit-making. In 1991 the average fee was said to be £1.51 for a 2–3 hour session. Half the groups offered some free places to children with special needs. While 67 percent of the groups had no Afro-Caribbean members and another 28 percent were less than half Afro-Caribbean, only 11 percent of London playgroups had no Afro-Caribbean or Asian members.[325] By 1992–93 the number of subsidized places was about 13,000. Total enrollment exceeded 800,000 in 1994. Approximately 230,000 of the children attending the playgroups were from families whose incomes derived from state benefits, a result made possible by low playgroup fees. Only about one-third of playgroups (but three-fourths of those in London) received external funding, this funding amounting to about 10 percent of the budgets of the groups receiving it, or less than 5 percent of the national expenditure by the groups, which totaled approximately £250 million.[326] In 1988 there 10 regional associations, 42 county associations, and 430 branches.[327]

In 1990, the report of the Rumbold Committee (the Committee of Inquiry into the Quality of the Educational Experience Offered to 3- and 4-Year Olds) found that the proportion of children from the managerial and professional groups in playgroups in 1988 was about 27 percent, as against 10 percent of children from semi-skilled and unskilled manual backgrounds. These discrepancies were in some measure offset by the fact that 16 percent of the semi-skilled group, but only 11 percent of the professional group, attended maintained nursery schools, an additional 6 percent of the professional group attending private nursery schools. Any view of playgroups as elite institutions is also dispelled by the fact that 23 percent of children of skilled nonmanual workers and 20 percent of those of skilled manual workers attend them.

By 1994 nursery education was a major political issue in Britain. The Liberal party estimated the cost of full provision of nurseries to all 3 and 4 year olds at £900 million, in addition to initial capital costs of £1.5 billion and £50 million in training costs. The recurring costs were equal to the yield of an additional one half of 1 percent of income tax. It was estimated that in 1994 28 percent of British 3–4 year olds were in nurseries, 21 percent in school reception classes, and 40 percent (42.7 percent in 1995) in playgroups. Central government subsidies to playgroups amounted to barely £1 million, or £1.50 per child. The P.P.A.'s formal training programs provided recognized credentials in child care and education, and the P.P.A. trained local authority nursery personnel in Kent,[328] having previously provided training to trainees referred by the Manpower Services agency. The P.P.A. offered a foundation course of 120[329] hours with approximately 8,200 students annually for playleaders stressing child development, educational play, and group organization, and awarding an attendance certificate but not giving examinations. Shorter courses of from 10 to 25 hours were given annually to approximately 30,000 parents. More elaborate courses of from 40 to 240 hours, followed by some local civil-service examinations, were provided to about 1,200 group organizers.[330] The P.P.A. developed elaborate accreditation schemes, launched in November 1992 for full-day playgroups and intended to be extended to sessional playgroups, and received a Department of Education grant for 19 additional training officers.[331] Its curriculum, published in 1991, was tailored to the requirements of Key Stage 1 of the national curriculum and was approved by the Department of Education.

The annual cost of ten sessions per week in a playgroup was estimated at £420 per year in 1987, as against £1039 in a nursery class and £1,500 in nursery school.[332]

In 1995, the Conservative government's proposals for nursery education provided for £1,100 vouchers for nursery education for 4 year olds to be distributed to parents, first in pilot districts and then nationally. Proposals to reimburse playgroups at half this rate were amended to provide full reimbursement, the bill passing in 1996. This approach has not escaped controversy, with feminist critics taking the view that playgroups are "facilities on the cheap, incorporating the unpaid labor of mothers themselves."[333]

The movement has spread to several other countries including The Netherlands, where playgroups for 2 and 3 year olds in 1986 enrolled 132,520 children in 3,313 playgroups, or 38 percent of the relevant population, and Ireland, where it is estimated that playgroup participants number approximately 20,000 in about 1,500 groups, 185 of them Gaelic speaking, and enroll about 15 percent of the relevant cohort.[334] The Dutch system, unlike the British, is heavily subsidized by the government. The 1989 New Zealand budget provided for vouchers for nursery care, usable at playgroups.[335] Similar mechanisms for cooperative day-care known as *anganwadi* have been created as a matter of government policy in India:

> Each center is staffed by a trained *anganwadi* worker who is usually recruited from the local community; she is assisted by volunteer helpers, most of whom are the mothers of children. The anganwadi workers are supervised by para-professional staff under the direction of the Child Development Project Officer who is usually a professionally qualified social worker.[336]

Even in Sweden, where state nursery provision is highly developed, recent years have seen the

> emergence of parental child-care cooperatives which by the end of 1992 involved about 25,000 children or some 6 percent of all child-care amenities. This type of care emerged in response to a shortage of child-care amenities and also because parents wanted to have a say in the organization of child care. Similar user cooperatives mainly in caring services for the elderly and disabled are now growing up in many municipalities.[337]

Day-care, and particularly cooperative day-care, is a civic amenity that lends itself to organization at the sublocal level and that is likely to call forth the amount of resident energy necessary to become effective. It is significant that a recent study negatively assessing the amount of civic energy generated by covenant-created village boards in a "new town" has identified day-care as the primary area in that such associations have been active.[338] Once again, this is a service which lends itself either to voucher funding, on the British pattern, or funding through a central-government tax credit, as already partially provided for in the United States. The internal governance of playgroups is provided for by model bylaws issued by the P.P.A. and its American analogues; there is no reason for the groups to be attached to local or sublocal governments; they probably function best as free-standing groups, with the government role confined to vouchers and subsidies and publicity to facilitate organization.

Local Transportation

The social isolation of the elderly and of many housewives and young people has not been a matter exciting great political interest in the United States: Lives of quiet desperation are just that. There have been expensive federal programs aimed at providing public transportation for the elderly and disabled; the problems of the young are incautiously addressed by widespread ownership of private automobiles and a low driving age, notwithstanding the ensuing accident rates.

Here too neighborhood organizations have a role to play. Although a number of American residential-community associations in communities made up of the elderly have begun providing demand-response and other local transportation services to their members, the use of amenity cooperatives or special-assessment districts for the purpose of providing such services has been little tried. Jitney transport, by cab or bus operators not operating on fixed routes, is in use in many foreign cities but has been outlawed in most American cities since the 1920s, with narrow exceptions relating to sharing of licensed taxicabs.[339] Recent British government proposals would permit parish councils to use their general revenues to provide car-sharing schemes, bus services, and concessionary taxi-fare schemes, thus recognizing the usefulness of organizing some local-transport services at the lowest possible level.[340]

Several studies have found that substantial savings can result from the privatization, and thus the devolution to small units, of both public transportation and school-bus services.[341] The economic problems of American central cities are in substantial part ascribable to the lack of transportation necessary to commute to available jobs. The organization and provision of such transportation facilities is an appropriate activity of sublocal governments and neighborhood community associations, as well as of a more deregulated private sector; their financing should appropriately come from user charges or modest special assessments on property owners.

Some British parishes have initiated ventures of this type, with government support, and the 1997 Local Government and Rating Act confers express authority on parish councils to do so.[342] It has been pointed out, most notably by Patrick Hare,[343] that the availability of such transit may enhance property values by diminishing the need of homeowners to invest in second cars, thereby increasing their ability to qualify for and service mortgages. To the extent that subsidies are necessary, they should take the form of formula or project grants from higher levels of government, since sublocal entities are not in a good position to engage in redistributive activities.

Delivery Services

The deliveryman—a member of an unskilled occupation— has all but vanished in the United States, notwithstanding the much-vaunted rising unemployment of the unskilled and uneducated. Seemingly only the pizza-delivery industry possesses the constellation of managerial skills necessary to employ what was once a familiar distribution device.

The recent proliferation of two-earner families and the resultant shortage of time for shopping activities suggests the possible usefulness of revived attention to home-delivery services and the role of neighborhood groups in organizing them by advising members of their availability or soliciting orders for them. Plainly, in the economic sense, these are private goods, though associations can play a role in the organization of demand for them.

Although home-delivery services by grocers were once commonplace, they began to be eliminated in the United States when the A&P food chain introduced economy stores in 1910: "Specific instructions were provided . . . prohibiting both credit and delivery. Stores ceased to have close contact with their customers."[344] A number of independent stores continued to maintain home-delivery for select customers.[345] Revived home-delivery services emerged in suburban areas, where

if the family had a means of transportation, the husband used it to commute to work, or the wife was not allowed or was unable to drive herself. . . . Most home-delivery companies limited sales to fewer than two hundred items. . . . Any goods that required special handling or refrigeration could not be sold profitably, and common goods, such as canned fruit and vegetables, were considered by company management too heavy for shipment and handling. . . . A home-delivery salesperson called about every two weeks on the same day of each week at approximately the same hour . . . promotional schemes using premiums attracted households to home delivery.[346]

Home delivery, the basis of the Jewel Tea chain in the United States, ultimately fell victim to increased automobile ownership (the two-car family), the rising size of supermarkets, which caused supermarkets offering home delivery to be located inconveniently far from many homes they served, and the increased use of refrigeration, which decreased the need for frequent shopping trips.[347] The direct-delivery operations of milk companies succumbed to grocery store competition in the United States,[348] though not as yet in Britain. As of 1980, about 85 percent of milk sold as such in the United Kingdom was still home delivered, as against 35 percent in The Netherlands and none in Denmark.[349] The success of home delivery by pizza shops and other fast-food operations, in both the United States and Britain,[350] suggests that there is a vacuum remaining to be filled, and speculative writing about "the smart store" includes speculation about the revival of home delivery.[351] In Britain, the fast-food home-delivery market is said to have grown 400 percent between 1989 and 1994, accounting for 26 percent of pizza sales as against 10 percent in 1985; the practice has now spread to fried chicken shops and Indian restaurants. It is said to have "low start-up costs and hence low barriers to entry" and to be growing since "home leisure-based activities are expected to account for a growing share of people's leisure time" and since it is "important as a value-for-money alternative to cooking at home."[352] Here also the activities contemplated are self-financing, and participation in them by association members being voluntary, there are minimal governance problems.

Domestic Service

The domestic servant, like the deliveryman, is assumed by Americans to be a creature of the past. What is unappreciated is that the entry of women into the professional labor force and the rising number of two-earner families in both the United States and Britain have resulted in a revival of domestic service, which had nearly died out in both countries. Much of this service involves informal private or neighborhood organization: the domestic servant no longer works for a single employer, but a group of neighbors. In Britain, for example, spending on domestic service increased from £1.45 billion, or 0.4 percent of total household expenditures, in 1985 to £3.89 billion, or 0.9 percent of total household expenditures, in 1995.[353] While the use of domestic servants as child-minders is not a social policy to be preferred to the creation of cooperative playgroups and nurseries, there has also been a revived demand for servants or employees to serve as house or apartment cleaners. In both countries, the new domestic workers have preferred to work as off-the-books independent contractors, being paid by the apartment or house rather than on an hourly basis.[354] This raises the possibility that residential community associations and neighborhood associations might regularize the employment of cleaners either by employing them for the benefit of members who would individually reimburse the association, or by operating clearing houses for their members. What has already been said about voluntary participation in purchasing groups applies here also.

NOTES

1. D. Eastwood, *Governing Rural England, 1780–1840*. Oxford: Clarendon, 1994, 33.
2. G. Harris, *Local Government in Many Lands*. London: King, 1933, 22, 37.
3. A. Leemans, *Changing Patterns of Local Government*. The Hague: IULA, 1970, 56n8.
4. *Local Government and Rating Bill*, 1996, secs. 27–31.
5. R. Tolley, *Traffic Calming in Residential Areas*. London: Beffi Press, 1995.
6. D. Appleyard, *Liveable Urban Streets*. Washington, DC: GPO, 1970.
7. *Built Environment*, 12 (1986), and E. Ben-Joseph, "Changing the Residential Street Scene," *J. Amer. Plan. Assoc.*, 61 (Autumn 1995).

8. S. Diamond, "Death and Transfiguration of Benefit Taxation," *J. Legal Studies*, 12, (1983), 201; D. Hagman and J. Miscynski, *Windfalls for Wipeouts*. Chicago: American Planning Association, 1978, 311–15, 612–14.

9. A. Moudon and Untermann, "Grids Revisited" in A. Moudon, *Public Streets for Private Use*. New York: Van Nostrand Reinhold, 1987, 148. See also R. Fitzgerald, *When Government Goes Private*. New York: Universe, 1988.

10. B. Ryan, *Street Vacations*, in Moudon, supra, at 284–85.

11. R. Oakerson, "Private Street Associations in St. Louis County," in Advisory Commission on Intergovernmental Relations, *Residential Community Associations*. Washington, DC: ACIR, 1989, 56 (hereafter *ACIR-RCA*).

12. M. Frazier, "Seeding Grass Roots Recovery," in *ACIR-RCA*, 63.

13. N. Elliott, *Streets Ahead*. New York: Whitney Library of Design, 1989.

14. R. Taylor and S. Gottfredson, "Environmental Design, Crime and Prevention," in A. Reiss and M. Tonry, *Communities and Crime* (Chicago: University of Chicago Press, 1986), 402; R. Taylor et al., "Block Crime and Fear: Defensible Space, Local Social Ties and Territorial Functioning," *J. Research on Crime and Delinquency*, 21 (1984), 303.

15. P. Wolf, "Rethinking the Urban Street: Its Economic Context" in S. Anderson, *On Streets* (Cambridge: MIT Press, 1978), 380–82.

16. R. Dilger, *Neighborhood Politics*. New York: NYU Press, 1992, 28–29.

17. K. Kolan, "Neighborhood Councils in the Nordic Countries," *Local Government Studies*, 17(3) (1991), 13.

18. L. Mumford, *The Culture of Cities*. New York: Harcourt Brace, 1938, 472.

19. See W. Fischel, *Regulatory Takings* (Cambridge, MA: Harvard University Press, 1994), sec. 2.3 on the difficulties of private land assembly.

20. J. Logan and H. Molotch, *Urban Fortunes* (Berkeley: University of California Press, 1987), 117–18, citing C. Trillin, "U.S. Journal: Atlantic City, N.J.," *Assemblage*, 54(47) and *New Yorker*, 44 (1979).

21. See Fischel, supra, secs. 2.10–2.18.

22. W. Dawson, *Municipal Life and Government in Germany*. London: Longmans, 1914.

23. Cmd. 6386 (1942), para. 143.

24. W. Doebele, ed., *Land Readjustment: A Different Approach to Financing Urbanization* (Lexington, MA: Lexington Books, 1982); M. Shultz and F. Schmidman, "The Potential Application of Land Readjustment in the United States," *Urban Lawyer*, 22 (1990), 197.

25. M. Walker, *Urban Blight and Slums* (Cambridge, MA: Harvard University Press, 1938), 192–95, 200–201, 208–10, 216–39; Architects' Club of Chicago, *Rehabilitating Blighted Areas* (Chicago: ACC, 1932); National Association of Real Estate Boards, *Act for Neighborhood Protective and Improvement Districts* (Washington, DC: NARB, 1935); C. Perry, *The Rebuilding of Blighted Areas* (New York: RPA, 1934); A. Holden, "A Basis for Procedure in Slum Clearance," *Arch. Record*, 73 (1933), 217; New York Private Housing Finance Code, sec. 201ff.

26. W. Doebele, "Introduction," in Doebele, supra, 7. On Adickes, see A. Sutcliffe, *Towards the Planned City* (New York: St. Martin's Press, 1981), 37ff; J. Sheehan, "Liberalism and the City in Nineteenth-Century Germany," *Past and Present*, 51 (1971), 116.

27. W. Doebele, "Synopsis," in Doebele, supra, 24–25. The statute was known as the Bundesbaugesetz. G. Larsson, *Land Readjustment: A Modern Approach to Urbanization* (Aldershot, UK: Avebury, 1993), 33. The 1960 legislation is in *Bundesgesetzblatt*, Part I, 341–88.

28. Baulandbeschaftundgesetz, 3 August 1953, *Bundesgesetzblatt* (1953), Part 1, 720–30, see J. Diefendorf, *In the Wake of War: The Reconstruction of German Cities After World War II* (New York: Oxford, 1993), 238–40.

29. See M. Miyazawa, "Land Readjustment in Japan," in Doebele, supra, 91.

30. Larsson, supra, 19–20.

31. Id., 21.

32. Id., 23

33. Larsson, supra, 25–26, 31. See generally Nakamura, "A Legislative History of Land Readjustment," in ed. L. Minerbi, *Land Readjustment: The Japanese System* (Cambridge, MA: Lincoln Institute, 1986), 17ff.; M. Shultz and F. Schmidman, "The Potential Application of Land Readjustment in the United States," *Urban Lawyer*, 22 (1990), 197, 224–27.

34. Shultz and Schmidman, supra, 227.

35. Larsson, supra, 72.

36. See Shultz and Schmidman, supra, 228–29.

37. Doebele, "Synopsis," supra, at 17.

38. R. Lee, "Agricultural Land Consolidation in Taiwan," in Doebele, supra, 57.

39. See R. Archer, "Land Pooling by Local Government for Planned Urban Development in Perth," in Doebele, supra, 29ff.

40. "Loi du 21 Juin 1865 relative aux associations syndicales," see Larsson, supra, 44 ff.

41. "Loi d'orientation fonciere du 30 Decembre 1967," div. 3, ch. 1.

42. Larsson, supra, 76.

43. Larsson, supra, 79.

44. Id., 54–63.

45. J. Buchanan and G. Tullock, *The Calculus of Consent.* Ann Arbor: University of Michigan Press, 1962, 57.

46. R. Nelson, "The Privatization of Local Government," in *ACIR-RCA*, 49.

47. *ACIR-RCA*, 4, 11, 12, 21.

48. E. Savas, *The Organization and Efficiency of Solid Waste Collection.* Lexington, MA: Lexington Books, 1977.

49. N.J. Code Ch. 40:67-23.2, *1993 New Jersey Laws*, 6.

50. S. McManus, "Decentralizing Expenditures," in R. Bennett, *Decentralization, Local Governments and Markets* (Oxford: Clarendon, 1990), 167.

51. R. Oakerson, "Residential Community Associations: Further Differentiating the Organization of Local Public Economies," in *ACIR-RCA*, 107.

52. J. Stiglitz, *Economics of the Public Sector*, 2d ed. New York: Norton, 1988, 192.

53. D. Mueller, *The Public Choice Approach to Politics.* Cheltenham, UK: Elgar, 1993, 91.

54. D. Rowat, ed., *International Handbook on Local Government Reorganization.* Westport, CT: Greenwood, 1980, 330.

55. F. Foldvery, *Public Goods and Private Communities: The Market Provision of Social Services.* Cheltenham, UK: Elgar, 1994, 25.

56. Id. at 48; see also H. Demsetz, "The Exchange and Enforcement of Property Rights," *J. Law and Economics*, 7 (1964), 11.

57. Boudreaux and Holcombe, "Government by Contract," *Public Finance Q.*, 17 (1989), 264.

58. See J. Gyford, *Citizens, Consumers and Councils.* London: Macmillan, 1991, 144–45.

59. H. Glennerster, "A Decentralized Housing Service," in ed. R. Bennett, supra, ch. 13; see O. Hill, *House Property and Its Management.* London: Allen & Unwin, 1921.

60. R. Kain, "Europe's Model and Exemplar Still?" *Town Planning Review*, 53 (1982), 403; F. Sorlin, "The French System for Conservation and Revitalization in Historic Centers," in ed. P. Ward, *Conservation and Development in Historic Towns and Cities* (Newcastle-on-Tyne, UK: Oriel Press, 1968), 221–34.

61. S. Humes and E. Martin, *The Structure of Local Governments Throughout the World.* The Hague: M. Nijhoff, 1961, 296.

62. G. Schwartz, "Logic of Home Rule and the Private Law Exception," *U.C.L.A. L. Rev.*, 20 (1973), 670, 687–90.

63. S. Barton and C. Silverman, "The Political Life of Residential Community Associations," in *ACIR-RCA*, 35, 37.

64. R. Nelson, "The Privatization of Local Government," in *ACIR-RCA*, 49.

65. J. Winokur, "Association-Administered Servitude Regimes," in *ACIR-RCA*, 85.

66. M. Maurel, "Small Communes and Rural Areas: Decentralization Reforms in France," in ed. R. Bennett, *Local Government in the New Europe* (London: Belhaven, 1993), 148.

67. Rowat, supra, 40.

68. W. Magnusson, "The New Neighborhood Democracy," in ed. L. Sharpe, *Decentralist Trends in Western Democracies* (London: Sage, 1979), 138.

69. See A. Rowe, *Democracy Renewed: The Community Council in Practice.* London: Sheldon Press, 1975.

70. *Research Study No. 9,* "Royal Commission on Local Government in England," Cmnd. 4040, 1969.

71. Local Government and Rating Bill, 1996, clause 22.

72. R. Bish and H. Nourse, *Urban Economics and Policy Analysis* (New York: McGraw-Hill, 1975), 277, citing O. Davis, "Economic Elements in Municipal Zoning Decisions," *Land Economics*, 39 (1963), 375.

73. R. Nelson, *Zoning and Property Rights.* Cambridge: MIT Press, 1977.

74. Fischel, supra, sec. 7.20.

75. G. Liebmann, "Suburban Zoning: Two Modest Proposals," *Real Prop. Probate and Trust L.J.*, 25 (1991), 1.

76. M. Castells, ed., *The Shek Kip Mei Syndrome: Economic Development and Public Housing in Hong Kong and Singapore.* London: Pion, 1990, 233.

77. Id., 260.

78. E. McKenzie, *Privatopia.* New Haven, CT: Yale University Press, 1994, 82.

79. A. de Tocqueville, *L'Ancien Régime* (tr. M. Patterson). Oxford: Blackwell, 1947, 169 (hereafter *"Ancien Régime"*).

80. E. Cubberley, *Public Education in the United States.* Boston: Houghton Mifflin, 1919, 43, 162, 235–40.

81. Y. Willbern, *The Withering Away of the City.* Tuscaloosa: University of Alabama Press, 1964, 111–15.

82. D. Friedman, "Comments on Peltzman," *J.Law and Economics*, 36 (1993), 371.

83. J. Tryneski, *Requirements for Certification of Teachers, Counselors, Librarians, Administrators for Elementary and Secondary Schools*, 61st ed. Chicago: University of Chicago Press, 1996.

84. *Agreement between the Baltimore Teachers Union . . . and the Board of School Commissioners, 1994–1996*, secs. 6.3, 7.9.

85. H. Lewis, *The French Education System.* New York: St. Martin's Press, 1985, 12.

86. D. Reed-Danahay, *Education and Identity in Rural France.* Cambridge: Cambridge University Press, 1996, 12.

87. W. Fraser, *Reforms and Restraints in Modern French Education.* London: Routledge, 1971, 152–53.

88. Reed-Danahay, supra, 169.

89. N. Beattie, *Professional Parents.* London: Falmer Press, 1985, 53.

90. H. Lewis, supra, 57; L. Elvin, ed., *The Educational Systems in the European Community: A Guide.* Windsor, UK: NFER-Nelson, 1981, 119–23.

91. R. Ballion, "A Changing Focus of Power: From the All-Powerful State to the User-Consumer," in A. Corbett and B. Moon, *Education in France: Continuity and Change During the Mitterand Years* (London: Routledge, 1995), 191.

92. Fraser, supra, 153.

93. Id., 58–59.

94. B. Holmes, ed., *International Handbook of Educational Systems: Europe and Canada.* Chichester, UK: Wiley, 1983, 317.

95. J. Derouet, "Lower Secondary Education in France: From Uniformity to Educational Autonomy," *European J. Education*, 26 (1991), 119.

96. N. Beattie, "Sex Education in France: A Case Study in Curriculum Change," *Comparative Education*, 12 (1976), 115.

97. Harris, supra, 21.

98. V. Krumm, "Expectations about Parents in Education in Austria, Germany, and Switzerland," in ed. A. Macbeth and B. Ravn, *Expectations about Parents in Education: European Perspectives* (Glasgow: University of Glasgow Computing Services, 1994), 17.

99. S. Fishman and L. Martin, *Estranged Twins: Education and Society in the Two Germanys*. New York: Praeger, 1987, 95.

100. Beattie, *Professional Parents*, 107–59.

101. Id., 107–60.

102. *A New Partnership for our Schools* (1977); R. Rogers, *Crowther to Warnock: How Fourteen Reports Tried to Change Children's Lives* (London: Heinemann, 1980), ch. 14; see also W. Bacon, *Public Accountability and the Schooling System* (New York: Harper & Row, 1978). See generally, Gyford, supra, 66–69.

103. M. Loughlin, *Local Government in the Modern State*. London: Sweet & Maxwell, 1986, 131–32, citing cases.

104. Loughlin, supra, citing Department of Education and Science, "Parental Influence at School," Cmnd. 9242 (1984), and "Better Schools," Cmnd. 9469 (1985).

105. R. Laughlin and J. Broadbent, "The Managerial Reform of Health and Education in the U.K.," *Political Quarterly*, 65 (1994), 152; A. Macbeth, ed., *Collaborate or Compete* (London: Falmer Press, 1995).

106. A. Wright, *Citizens and Subjects: An Essay on British Politics* (London: Routledge, 1994), 108. See also *Self-Governing Schools (Scotland) Act*, 1989; Department of Education, *The Implementation of Local Management of Schools* (1992); R. Dale, *The State and Educational Policy* (Milton Keynes, UK: Open University Press, 1989); and for criticism, R. Deem, *Active Citizenship and the Governance of Schools* (Buckingham, UK: Open University Press, 1995).

107. Loughlin, supra, 135.

108. *Times Educational Supplement*, 22 October 1976.

109. See [New Zealand Department of Education] "Task Force to Review Educational Administration, Administering for Excellence [Picot Report]," *Tomorrow's Schools* (Wellington, NZ: Government Printer, 1988); B. Cusack, "Political Engagement in the Restructured School: The New Zealand Experience," *Education Management and Administration*, 21 (1993), 107; and for criticism, L. Gordon, "Educational Reforms in New Zealand," *Comparative Education*, 28 (1992) 281.

110. See D. Gamage, "School-Centered Educational Reforms of the 1990s: An Australian Case Study," *Education Management and Administration*, 20 (1992), 5; R. MacPherson, "Administrative Reforms in the Antipodes," *Education Management and Administration*, 21 (1993), 49; R. Dale, "Whither the State and Educational Policy: Recent Work in Australia and New Zealand," *Brit. J. Sociology Education*, 13 (1992), 387.

111. Quoted in D. Brown, *Decentralization and School-Based Management* (London: Falmer Press, 1990), 91; P. Hughes, "Parents and School Government in Australia," in ed. G. Baron, *The Politics of School Government* (Oxford: Pergamon, 1981), 131.

112. W. Wickwar, *The Political Theory of Local Government*. Columbia: University of South Carolina Press, 1970, 65.

113. A. Norton, *International Handbook of Local and Regional Government* (Aldershot, UK: Elgar, 1994), sec. 6.12; see also P. Bogason, "Danish Local Government," in ed. J. Hesse, *Local Government and Urban Affairs in International Perspective* (Baden-Baden: Nomus, 1991), 280–81; Holmes, supra, 215; K. Struwe, "Schools and Education in Denmark," in Holmes, supra, 66; Elvin, supra, 55.

114. J. Lauglo, "Scandinavian School Governance," in Baron, supra, 265–68.

115. Id., 277.
116. Elvin, supra, 139.
117. R. Martinez et al., "Expectations about Parents in Education in Portugal and Spain," in Macbeth and Ravn, supra, 44.
118. F. Smit and W. van Esch, "Opportunities for Parents to Influence Education in The Netherlands," in Macbeth and Ravn, supra, 59.
119. Id., 175–77.
120. N. Beattie, *Professional Parents*, 83.
121. Id., 99–100.
122. P. Pridham, "The Introduction of School Councils in Italy," in Baron, supra, 225.
123. V. Krumm, "Whose School Is It Anyway?" *Intl. J. Educational Research*, 15 (1991), 265.
124. B. Barber, *The Death of Communal Liberty* (Princeton, NJ: Princeton University Press, 1974), cites Articles 40 and 41 of the Graubunden Cantonal Constitution.
125. J. Bryce, *Modern Democracies* (London: Macmillan, 1921), 375; R. Brooks, *Civic Training in Switzerland* (Chicago: University of Chicago Press, 1930), 206n58.
126. Bryce, supra, 36.
127. Council of Europe, "Participation by Citizen-Consumers in the Management of Local Public Services," in *Local and Regional Authorities in Europe*, no. 54 (1994), 39.
128. B. Ravn, "Expectations about Parents in Education in the Scandinavian Countries," in Macbeth and Ravn, supra, 68; J. Lauglo, "Scandinavian School Governance," in Baron, supra, 261.
129. B. Cooper, "Parental Involvement and Public Choice in Education," *Intl. J. Educational Research*, 15 (1991), 235, 244.
130. R. Jennings, "School Advisory Councils in America: Frustration and Failure," in Baron, supra, 23, 35.
131. N. Beattie, "Politicians and Parents: Recent Legislation in England and Wales and Massachusetts," *Intl. J. Educational Research*, 15 (1991), 293, citing J. Goodlad, *A Place Called School* (1984), and T. Sizer, *Horace's Compromise: The Dilemna of the American High School* (1984).
132. B. Lucas and C. Lusthaus, "Public Involvement in School Governance in Canada," in Baron, supra, 53.
133. Brown, supra, 71.
134. Quoted in M. Keating and P. Hainsworth, *Decentralization and Change in Contemporary France*. Aldershot, UK: Gower Publishing, 1986, 26.
135. M. Walzer, *Radical Principles*. New York: Basic Books, 1979, 66.
136. Id., 126, reprinted from M. Walzer, *The University and the New Intellectual Environment* (1968).
137. Id., 51.
138. Leemans, supra, 120.
139. Rowe, supra, 14. See also J. Duncan, "Community Councils in Glasgow," *Local Government Studies*, 16 (1990), 8.
140. See R. Honeywell, *The Educational Work of Thomas Jefferson*. Cambridge, MA: Harvard University Press, 1937, appendix.
141. P. Berger, *Facing Up to Modernity*. New York: Basic Books, 1977, 139.
142. B. Barber, *Strong Democracy*. Berkeley: University of California Press, 1974, 146n8.
143. 20 U.S.C. secs. 1701(a), 1705, 1714.
144. Equal Access Act of 1984, 20 U.S.C. sec. 4071 upheld against establishment clause challenge in *Board of Education v. Mergens*, 496 U.S. 226 (1990). See also U.S. Bureau of Education, Proposed Community Forum Bill (1922); E. Glueck, *Community Use of Schools* (Baltimore: Williams & Wilkins, 1927).
145. C. Faher, "Is Local Control of Schools Still a Viable Option?" *Harvard J. Law and Public Policy*, 14 (1991), 447, 467–72; *Ky. Rev. Stat.*, 160.155, 160.345 (Baldwin supp. 1990).

146. *Fumarolo v. Chicago Board of Education*,142 Ill. 2d 54, 566 N.E. 2d 1283 (1990), criticized in J. Evans, "Let Our Parents Run," *Hastings Const. Law Q.*, 19 (1992), 963; and in R. Briffault, "Who Rules at Home?: One Man, One Vote and Local Government," *Univ. Chi. Law Rev.*, 60 (1993), 339. See also "Comment," *Univ. Chi. Law Rev.*, 39 (1972), 639. Parent boards were recommended in Carnegie Foundation for the Advancement of Teaching, *An Impeded Generation* (1988), ch. 2. On the background of the Chicago proposal, see M. Raywid, "Evolving Effort to Improve Schools," *Phi Beta Kappan*, 72 (1990), 139.

147. R. Dahl, *After the Revolution.* New Haven, CT: Yale University Press, 1970, 44.

148. J. Hannaway, "The Organization and Management of Public and Catholic Schools," *Intl. J. Educational Research* (1971), 463, 477.

149. Wickwar, supra, 69.

150. B. Hamilton, "Zoning and Property Taxation in a System of Local Governments," *Urban Studies*, 12 (1975) 205; Fischel, supra, sec. 7.4.

151. Fischel, supra, sec. 7.5.

152. Logan and Molotch, supra, citing P. Rossi, *Why Families Move* (1955).

153. Id., 42.

154. Stiglitz, supra, 639, citing R. Ebert, "Jurisdictional Homogeneity and the Tiebout Hypothesis," *J. Urban Econ.*, 10 (1980), 227, and H. Pack, "Metropolitan Fragmentation and Local Public Expenditure," *Natl. Tax J.*, 31 (1978), 349.

155. S. Beer, "A Political Scientist's View of Fiscal Federalism," in W. Oates, *The Political Economy of Fiscal Federalism* (Lexington, MA: Lexington Books, 1977), 34.

156. Deem, supra.

157. T. Clark, *Comparative Community Politics.* Beverly Hills, CA: Sage, 1974, 34.

158. R. Musgrave and P. Musgrave, *Public Finance in Theory and Practice*, 5th ed. New York: McGraw-Hill, 1988, 182.

159. R. Wood, "A Service for Children," *Soc. Services Q.*, 28 (1954), 132; J. Whidbourne, "The Children's School Care Committees," *Soc. Services Q.*, 25 (1951), 20; H. Bosanquet, *Social Work in London* (Reprint, Brighton, UK: Harvester Press, 1973), 253–56.

160. *Report of the Committee on Local Authority and Allied Personal Services* (Seebohm Report, Cmnd. 3703, 1968), para. 1034.

161. Id., para. 241.

162. Id., para. 250.

163. Id., para. 927.

164. A. Wimble, "The School Care Service" in M. Craft, *Linking Home and School*, 2d ed. (London: Longmans, 1972), 187–89; Social Research Unit of Bedford College, *The Social Welfare Services of the Inner-London Education Authority* (Jeffreys Report) (1970).

165. An early description appears in A. Shaw, *Municipal Government in Continental Europe* (New York: Century, 1895), 123.

166. Id., 375, 432.

167. Advisory Commission on Intergovernmental Relations, *Model State Legislation, Neighborhood Subunits of Government*; 1970 ACIR Cumulative State Legislative Program (1969); *Fiscal Balance in the American Federal System* (1962), 16–17.

168. Norton, supra, sec. 9.12.

169. K. Kolan, "Neighborhood Councils in the Nordic Countries," *Local Government Studies*, 17, no. 3 (1991), 13.

170. A. de Tocqueville, *Democracy in America*, vol. 2. London: Everyman, 1994, 300.

171. Id., 318.

172. M. Morris, *Voluntary Work in the Welfare State.* London: Routledge, 1969.

173. G. Finlayson, *Citizen, State and Social Welfare in Britain.* Oxford: Oxford University Press, 1994, 406.

174. L. Jackman, "The Future Development of the CAB Service," *Soc. Services Q.*, 55 (1977), 246.

175. *London Times*, Jan. 18, 1984, 2.
176. *New Society*, June 5, 1987, 22.
177. *Guardian*, April 20, 1991, 18.
178. *Independent*, June 27, 1992, 25.
179. Jackman, supra, 246.
180. *Parliamentary Debates* (Commons), Sixth Series, 40, 676–84; 41, 576–82, 875–80; *Parliamentary Debates* (Lords), 441, 115–22, 940–45; 442, 158–76.
181. Cmnd. 3139 (1984).
182. *London Times*, Jan. 17, 1988, A7.
183. *Sunday Times*, Sept. 26, 1986.
184. *Times*, May 13, 1993, 12.
185. *Independent*, May 15, 1994, 13.
186. *Paras.*, 191, 197.
187. *New Society*, Nov. 10, 1983, 50.
188. *New Society*, May 24, 1984, 328.
189. *New Society*, Oct. 11, 1985, 80.
190. M. Brasnett, *Voluntary Social Action.* London: National Council of Social Service, 1969, 264.
191. C. Mowat, *Charity Organization Society* (London: Methuen, 1977), 191. On the history of the CAB, see generally, J. Richards, *Inform, Advise, and Support* (London: Lutterworth Press, 1989).
192. Eastwood, supra, 213.
193. J. Toulmin Smith, *Local Self-Government and Centralization.* London: Chapman, 1851, 369.
194. B. Disraeli, *Coningsby*, 118, 316, quoted in Eastwood, supra, 265.
195. C. Steedman, *Policing the Victorian Community.* London: Routledge, 1984.
196. M. Zuckerman, *Peaceable Kingdoms.* New York: Knopf, 1970, 87.
197. Id., 117.
198. Id., 236.
199. Id., 241.
200. 13 Edward I, stat 2 (1285). In pertinent part, the statute read: "in every city, six men shall keep at every gate, in every borough 12 men,every town 6 or 4 according to the number of inhabitants of the town, and shall watch the town continually all night . . . and if they will not obey the arrest they shall levy the hue and cry upon them and such as keep the town shall follow with hue and cry with all the town, and hue and cry shall be made from town to town . . . in every hundred or franchise two constables shall be chosen to make the view of armor . . . view of armor shall be made every year two times . . . every man between 15 years of age and 60 years shall be assessed and sworn to armor according to the quantity of their lands and goods . . . they shall follow the cry with the country . . . the defaults shall be presented by the constables to the justices assigned."
201. 27 Henry II (1185).
202. 10 George IV, c.449 (1829).
203. D. Hay and F. Snyder, eds., *Policing and Prosecution in England, 1750–1850* (Oxford: Clarendon, 1989). See also M. Greenberg, *Auxiliary Police: The Citizen's Approach to Public Safety* (Westport, CT: Greenwood, 1984), ch. 1.
204. See *The Federalist*, No. 45.
205. O. Handlin, "'Preface' to Lane, *Policing the City* (Cambridge, MA: Harvard University Press, 1967)" See J. Bryce, *American Commonwealth* (New York: Macmillan, 1888), 2, 569–70.
206. See *ACIR-RCA* (the best survey of the incidence and function of such associations).
207. *Much Ado About Nothing*, act IV, scene 2. On early American constables, see H. Adams, *Norman Constables in America* (Baltimore: Johns Hopkins University Press, 1883).

208. Jefferson to Joseph Cabell, Feb. 2, 1816, in *Autobiographical Writings*, vol. XIV. New York: Putnam, 1904, 419.

209. R. Storch, "Policing Rural England Before the Police," in Hay and Snyder, supra, 212n4.

210. J. Skolnick and D. Bayley, "Theme and Variation in Community Policing," in M. Tonry and N. Morris, *Crime and Justice* (Chicago: University of Chicago Press, 1988), 1–38.

211. On Japanese neighborhood association chairmen serving similar functions for groups of about 30 homes (*Bohan Kyokai*), see R. Thornton, *Preventing Crime in America and Japan* (Armonk, NY: M.E. Sharpe, 1992), 61–62; C. Fenwick, "Law Enforcement, Public Participation and Crime Control in Japan," *Amer. J. Police* (1983), 83–109.

212. R. Fogelson, *Big City Police* (Cambridge, MA: Harvard University Press, 1977), 305. On the *koban* system of the Japanese police, said to have been borrowed from German practice during the Meiji restoration, see Thornton, supra, 43–45; W. Ames, *Police and Community in Japan* (Berkeley: University of California Press, 1981), ch. 1. See also L. Lambert, "Police Mini-Stations in Toronto," *R.C.M.P. Gazette*, 50 (1988), 6. On neighborhood patrols, see J. Shapland and J. Vagg, *Policing by the Public* (London: Routledge, 1988); R. Yin et al., *Citizen Patrol Projects; National Evaluation Program; Phase One Summary Report* (1977); S. Smith, *Crime, Space and Society* (Cambridge: Cambridge University Press, 1986).

213. *Economist*, July 25, 1992, 25.

214. See L. Johnston, *The Rebirth of Private Policing*. London: Routledge, 1992, 176–77.

215. For a survey of association activities, see G. Liebmann, "Devolution of Power to Neighborhood and Block Associations," in *Proc. Intl. Assoc. of Housing Sciences* (1992), 668–94.

216. E. Monkkonen, *Police in Urban America, 1860–1920* (Cambridge: Cambridge University Press, 1981). See also S. Walker, *Popular Justice:A History of American Criminal Justice* (New York: Oxford University Press, 1980), 18–24.

217. Dahl, supra, 130.

218. Blue, "High Noon Revisited," *Yale Law J.*, 101 (1992), 1475. Contrast the reference to the *posse comitatus* in *The Federalist*, No. 29 (Hamilton): "It would be . . . absurd to doubt that a right to pass all laws necessary and proper to execute declared powers would include that of requiring the assistance of the citizens to the officers who may be entrusted with the execution of those laws."

219. J. Wilson, *Thinking about Crime* (New York: Vintage, 1985), 87. McChesney, "Government Prohibition of Volunteer Firefighting in 19th-Century America," *Journal of Legal Studies*, 15 (1976), 69.

220. See R. Ahlbrandt, "Efficiency in the Provision of Fire Services," *1973 Public Choice* 16.

221. Mueller, supra, 61.

222. See, for example, R. Neely [Chief Justice of West Virginia], *Take Back Your Neighborhood* (New York: D.I. Fine, 1990). On neighborhood watch programs, see T. Hope and M. Shaw, *Communities and Crime Reduction* (London: HMSO, 1988); J. Bennett, *Evaluating Neighborhood Watch* (Aldershot, UK: Gower, 1990); S. Mukherjee and P. Wilson, "Neighborhood Watch" in P. Wilson, *Issues in Crime, Morality and Justice* (Canberra: Australian Institute of Criminology, 1992), and K. Whitehead, "Wonder Scheme or White Elephant," *Police Review* (1989), all dealing with the English experience. Also see W. Skogan, *Disorder and Decline* (New York: Free Press, 1991); D. Lewis, *Social Construction and Reform: Crime Prevention and Community Associations* (New Brunswick, NJ: Transaction Books, 1988).

223. See McChesney, supra (exemption from jury service, militia duty, and road taxes).

224. See generally, Koven, "Co-Production of Law Enforcement Services," *Urban Affairs Q.*, 27 (1992), 457; Institute for Local Self Government, *Alternatives to Traditional Public-Safety Services* (1977).

225. See N. Morris and G. Hawkins, *Letter to the President on Crime Control*. Chicago: University of Chicago Press, 1971, 30.

226. L. Sherman, "Policing Communities: What Works," in Reiss and Tonry, supra.

227. W. Skogan, "Community Organizations and Crime," in Tonry and Morris, supra, 39, 68.

228. See O. Newman, *Community of Interest* (Garden City, NY: Doubleday, 1972); Shaftoe et al., "Crime, Design and Management," in *Proc. Intl. Assoc. for Housing Sciences* (1992), 692–703; R. Taylor and S. Gottfredson, "Environmental Design, Crime, and Prevention," in Reiss and Tonry, supra, 387.

229. Summerson, "The Structure of Law Enforcement in Thirteenth-Century England," *Amer. J. Legal History*, 23 (1979), 313.

230. J. Austen, *Northanger Abbey*, ch. 24.

231. J. Hall, "Legal and Social Aspects of Arrest without a Warrant," *Harvard Law Rev.*, 49 (1936), 571.

232. E. Chadwick, "Preventive Police," *London Review*, 1 (1829), 285, quoted in J. Styles, "Print and Policing," in Hay and Snyder, supra, 56n4. See P. Pringle, *Hue and Cry: Henry and John Fielding* (London: Dobson, 1968).

233. See de Tocqueville, *Democracy in America*, 99.

234. L. Sherman, "Policing Communities: What Works," in Reiss and Tonry, supra, 351; see D. Rosenbaum, *Crime Stoppers: A National Evaluation of Program Operations and Effects* (Washington, DC: U.S. Justice Dept., 1985).

235. K. Carriere and R. Erickson, *Crime Stoppers: A Study in the Organization of Community Policing*. Toronto: University of Toronto Press, 1989.

236. See D. Rosenbaum, *Evaluating Community Crime Prevention* (Beverly Hills, CA: Sage, 1986), ch. 13, on present-day anticrime newsletters, and see K. Carrierre, "The Organization of Community: Crime-Time Television," *F.B.I. Law Enforcement Bull.*, 58 (1989), 8, and T. Baxter, "Video Time to Stop Crime," *Law and Order*, 35 (1987), 9, on the use of television for criminal apprehension, more common in Europe than in the United States.

237. *Ancien Régime*, 216.

238. 1 Stat. 271 (1792). See the present 10 U.S.C. sec. 311: "The militia of the United States consists of all able-bodied males at least 17 years of age and . . . under 45 years of age."

239. 1 *Annals of Congress* 933 (1790).

240. See M. Clinard, *Cities with Little Crime: The Case of Switzerland*. Cambridge: Cambridge University Press, 114–15.

241. J. Story, *Commentaries on the Constitution*. Boston: Hilliard, Gray, 1833, 746–77.

242. J. Jacobs, "Exceptions to a General Prohibition," *Law and Contemporary Problems*, 49 (1986), 5, 34.

243. D. Kates, "Value of Civilian Arms Possession," *Amer J. Criminal Law*, 18 (1991) 113, describing such an effort in Florida. For a survey of gun-control studies, see J. Wright, *Under the Gun* (New York: Aldine, 1990), 259, referring to a Dade County, Florida, scheme conditioning a purchase permit on completion of a handgun-safety and firearms-law course. See also G. Kleck and K. McElrath, "Effect of Weaponry on Violence," *Social Forces*, 69, no. 3 (1991) 669–92; *F.B.I. Law Enforcement Bull.*, (1991), 60–68. C. Bakal, *No Right to Bear Arms* (New York: Paperback Library, 1968), ch. 13, notes that Connecticut, New York, and Rhode Island conditioned grant of hunting licenses to adults on completion of a firearms-safety course, and that the rate of accidental gun deaths in these jurisdictions was about one-third the national rate. Ten additional states require such courses for minor licensees.

244. See Greenbers, supra, ch. 16, describing auxiliary police programs providing 52 to 381 hours of training in several cities, including use of uniforms, handcuffs, nightsticks, and two-way radios; R. Sundeen and G. Siegel, "The Uses of Volunteers by the Police," *J. Police Science and Admin.*, 14 (1986), 49.

245. Police Act, 1964 (Laws, 1964, c.48, secs. 16, 34, 1965 S.I. 536, 1992 S.I. 526). See M. Gill and R. Mawby, *A Special Constable: A Study of the Police Reserve* (Aldershot, UK:

Avebury, 1990); C. Leon, "The Special Constabulary," *Policing* (1989), 514; M. Gill and R. Mawby, *Volunteers in the Criminal Justice System* (Washington, DC: U.S. Justice Dept., 1990), 57–75. For proposals for security courses for the public, see M. Greenberg, "Volunteer Crime-Prevention Programs," *Police Chief*, 44 (1977), 60–61; see generally, J. Duncan, *Citizen Crime Prevention Tactics: A Literature Review and Selected Bibliography* (Washington, DC: National Institute of Justice, 1980).

246. G. Berkley, *The Democratic Policeman* (Boston: Beacon Press, 1969), 175–78, describes the 43,000 strong British special constabulary, one-third as numerous as the regular force, who receive 24 hours of training, and the 6,000-strong Berlin auxiliary police, who receive 52 hours of instruction, as well as the Baden-Wurtemburg auxiliary police, who serve for 6 hours per month after receiving 92 hours of training and who carry pistols on shift.

247. J. Weber, "The King's Peace," *Amer. J. Legal History*, 10 (1989), 135, quoting Mumford, supra, 29.

248. Styles, supra, 94–95n26.

249. Humes and Martin, supra, 372 (Turkey); 369 (Lebanon).

250. Shaw, supra, 16.

251. Id., 35, 111.

252. Id., 42.

253. Id., 41.

254. J. Toulmin Smith, supra, 361.

255. Bish and Nourse, supra, 195.

256. R. Kania, "The French Municipal Police Experiment," *Police Studies*, 12 (1989), 125; Johnston, supra, 135–36.

257. J. Midgely, *Community Participation, Social Development and the State* (London: Methuen, 1986), 130, citing W. Clifford, "Training for Crime Control in the Context of National Development," *International Review of Criminal Policy*, 24 (1966), 1.

258. *Report of the Departmental Committee on Training, Appointment and Payment of Probation Officers*, Cmd. 1601 (1922).

259. W. Bolt, "Letter," *British J. Delinquency*, 8 (1957), 232.

260. Working Party on the Place of Voluntary Service in After Care, *The Place of Voluntary Service in After Care*. London: HMSO, 1967.

261. A. Holme and J. Maizels, *Social Workers and Volunteers*. London: Allen & Unwin, 1978.

262. Home Office, *Probation Service in England and Wales: Statement of National Objectives and Priorities* (1984); *Community Work and the Probation Service* (1991). The earlier history is reviewed in Gill and Mawby, *Volunteers in the Criminal Justice System*, 30–31.

263. Home Office, *Crime, Justice and Protecting the Public* (1990); *Punishment, Custody and the Community* (1988).

264. On the United States, see the articles in *Federal Probation*, 33 (1969), 41; *Federal Probation*, 34 (1970), 12; *Federal Probation*, 35 (1971), 46; *Federal Probation*, 47 (1983), 57.

265. European Assembly for Probation and After-Care, *Probation in Europe*. Hertogenbosch, The Netherlands: EAPAC, 1981, 72.

266. Id., 44.

267. H. Becker and E. Hjellemo, *Justice in Modern Sweden*. Springfield, IL: Thomas, 1976.

268. European Assembly for Probation and After-Care, *Probation in Europe*, 412.

269. A. Hess, "The Volunteer Probation Officers of Japan," *Intl. J. Offender Therapy*, 14 (1970). See also Ames, supra; W. Clifford, *Crime Control in Japan* (Lexington, MA: Lexington Books, 1976), 109.

270. Gill and Mawby, *Volunteers in the Criminal Justice System*, 31.

271. European Assembly for Probation and After-Care, *Probation in Europe*, 110.

272. L. Lipson, "Law: The Function of Extra-Judicial Mechanisms in the USSR," in ed. D. Treadgold, *Soviet and Chinese Communism* (Seattle: University of Washington Press, 1967),

144–67; T. Friedgut, *Political Participation in the USSR* (Princeton, NJ: Princeton University Press, 1979), 249–57.

273. R. Woodson, *A Summons to Life*. Cambridge, UK: Ballinger, 1987.

274. Stiglitz, supra, 163.

275. Mueller, supra, 464.

276. Id., sec. 3.12.

277. Id. sec. 4.12.

278. Id., sec. 5.12, citing Kolam, "Neighborhood Councils in the Nordic Countries," *Local Government Studies*, 17, no. 3 (1991).

279. F. Kjellberg, "A Comparative View of Municipal Decentralization," in ed. L. Sharpe, *Decentralist Trends in Western Democracies* (London: Sage, 1979).

280. Id., 106.

281. Mueller, supra, 103.

282. de Tocqueville, *Democracy in America*, 324.

283. Id., 60–61.

284. K. Messere, *Tax Policy in OECD Countries* (Amsterdam: IBFD Publications, 1993), 47. See also W. Pommerehne, "Quantitative Aspects of Federalism: A Study of Six Countries," in Oates, supra, 275.

285. W. Pommerehne and F. Schneider, "Unbalanced Growth Between Public and Private Sectors," in ed. R. Haveman, *Public Finance and Public Employment* (1982), 309–26, quoted in Mueller, supra, 393.

286. W. Magnusson, "The New Neighborhood Democracy," in Sharpe, supra, 135.

287. Dahl, supra, 126.

288. Id., 141n13, citing studies collected in R. Dahl, "The City in the Future of Democracy," *Amer. Political. Science. Rev.*, 61 (1967), 953, 966n14.

289. Zuckerman, supra, 128.

290. M. Hechter, *Principles of Group Solidarity*. Berkeley: University of California Press, 1987, 146–67.

291. R. Axelrod, *The Evolution of Cooperation*. New York: Basic Books, 1984, 20.

292. Rowat, supra, 300.

293. Mueller, supra, 93.

294. Id., 94.

295. A. Downs, *An Economic Theory of Democracy*. New York: Harper & Row, 1957, 258–59.

296. Rowat, supra, 320.

297. J. Stewart and M. Clarke, "Elected Special Purpose Authorities," *Local Government Studies*, 22 (1996), 1.

298. G. Gomme, *Lectures on the Principles of Local Government*. Westminster, UK: Constable, 1897, viii.

299. H. Mendras and A. Cole, *Social Change in Modern France*. Cambridge: Cambridge University Press, 1991, 129, 142.

300. Swiss Constitution, Art. 59; see J. Steinberg, *Why Switzerland?* (Cambridge: Cambridge University Press, 1996), 79.

301. J. Stiglitz, "The Theory of Local Public Goods," in G. Zodrow, *Local Provision of Public Services* (New York: Academic Press, 1983), 17, 52.

302. C. Arnold-Baker, *Municipal and Public Services Journal* (July 25, 1969), quoted in B. Rose, *England Looks at Maud* (Chichester, UK: Justice of the Peace, 1970), 97.

303. P. Self, *Government by the Market*. Boulder, CO: Westview, 1993, 269.

304. Lock, "Ideology and Female Midlife," *J. Japanese Studies*, 25 (1994), 46–51; see also A. Ernst, "A Segmented Welfare State," *J. Institutional and Theoretical Economics*, 138 (1982), 545; J. Ogawa, "Population Aging and Medical Demand: The Case of Japan," in U.N.

Department of International Economic and Social Affairs, *Economic and Social Implications of Population Aging* (1988), 254–75.

305. Lock, supra, note 1; see also Y. Kinoshita, "The Political Economy Perspective of Health and Medical Care Policies for the Aged in Japan," in S. Ingman, *Eldercare* (Albany: SUNY Press, 1995); W. Coaldrake, "The Architecture of Reality: Trends in Japanese Housing 1985–89," *Japan Architect* (October 1989), 61, 66.

306. Castells, supra, 136–38; A. Wong and S. Yeh, *Housing a Nation: Twenty-Five Years of Public Housing in Singapore* (Singapore: Maruzen Asia, 1985), 272.

307. The resulting system is described in a number of works in English; for example, in E. Ben Ari's *Changing Japanese Suburbia* (London: Kegan Paul, 1991).

308. Id.

309. Wickwar, supra, 82.

310. See generally, T. Campbell, "The Old People Boom and Japanese Policymaking," *J. Japanese Studies*, 5 (1974), 321; J. Campbell, *How Policies Change* (Princeton, NJ: Princeton University Press, 1992); S. Linhart, "The Search for Meaning in Old Age: The Japanese Case," *Intl. Cong. of Gerontology*, 12 (1981); D. Maeda, "Decline of Family Love and the Development of Public Services," in ed. J. Eekelaar, *An Aging World: Dilemmas and Challenges for Law and Social Policy* (Oxford: Clarendon, 1989), 313.

311. Castells, supra, 136–38; A. Wong, "The Hong Kong Neighborhood Associations," *Asian Survey*, 12 (1972), 587; "Hong Kong: Issues in Social Policy," *Asian J. Public Administration*, 8 (1986); Hong Kong Government, *Services for the Elderly* (1977).

312. K. Kolan, "Neighborhood Councils in the Nordic Countries," *Local Government Studies*, 17, no. 3 (1991), 13.

313. F. Kjellberg, "A Comparative View of Municipal Decentralization," in Sharpe, supra, 97.

314. S. Benstead, "The Village Warden: A New Concept in the Care of the Elderly," *Local Council Review* (summer 1984), 27.

315. Wickwar, supra, 64.

316. Shaw, supra, 107, 202.

317. Id., 367.

318. J. Statham, *Playgroups in a Changing World*. London: HMSO, 47.

319. H. Jarecki, *Playgroups*. London: Faber, 1990.

320. *New Society*, June 22, 1967, 923.

321. *Committee of Inquiry into the Quality of the Educational Experience Offered to Three- and Four-Year Olds* (Rumbold Report), para. 21.

322. Central Education Advisory Committee for England and Wales, *Children and Their Primary Schools* (1968).

323. *Parliamentary Debates* (Commons), Sixth Series, Jan. 18, 1989, 397–98.

324. *New Society*, May 27, 1987, 22; Sept. 19, 1986, 22.

325. *New Society*, Sept. 19, 1986, 22.

326. J. Brophy, *Playgroups in Practice:Self-Help and Public Policy*. London: HMSO, 1992, 93.

327. Id., 6.

328. *London Times*, Nov. 4, 1992, 10; *Times Educational Supplement*, Nov. 6, 1992, 3.

329. D. MacLeod, "Swings and Roundabouts," *Guardian Education*, Oct. 4, 1994, 2.

330. *New Society*, May 29, 1987, 22.

331. Statham, supra, 7.

332. Rumbold Report, supra, 23; Preschool Playgroups Association, *Playgroups Go Forward* (London: PPA, 1995).

333. J. Finch, "The Deceit of Self-Help, Pre-School Playgroups and Working-Class Mothers," *J. Social Policy*, 13 (1984), 1; G. Dalley, *Ideologies of Caring: Rethinking Community and Collectivism* (1988). Both are quoted in Gyford, supra.

334. Statham, supra, 16.

335. J. Statham, *Playgroups in Three Countries* (London: University of London Press, 1989); Brophy, supra, 47.

336. Midgely, supra, citing Indian Ministry of Social Welfare, *Integrated Child-Development Service Scheme* (1980) and Indian Ministry of Social Welfare, *Report* (1983).

337. Council of Europe, *Participation by Citizens-Consumers in the Management of Local Public Services, Local and Regional Authorities in Europe*, no. 54 (1994), 40.

338. R. Brooks, *New Towns and Communal Values*. New York: Praeger, 1974, 133–34.

339. Bish and Nourse, supra, 356–57, 376–77, citing E. Kitch et al., "The Regulation of Taxicabs in Chicago," *J. Law and Economics*, 14 (1971), 285; R. Eckert and G. Hilton, "The Jitneys," *J. Law and Economics*, 15 (1972), 294; R. Farmer, "Whatever Happened to the Jitney?" *Traffic Quarterly*, 19 (1965), 263.

340. Local Government and Rating Bill, 1996, clauses 27–31.

341. R. McQuire and N. Van Cott, "Public v. Private Activity: A New Look at School Bus Transportation," *Public Choice* (1984), 43; J. Perry and T. Babitsky, "Comparative Performance in Urban Bus Transit," *Public Administration Rev.* (Jan.–Feb. 1986); E. Marlock and P. Viton, "The Comparative Costs of Public and Private Transit," in ed. C. Love, *Urban Transit: The Private Challenge to Public Transit* (1985), cited in Stiglitz, supra, 196.

342. "Parish Voluntary Car Service," *Local Council Rev.* (summer 1981), 56.

343. P. Hare, *Making Housing Affordable by Reducing Second-Car Ownership* (Washington, DC: Patrick H. Hare Planning and Design, 1995); P. Hare, "Junking the Clunker," *Western City* (October 1992), 3.

344. W. Walsh, *The Rise and Decline of the Great Atlantic and Pacific Tea Co.* (Secaucus, NJ: Lyle Stuart, 1986), 27; R. Mueller, *A & P* (New York: Progressive Grocer Magazine, 1971), 18.

345. W. Marnell, *Once Upon a Store*. New York: Herder & Herder, 1971, 80–81.

346. W. Gerbosi, "What about Wagon Route Selling?" in ed. P. Sayres, *Foodmarketing* (New York: McGraw-Hill, 1950), 88–94.

347. J. Mayo, *The American Grocery Store*. Westport, CT: Greenwood, 1993, 132–33.

348. W. Greer, *America the Bountiful*. Washington, DC: Food Marketing Inst, 1986, 154–55.

349. C. Groves, *Marketing of Milk Products in the U.K.* Ayr: West of Scotland Agricultural College, 1981, 32–35.

350. Z. Raitcliff, ed., *Fast Food and Home-Delivery Outlets*. London: Market Assessment Publications, 1995.

351. Mayo, supra, 243.

352. Raitcliff, supra, 4, 41, 52, 55–56.

353. *Economist*, December 14, 1996, 28.

354. See as to Britain, N. Gregson, *Servicing the Middle Classes* (New York: Routledge, 1994); and as to the United States, M. Romero, *Maid in the U.S.A.* (New York: Routledge, 1992).

CHAPTER 2

Enfranchising Citizens

It is important to the wise exercise of newly conferred powers that they be subject to adequate controls, both internal and external. A discussion follows of some of the most widely utilized methods of control that have a bearing on sublocal governments and associations, whose basic premise is that the franchise, in sublocal as well as larger contexts, is a right protective of all rights.

ELECTION TECHNIQUES

In Colonial Massachusetts, "Governor Shirley attempted the substitution of triennial elections for the annual ones to which the men of Massachusetts were accustomed. . . . By 1776 the importance of annual elections was so well established that John Adams could claim that there was not in the whole circle of the sciences a maxim more infallible than this: "Where annual elections end, there slavery begins."[1]

By contrast, prewar Swedish communal councils, though elected by public meetings of all citizens, were elected for terms of four years.[2] British parish councils are normally elected for four-year terms.[3]

Most American residential-community associations employ staggered three-year terms with annual elections for one-third of the board;[4] the street associations of St. Louis employ one-year terms.[5] Annual election of officers and at least part of the board does not impose undue organization costs on very small organizations and is important to allow self-correction while the skills and attributes of neighbors are being discovered.

The possibility of early change has a dampening effect on political grievances and passions; in addition, frequent replacement of representatives gives a larger number of persons experience of office-experience that itself may moderate opinions.

Unanimity Requirements

The benefit of unanimity requirements has been summarized by Jane Mansbridge:

Requiring consensus directs members' attention to the common good. It intensifies the tendency of any face-to-face group to focus attention and communication on dissidents, trying to draw them into the group. It encourages people to listen carefully to both the emotional tone and the intellectual content. It helps bring out information, forges commitment, discourages factions.[6]

Unanimity requirements, however, "benefit those whose interest lies with the status quo . . . who can make things happen outside the consensual process and who therefore set the boundaries . . . who have the inner strength to stand up to group pressure. . . ."[7]

It is possible to supply artificial incentives to unanimity. Mansbridge notes that "the [pre-1640] British Parliament would defer issues in the hope of reaching unanimity or reconsider a question after the vote was taken."[8] A modern Indian legislature provided an enhanced grant to villages electing their chairmen and 80 percent of their council by unanimous vote.[9] Consent calendars in the U.S. House and Senate make possible fast progress of legislation where unanimity exists. An inducement to compromise could be provided by the converse: a mandated period of delay for nonunanimous legislation.

However, unanimity is usually conceived of as a self-protective mechanism, as in the old Polish Diet and Aragonese Cortes. This feature of it is dramatized by Dennis Mueller's observation that "no over-centralization problem would exist if the national legislature made decisions under the unanimity rule."[10] Buchanan and Tullock in *The Calculus of Consent* assert that it encourages stubbornness, bluffing, and the pretense of unreasonableness, leading to the comment that "their image of unanimity is the Big Five veto in the U.N. Security Council."[11] They are criticized for failing to recognize that "the way a group makes decisions can alter the members' goals."[12] To this, the public-choice theorists rejoin by rejecting "the implicit assumption that the individual must somehow shift his psychological and moral gears when he moves between the private and the social aspects of life."[13] It is conceded, however, that the application of economic models to political behavior is limited by the fact that the outcomes of individuals' political acts are more uncertain and that the diffused nature of politics produces less of a sense of decision-making responsibility.[14] Public-choice theorists do not deny that "moral restraint is a substitute for institutional–constitutional restraint, and in a society with more of the former there will be less need for the latter, and vice-versa."[15] Mancur Olson is less dogmatic than Buchanan and Tullock: "More bargaining is likely in any situation where 100 percent participation is required than when some smaller percentage can undertake group-oriented activity."[16]

The value of unanimity would seem greatest in small, limited-purpose organizations; in Mansbridge's words:

Interests are least likely to conflict in very small polities . . . decentralization works best when the scope of the decision need not be broad and when accuracy, speed, and adaptability are at a premium.[17] Small size promotes conformity. . . . If even one person supports a dissenter against a group, the chance of the dissenter's conforming drops drastically . . . members of small communities tend to avoid conflict because of the greater sanctions their neighbors can wield.[18]

However,

the costs of reaching agreement on decisions rises quite sharply as the unanimous support of the whole group is approached. . . . The reduction in expected costs that may be secured by the change from the unanimity rule to, say, a 90 percent rule, may more than offset the increase in total expected costs involved in discounting possible adverse decisions when the individual falls in the minority 10 percent.[19] If small size does promote empathy, the effect may well disappear by the time a political unit contains 1,000 people.[20]

The demand for government action not based on unanimous consent rises as groups grow larger; in small groups

[a]ll externalities, negative and positive, will be eliminated as a result of purely voluntary arrangements that will be readily negotiated among private people. . . . The costs of interdependence include both external costs [from having to yield one's preferences to majority views] and decision-making costs, and it is the sum of these two elements that is decisive in the individual constitutional calculus.[21]

Bargaining costs [to achieve unanimity] might approach infinity in groups of substantial size.[22]

It is said that in small French communes

the mayor establishes himself as a person who may "speak for the community" by suppressing political conflicts where they occur . . . this is achieved in the smaller communes through establishing personal contacts with citizens, placating enemies by means such as getting their children into a desired school, pouring oil on troubled waters, and resolving differences over a cup of tea.[23]

Supermajority Requirements

In suggesting supermajorities as a check on neighborhood assemblies, Benjamin Barber observes: "Civic communities act with the greatest caution in the face of dissent because dissent is a signal that the community itself is in jeopardy. . . . In this spirit, neighborhood assemblies might want to experiment with requiring near-unanimous consensus in matters of local jurisdiction. . . ."[24] In any event, according a minority a veto is not to be deemed inconsistent with democratic principles:

Many scholars seem to have overlooked the central place that the unanimity rule must occupy in any normative theory of democratic government. . . . At best, majority rule should be viewed as one among many practical expedients made necessary by the costs of securing widespread agreement on political issues when individual and group interests diverge.[25]

The last proposition as to majority voting has been disputed on the basis that majority rule "minimizes the chances of supporting an issue that fails and opposing an issue that passes."[26]

Small political entities can more readily resort to supermajority requirements than large ones:

The expected costs of organizing decisions, under any given rule, will be less in the smaller unit than the larger. . . . From this it follows that, for those activities which are collectivized . . . the smaller unit will normally have a more inclusive decision-making rule than the larger unit. . . . One means of reducing . . . costs [of reaching agreement] is to organize collective activity in the smallest units consistent with the extent of the externality that the collectivization is designed to eliminate.[27]

Supermajority requirements minimize the need for judicial review: "The larger the majority required to pass laws restricting individual freedom, the less need there is to protect individual rights in the constitution."[28] Economists assert that they limit logrolling and "gross privilege seeking."[29]

In the towns of Colonial Massachusetts "unanimity was . . . demanded almost as a matter of social decency, so that a simple majority commanded little authority at the local level and scarcely even certified decisions as legitimate."[30] "A politics of consensus was a politics of the compromises necessary to come to a consensus."[31] "[D]iscussion and practice both reflected the assumption that legitimacy was a consequence not of royal assent but of the consent of the governed . . . a change in the American view of the derivation of authority."[32]

The Uniform Common Interests Act regulating condominium and homeowners' associations—variants of which have been adopted thus far in six states since its promulgation in revised form in 1994—requires an 80 percent supermajority to terminate an association, noting that "unanimous consent from all property owners would be impossible to secure as a practical matter in a project of any size." There is also a requirement of the assent of 80 percent of all members to impose new use and occupancy restrictions, and a further requirement that existing uses be grandfathered, on the premise that restrictions should be imposed "only by a supermajority and only after providing for protection for those whose use or occupancy may be affected," an approach reminiscent of an early New England town-meeting.[33] The 1994 changes should bring to an end a major source of criticism of residential-community association rules: That strange and petty aesthetic and behavioral regulations may be imposed on homeowners. In fact, considering the tens of millions of residents of such associations, the amount of litigation generated by such restrictions has been remarkably small.

In addition, use restrictions may not be imposed unless the proscribed use adversely affects other owners.[34] Adoption of the budget requires 67 percent of all members, except that the budget proposed by the board of directors takes effect unless a majority of all members rejects it—in effect an executive budget system making both upward and downward departures difficult.[35]

Similar attachment to consensus survives in many Asian communities. It has been observed that "[D]ecision making, Japanese style, is based on consensus. There is still a deep feeling in many quarters that it is immoral and 'undemocratic' for a majority to govern, for decisions to be reached without compromise with the minority," and further that [in Java] "matters are not decided by voting. The aim is to secure essential unanimity."[36] One Western commentator states categorically: "A decision by consensus cannot be reached in a council where active members number more than about 15. A unanimous decision in a council of one hundred men is, in fact, an act of acclamation or legitimation: the actual decision has been taken elsewhere."[37] The same writer urges the thesis that "conflicts will tend to be resolved by a compromise if the majority knows that the minority must be carried with them on pain of taking no action at all" as where the members of a body execute their own decisions. In addition "'horse-trading' negotiations which can lead to consensus are only possible when there is a frequency of interaction." Further, in "elite councils," "closing of the ranks [may be] an act of fusion consequent upon the opposition between . . . guardians and their subjects . . . or in opposition to a body outside itself and its public." All these factors favor unanimity rules in small associations.

Prewar Swedish communes required a two-thirds majority in their councils for purchase or sale of real property, new programs, rate assessments above a specified minimum, or remission of rates.[38] It has been said of American residential-community associations that

[U]ntil recently, the primary concern of state law governing CIDs has been protection of individual owners from majority rule, with requirements for supermajorities to raise assessments or change association rules. More recently, California law has recognized that allowing a recalcitrant majority to block board decisions may in fact violate important rights of other individual owners and lead to physical deterioration.[39]

The requirement of unanimity to relax restrictions in many early RCA covenants has been criticized; more recent covenants tend to adopt the suggestion that

[t]he developer might be allowed to designate an initial set of amenity regulations to be incorporated in the deed but also be required to enable an association to relax the restrictions by some extraordinary-majority vote after a designated period of time. This would create . . . a limited public capability on the part of the association to modify private property rights, analogous to municipal zoning powers but with the reverse effect.[40]

A two-thirds majority provision is said to obviate the possibility of cyclical strategic voting on successive issues, thereby providing stable majorities.[41] Robert Dahl has enunciated the general principle that

the greater the difference in competence among members, the weaker the case for political equality; the greater the amount of disagreement among members, the weaker the case for majority rule. . . . For the state . . . one may reasonably opt for political equality and at the same time a system that . . . limit[s] what simple majorities . . . can do.[42]

French communal elections traditionally required successful candidates to obtain a majority of votes cast, and one-fourth the total electorate; upon a second ballot, a plurality sufficed.[43]

Use of supermajority requirements for major actions seems entirely appropriate in small associations, and something like the French approach is appropriate in connection with the election of their officers.

Sortition

Sortition, or choice of representatives by lot, was a device of ancient Greek democracy that survives in contemporary culture in the choice of juries. The Athenian council, which usually consisted of four to six hundred members, was elected or chosen by lot in and from the subdivisions of the state. In this way, a domination of the countryside by the town was avoided, and sortition prevented as far as possible any tampering with the election.[44]

Appointment by lot excluded influence of any kind and any regard for persons; in combination with the prohibition of re-election it . . . emphatically served the principle of democratic authority. . . . Sortition was regarded as an entirely normal way of appointing officials in a democracy and it worked.[45]

Montesquieu observed "the suffrage by lot is natural to democracy, as that by choice is to aristocracy."[46] The device is said by Benjamin Barber to have been employed in Venice and Florence. In fourteenth-century Florence, fifty citizens were selected by drawing lots every two to four months to fill magistracies and boards.[47]

In contrast, a plurality system tends to select representatives whose views are near the "center" of the distribution of preferences, leaving those with minority views unrepresented. A representative in Florence did not have to run for reelection and was therefore less closely tied to the geographically defined interests of his quarter.[48]

The pool from which officers are drawn can be a volunteer pool, supported or not supported by official salaries; training can be supplied to candidates, and there can be recall provisions.[49] The Athenian system was subject to the safeguard of the *dokimasia*, or scrutiny requiring those drawn to show that they had paid taxes, performed military service, and treated their parents with respect.[50]

As late as the early nineteenth century, foreigners were impressed by the extent to which obligatory service employing sortition was the practice in England not only for juries, but for sheriffs, constables, and the militia.[51] The principle has been applied more recently for a time in the United States in connection with the military draft, and continues to be so employed in foreign countries.

Public-choice theorists have suggested a revival of the process to select an advisory legislature: The major requirement is to establish institutional structures in which the decision-makers are not responsible for deciding issues that have a significant short-range impact upon themselves. Delegates . . . might be drawn from the old (as many Indian societies do), from another community, or at random from the population. Sortition has been suggested as a substitute for the national "electronic town meetings" proposed by some; it has the advantage of limiting the "value of the time the polity would have to expend in becoming reasonably well informed." Where the number of delegates is small, it is subject to the objection that "the probability will approach 100 percent over time that in a draw of the legislature a set of representatives which reflect only a small part of the underlying population will dominate."[52] Sortition has even been suggested for legislative acts: "A lottery in which the probability of a proposal's victory is the fraction of votes in the parliament of the party which proposes it [would encourage] . . . a mutually beneficial compromise."[53]

The usefulness of sortition in small associations is probably greatest in connection with the rendition of services rather than the election of officers, who in most instances will be quasi-volunteers. Sortition is the device customarily used to keep up participation in preschool playgroups and neighborhood security patrols.

Term Limits

In the Athenian Council, "[T]he turnover within the whole body of citizens was ensured by having each man elected for a fixed period only (mostly a year and never more) and by restricting re-elections in Athens . . . no one could be councillor more than twice in his life."[54] It has been said that

[I]t is a mistake to suppose that it was basically *sortition* which kept the democracy in being. More fundamental by far was the principle of rotation—that no citizen should hold any one office more than once in his lifetime. . . . The use of the lot and the diminution in the authority of the magistracy were both alike the logical corolaries of rotation, a principle which rendered it inevitable that the competence of a candidate should not be a determining factor in his selection.[55]

Similarly, "the communities of provincial Massachusetts . . . converted the most trivial tasks into public functions exercised by elected agents."[56] In this light, one of the stranger criticisms of residential community associations is Evan McKenzie's complaint that RCAs are unique in

placing the fate of the experiment in the hands of untrained, uncompensated amateurs; establishing no qualifications for their participation; creating no public institutional support structure for on-the-job training; and leaving the directors essentially free of public regulation. . . .[57]

It can be argued that annual terms for officers serve a purpose similar to term limits, re-eligibility restrictions, and required rotation, but they may not be sufficient. If a significant number of members of the association have not been involved in active management the performance of the association may suffer, and civic apathy may be the product of prolonged delegation of functions to an officer, however qualified and skilful he may be. There are values in local participation; we may recall Tocqueville's observation that

[i]f the French ... had continued to busy themselves daily in the administration of the country in the provincial assemblies, they would certainly never have let themselves be inflamed, as they then were, by the ideas of the writers; they would have kep[t] a touch on practical business which would have saved them from pure theory.[58] As the general liberties perished, dragging with them in their ruin local liberties, the townsman and the gentleman ceased to have contact in public life ... these two men never met except by mere chance in private life. The two classes were not only rivals, they were enemies.[59] Thus Paris had become the master of France, and the army, that was to make itself mistress of Paris, was already assembling.[60]

Secret Ballots

In Athens, "the debate led up to the vote in which numbers were decided either by show of hands or in secret ballot by voting pebbles ... the introduction of the ballot was a very important step in the development towards democracy."[61] It has been questioned, however, whether the pebbles were cast secretly.[62] In the courts, however, the casting was secret.[63] John Stuart Mill, on the other hand, argued against the secret ballot in his *Representative Government*, on the ground that electors had a duty of public justification, on the non–Madisonian theory, earlier expressed by Burke, that

each is under an absolute moral obligation to consider the interest of the public, not his private advantage, and give his vote to the best of his judgment, exactly as he were bound to do if he were the sole voter, and the election depended on him alone.

Where a representative body is chosen by election, open voting by its members is necessary for members to be accountable to their constituents. If such a body were selected by sortition, secret voting would be appropriate to insulate the otherwise unaccountable members from corruption, since it "increases uncertainty in vote buying."[64] It is provided for in the election of the German president to insulate parliamentarians from party pressures.

In Colonial Massachusetts, secret ballots were used in town elections: "Secrecy was essential for the prevention of town dissension and the preservation of group solidarity."[65] Ten percent of those in attendance at a British parish meeting can require that it be polled by ballot.[66]

The appropriate principle for small community associations would appear to involve a secret ballot for elections of officers and open voting at meetings of the governing board. Other questions arising at membership meetings might be decided by secret ballot upon request.

District Elections

"In Athens, probably from the time of Cleisthenes, councillors were drawn by lot in the *demes* of each *phyle* in approximate relation to the number of citizens in each *deme*."[67] The theory, however, was not that of representative government. The representation of the will of some body within the state (*deme* or *phyle*) by an individual—naturally elected and not chosen by lot—and the gathering of such individuals into a body to represent the general will—this was something the *polis* never knew and, perhaps, being what it was, never could know.[68] Early Massachusetts town meetings stood in marked contrast to the *polis* in that the persons they sent to the state General Court were sent as representatives, were required to reside in the town, and were given detailed mandates making them mere agents for the town meeting, and were required to render reports to it.[69]

The argument against functional representation of economic groups or proportional representation has been succinctly stated by Mancur Olson: "One shortcoming of . . . a pressure-group parliament is that no one legislator can feasibly trade off one interest in favor of another, and therefore the degree of compromise necessary to a continuing democracy may be unattainable."[70] On the other hand, it has been alleged that district representation produces a link between political power and concentrated economic interests.[71]

Proportional representation, and consequent coalition government with principal parties sharing offices in a stable pattern, has been common in local and national government in Switzerland, Austria, Belgium, and The Netherlands. The advantage of this system is said to be that

[a]ll voters, not just the majority of each constituency, are represented in the legislature. Consequently a majority of the legislature represents a majority of the voters, not just one fourth plus as may be the case . . . when the members are elected from single-member constituencies.[72]

In addition, it has been urged by Dennis Mueller that "the tendency for centralization should be weaker when representation in the national legislature is not geographically based" since proportional representation fosters loyalty to party rather than constituency and thereby discourages "geographic redistribution through logrolling."[73]

In defending district elections, Lord Salisbury urged:

So long as men sit by a number of tenures, a tyrannous majority is impossible. One man sits because he is locally popular, another because he is friends with the powerful men of his district; a third because he has sat for a long time and does parliamentary business well; a fourth because he is a good Catholic; a fifth because he is a good Protestant; a sixth because he understands the particular trade of his locality.[74]

Madison, in *The Federalist* (No. 10), in arguing for large republics, used language that could also be used in support of district elections within small republics:

You take in a greater variety of parties and interests; you make it less probable that a majority of the whole will have a common motive to invade the rights of other citizens; or, if such a common motive exists, it will be more difficult for all who feel it to discover their own strength and act in unison with each other.

The arguments for geographic representation are pragmatic:

Geographic representation . . . falls somewhere between the two extreme models—between purely randomized representation and purely functional representation. . . . Within single constituencies there is normally to be found a reasonably wide range of voter interests, but there also remain many political issues which involve differential geographical impact. . . . Geographical representation is similar to majority voting in that, a priori, there is nothing that can be said for it as regards superiority over other possible bases.[75]

British parish councils may be divided into wards for the election of councillors upon application of the parish council or 30 of the electors of a parish.[76]

French arrondisement councils in the three major cities have two-thirds of their members elected by proportional representation, the remainder being the city councillors.[77] The use of city-wide lists for the municipal council was defended by an early commentator on the basis that it aids in "securing men of acknowledged note and standing for candidates";[78] proportional representation has as one of its merits the fact that it is a form of indirect election. Madison would have approved of this, but disapproved of the system's tendency to multiply factions. The arrondisements have been immune from the American disease of reapportionment, since "it will be found by far more convenient to assign additional members to the more populous arrondisements than to recast the lines in order to create districts of equal population."[79]

In very small organizations, a case can still be made for district representation as a means of discouraging factions, possibly combined with some at large election or co-optation to recruit specially talented persons. District representation should be on a block-by-block or building-by-building basis as appropriate, thus insuring that representatives can be easily contacted. The follies of reapportionment should be avoided in the interests of stable constituencies unless required by the courts, in which case weighted voting, retaining existing lines, should be resorted to.

Property Qualifications

Limited-purpose governments have traditionally restricted their franchise to those with the largest interest in their activities, who bear the burden of them. It was not until 1948 that nonratepayers were accorded a vote in British local-government elections, and the decline of British local government according to some observers can be measured from that date.[80] The history of American municipal government is quite similar in that the municipal franchise was liberalized less rapidly than the parliamentary franchise, though at a much earlier date than in Britain.[81] It is interesting to observe the revival of organizations with ownership-based franchises, such as residential community associations and business-improvement districts, in response to felt need. It is possible to have too wide, as well as too narrow, a franchise for limited-purpose organizations. Even the most committed egalitarians do not favor giving commuters and tourists the vote in municipal elections.[82] If taxation without representation is tyranny, so is its reverse.

It is only when limited-purpose organizations are accorded general taxing powers that there is a case for general enfranchisement. James Bryce observed of American local government in 1921: "A government controlled by those who have no interest in economy will not be economical. . . . Here was representation without taxation."[83] Shortly earlier, President Frank Goodnow of Johns Hopkins noted:

By not providing for either property or educational qualification, and by requiring only a short term of residence, the United States city election laws thus generally bring it about that the number of voters at city elections is from eight to fifty percent greater than elsewhere. Finally the fact that these laws do not accord the vote to nonresident taxpayers prevents the exercise of a possible conservative influence on city elections.[84]

The insights of game theory have been invoked to support the proposition that, where discriminatory taxation is resorted to,

there are no effective limits to resource wastage. . . . Any project yielding general benefits, quite independently of cost considerations, will be supported by the dominating majority if they are successful in imposing the full tax financing of the project onto the shoulders of the minority . . . all projects yielding any benefits at all to the majority coalition members, and costing no more than the maximum taxable capacity of the minority, will be adopted without question.[85]

This may seem an overstatement, but there is experience that suggests that it is not—notably that of municipalities supported by property taxation in which ratepayers make up only a small fraction of the electorate. The extravagances of the so-called "looney left" councils in London boroughs with few owner-occupiers gave rise to the Thatcher government's efforts at "rate capping" of local authorities and ultimately to its misbegotten effort to impose a capitation tax rather than rates.[86] Similarly, the extravagances of municipal governments in New York and Washington, D.C.—both cities with unusually large proportions of renters and unusually few owner-occupiers led higher-level governments to impose appointed boards with the authority to veto or curtail locally approved expenditures.

While more than 65 percent of American housing is owner-occupied, the percentage of owner-occupied housing in New York State is 52 percent and in the District of Columbia 37 percent, rendering these jurisdictions very different polities. The privatization of public housing carried on by the Thatcher government in Britain had as one of its aims the creation of a more "responsible" electorate in poorer subdivisions. The economist Joseph Stiglitz, by way of explanation, has noted "the absence of appropriate incentives for renters for voting for efficient public goods tax packages" and has observed:

The sole concern of the renter in evaluating any program is whether it raises rents by less than it improves his welfare . . . renters have no incentive to ensure that public services are provided efficiently, and have perverse incentives with regard to the choice of quality and quantity of public goods.[87]

Colonial Massachusetts imposed a property qualification for voting at town meetings.[88] Its main purpose was the exclusion of tenants on the ground that "they have not sufficient discretion, or are so situated as to have no wills of their own."[89] When the franchise for British parish councils was widened to include agricultural laborers in 1894:

No direct objection of any kind was made against the introduction of a democratic franchise. . . . But loud voices were raised . . . against a danger . . . that local expenditure might come to be controlled by a majority of persons who would contribute but little to the local revenues . . . [the bill] was studded with . . . provisions to limit the expenditure and define the functions of parish . . . councils.[90]

It was said to have been a vice of the Elizabethan Poor Law when it came under pressure as a result of the depression following the Napoleonic Wars that in some parishes the "poor themselves predominated . . . and could fix the terms and rates of relief as they saw fit, without thought for the interests of the ratepayers."[91] The Parish Vestries Act of 1818 therefore limited the franchise to ratepayers and introduced a system of plural voting, corporations and nonresident property owners being enfranchised in the following year.[92] There are currently no property qualifications for voting in parish elections other than for nonresident property owners, who must have property with a yearly value of ten pounds.[93]

In France, a citadel of owner-occupiers, property qualifications for communal elections were eliminated in 1884. However, the principal source of local revenue was not a property tax but a system of excises administered by local customshouses that fell on all electors, not merely property owners. Even today, an unorthodox source of revenue, the *taxe professionelle* on business rental values and payroll, supplies about a third of French local-government expenditure.[94] Nonresident property owners continue to be permitted to vote in France, but are required to choose between the location of their property and their place of residence, and were prohibited from voting in both places.[95] "Small peasant and artisan property in cottages and plots was widely diffused in Western Europe, where democracy appeared to have been effectively tamed. A plebiscatory universal franchise became the bulwark of authority, first in Napoleon III's France. . . ."[96] In this view, widespread ownership of taxable property is a prerequisite to effective local democracy, a condition that does not obtain in cities or portions of cities where the proportion of rental housing is unusually high and revenue sources are limited to grants and property taxes, as in the District of Columbia, most of New York City, and some London boroughs. As Tocqueville observed: "The extravagance of democracy is less to be dreaded . . . as the people acquire a share of property, because, on the one hand, the contributions of the rich are then less needed, and on the other, it is more difficult to impose taxes that will not reach the imposers."[97]

The continued recourse to village or other sublocal units in underdeveloped countries has led to the observation that: "There is good reason to believe that preservation of the small commune in many developing countries may entail the continuation of the formal or informal predominance of the rural aristocracy."[98]

Concerns about the ability of enfranchised nonratepayers to heavily tax business property as well as a desire to foster equalization of revenues have led in our time to "restrictions on local business tax in Germany, the removal of local discretion on commercial property taxation in Britain, and the limitation of the rating powers of local councils on business tax in France,"[99] as well as provisions in Minnesota for sharing of the yield of the commercial property tax.

An opposite concern has been expressed about the condition that would arise if the local income tax were the sole local revenue source: "A local income tax without a local property tax infringes accountability in inviting those below the income tax threshold to vote for higher local spending in the knowledge that they would not be contributing to its costs."[100]

American residential community associations characteristically exclude tenants from voting. In homeowner associations, there is usually one vote per unit; in condominium associations votes are frequently based on the size of units. Plural voting and nonresident voting are thus provided for. The associations that permit tenant voting usually bar tenants from voting on financial matters. It has been implied that a restricted franchise in RCAs disadvantages blacks, who tend to be renters. This argument overlooks the continuing growth in black homeownership in the United States: in 1995, 69.2 percent of whites and 43.6 percent of blacks were owner-occupiers.[101] The home ownership rate for all races was 41 percent in 1940—the black rate today.[102] The Uniform Common Interests Act as amended in 1994 permits but does not require[103] associations to allow tenants to vote on certain issues, noting that

it may be desirable to give lessees, rather than lessors, of units the right to vote on issues involving day to day operation both because the lessees may have a greater interest and because it is desirable to have lessees feel they are an integral part of the common interest community.[104]

There are conflicts among various interests:

Tenants may not wish to see property values increase because that might result in rent increases. Absentee owners may have less interest in quality-of-life issues than do resident homeowners and tenants. Absentee owners may cast their votes against special assessments for certain community facilities, against certain rules of behavior . . . or against community plans to oppose development in surrounding areas.[105]

Two commentators have urged a "split vote," half cast by the nonresident owner and half by the tenant.[106] One critic of RCAs has alleged, without empirical evidence, that "the ideal was that of self-governing local communities. . . . The reality, too often, was an undemocratic oligarchy in which an apathetic body of residents was governed by a few dedicated or overly zealous neighbors who were for the most part told what to do by property managers and lawyers."[107] But most governments of any kind are led by the "dedicated" and "zealous" who are told what to do by "lawyers" and "managers"; they are not stigmatized as "undemocratic" on that account. And RCAs, unlike most governments, characteristically have annual elections.

A new device—the parallel taxing district—has allowed RCAs to escape the restrictions imposed on them by a property-owners' franchise. New functions, such as local legislation, the operation of schools and the receipt of large quantities of public funds, which might subject them to one-man, one-vote rules, can be carried on by a special taxing district with manhood suffrage and the same boundaries. For the normal functions of an RCA, there would seem to be no need to depart from a property-owners' franchise. The capitalization of property assessments renders minimal any impact of them on renters, the areas governed are homogeneous, and the functions paid for are limited and closely relate benefits to assessments bringing the associations, and like organizations such as business-improvement districts within the rule of the cases upholding property franchises in special districts,[108] and a delay in the effectiveness of nonunanimous regulations would encourage efforts to compromise with dissenters.

PARLIAMENTARY SAFEGUARDS

We here consider such devices as referenda, publication of agendas, rotation of chairmen, quorums, and delayed effective dates.

Referenda

Jane Mansbridge has observed:

When individuals do not have equal power, a polity whose goal is the equal protection of interests must redistribute power—by instituting referenda, for example.[109] When a group grows larger or more diverse it must find a substitute for discussion and genuine persuasion . . . a combination of referenda, representation and either majority rule or an emphasis on proportional representation . . . democracies as large as the modern nation state [must] be primarily adversary democracies . . . efforts to create a unitary "moral equivalent of war" lose their glamour after a year or two.[110]

Indeed, the case has been made that apathy is an almost inevitable consequence of the large size of organizations:

[C]lass-oriented action will not occur if the individuals that make up a class act rationally . . . the rational thing [in a large state] to do is to ignore . . . class interests and to spend . . . energies on . . . personal interests. . . . Crane Brinton has shown that the major revolutions, communist or otherwise, were carried out by strikingly small numbers of people.[111]

The use of referenda as a form of direct democracy has recently become popular in Western Europe, in part as a reaction to the large size of urban and suburban governments. Switzerland has long had referenda and several German Lander (usually on 10 percent petition) have recently enhanced the availability of local referenda, and advisory local referenda have been newly provided in Finland (on 2 percent petition), Luxembourg (on 20 percent petition), Austria (in several Lander), France, and Italy.[112] Traditionally, referenda were available in the United Kingdom[113] and Norway to determine a limited number of local questions (the new British Labor government has proposed their use as a substitute for local rate-capping), and are extensively used in most jurisdictions in the United States and Canada.[114] Japan has provisions, introduced at American request after the war, for referenda on petition of one-fifth of citizens for recall of officers or ordinances (other than those for taxes and charges) or for audits of enterprises. Recall of officers requires a petition signed by one-third of the electorate.[115] In Switzerland, at the national level, "there are only four instances in Swiss history where popular initiatives have been accepted contrary to the advice of the government. Rather the referendum has acted as a brake on the wishes of government and parliament,"[116] and is credited with limiting the level of taxation.[117] One of its supporters observed: "the most straightforward method for allowing voters to reveal their preferences for public goods would be to present each issue along with a tax formula for financing it, a procedure recommended by Wicksell."[118] This device was applied to school appropriations in Ohio by legislation sponsored by Senator Robert Taft in his days in the Ohio legislature and is credited with limiting the tax burden of education in that state.

Referenda speak to a recurrent problem of representative government, at high levels or low: "If only some citizens participate in political life, it is essential that they always remember and be regularly reminded that they are . . . only some."[119] The criticism of referenda stresses "the greater informational efficiency" inherent in representative government[120] and the alleged fact that "the ballot does not easily register intensity of interest as the legislative process does."[121]

In the case of sublocal governments and RCAs the costs of referenda are slight, and availability of the device on petition of a specified percentage of members obviates the need to minutely monitor the frequent meetings of boards.

Published Agendas

Prewar Belgian communes were required to hold public meetings on financial matters, unless two-thirds of the members found that the public interest requires a private meeting.[122] British parish council meetings are required to be public unless closed by majority vote for a particular occasion for a reason stated in the resolution closing the meeting.[123] French communal council meetings have been required to be public since 1884.[124] Most American sublocal governments and RCAs have their councils subject to open-meeting provisions, in fulfillment of Justice Brandeis's conception that "sunlight is the best disinfectant; electric light the best policeman."

In the Athenian state,

every decree of the people must be preceded by a preliminary decision of the Council. In this way the debate in the popular assembly was generally directed. Still, it was always possible to tell the Council what they should produce, to decline it or to change it by amendments till it could be reversed; this gave the *Ecclesia* a good part of its power back.[125] The requirement that every ordinary meeting must be announced some days in advance and the impossibility of holding an extraordinary meeting without express summons provided some safeguard against any caprice or overhastiness of the masses.[126]

Meetings "took place monthly or even more frequently (Athens eventually had 40 during the year)."[127]

Colonial Massachusetts allowed much variation in notice and in the setting of meeting times, but there too "the insistence on full warning was an insistence on inclusiveness."[128] Warrants of meetings prohibited action on matters not on the agenda. British parish councils are required to meet at least four times annually, and a public notice must be posted at least three days ahead of time.[129] Under the Uniform Common Interests Act, 14-to-30-days notice must be given of budget meetings, and similar provisions apply to other meetings. These provisions are necessary safeguards against surprise and the packing of meetings, and allow problems to surface and be ironed out in advance of them.

Rotation of Chairmen

"Daily change of chairmen, such as we find in Athens and elsewhere, prevented any permanent influence either way between the *Ecclesia* and its leader."[130] A rotating executive is a feature of the Swiss Constitution; in Colombia the presidency alternates between political parties. British parish councils select their chairmen annually, even though their members have four-year terms.[131] The considerations bearing on term limits are equally applicable here; for most purposes, annual rotation appears sufficient. The modern left has a tendency to forget Aristotle's description of democracy as including

election of officials by all from all, government of each by all, and of all by each in turn; election by lot to all magistracies or to all that do not need experience and skill ... no office to be held twice, or more than a few times, by the same person, or few offices except the military ones; short tenure either of all offices or of as many as possible; judicial functions to be exercised by all citizens, that is, by persons selected from all, and on all matters, or on most and the greatest and most important, for instance, the audit of official accounts, constitutional questions, private contracts; the assembly to be sovereign over all matters, but no official over any or only over extremely few; or else a council to be sovereign over the most important matters.... And in respect of the magistracies it is democratic to have none tenable for life....[132]

Quorums

In Greece, "so large a part of the citizens were often missing that quorums had to be introduced to make decrees valid."[133] Other means of fostering the same purpose have been outlined by Jane Mansbridge:

In trying to ensure that the "volunteers" who attend represent the entire group, three specific strategies might be helpful. First, altering the time and duration of meetings, making meeting days legal holidays, paying members to attend, and providing child care and transportation. Second, occasional referenda. Third ... [imposing] the obligation to consider ... the interests of those not present.[134]

The quorum for British parish-council meetings is one-third of the membership.[135] Traditionally, in vestry meetings "the major part of those present concludes all that are absent."[136] The quorum of a parish meeting is two (three for execution of documents).[137] The Uniform Common Interests Act imposes only a 20 percent quorum requirement by reason of the fact that it applies to many resort communities; it also permits proxy voting, but requires supermajorities of all members for nonroutine actions.[138] This approach seems appropriate for most purposes, particularly if the further check of a referendum is provided on demand of a specified portion of voters.

Delayed Effective Dates

One method proposed for limiting drastic constitutional change or possible oppression by temporary majorities is a requirement of delayed effective dates for significant changes as a means of inspiring disinterestedness in those proposing them. Under this scheme, new rules might "not take effect for five, ten, or even twenty-five years . . . restrictions could be placed on the frequency with which . . . decisions could be reversed, as well as the majorities necessary to reverse them."[139] Delays of this magnitude may tax the institutional memory of small associations; a one-year delay, however, would allow time for second thoughts and an intervening election, and a delay in the effectiveness of nonunanimous regulations would encourage efforts to compromise with dissenters.

SECESSION

Robert Nozick has observed:

It is not a general principle that every community or group must allow internal opting out when that is feasible. For sometimes such internal opting out would itself change the character of the group from what is desired. In a face-to-face community, one cannot avoid being directly confronted with what one finds to be offensive. How one lives in one's immediate environment is affected. Must the great majority cloister themselves against the offensive minority?[140]

An example was given by Sir Henry Maine, writing of Indian village communities, who observed:

If English influence has had anything to do with arresting customs of re-partition, which are, no doubt, quite alien to English administrative ideas, it is a fresh example of destructive influence, unwillingly and unconsciously exercised. . . . The partition of inheritances and execution for debt levied on land are destroying the communities—this is the formula heard nowadays everywhere in India.[141]

Face-to-face communities with common ownership have their economic limitations. Maine also observed:

Their admirers certainly do not claim for them that they readily adopt new crops and new modes of tillage, and it is often admitted that they are grudging and improvident owners of their waste land. . . . Gradually the assumption of the right to get the best price has penetrated into the interior of these groups, but it is never completely received so long as the bond of connection between man and man is assumed to be that of family or clan-connection. The rule only triumphs when the primitive community is in ruins.[142]

Writing of the postwar movement to the suburbs, Hadley Arkes noted:

> The current in recent years has been in the direction of smaller communities, where there may be a larger possibility for the sharing of public purposes. If public policy becomes unacceptable on any decisive point, there is the prospect of moving to another community, and so the problem of moral discordance may be softened by a combination of freedom of choice and the powers that are still preserved in local communities to determine their own character.[143]

Buchanan and Tullock similarly point out

> choice among alternative collective units limits both the external costs imposed by collective action and the expected costs of decision-making . . . the limit to damages expected [and] of individual investment in bargaining [is] the cost of [an individual] shifting to a more agreeable collectivity . . . decentralization . . . introduces elements into the political process that are not unlike those found in the operating of competitive markets.[144]

Conflict in early Massachusetts towns was frequently dealt with by allowing dissenters to secede and form a new town.[145] It is worth remembering that, as Tocqueville reminded us, the New England colonies were formed by "allowing a certain number of emigrants to form themselves into a political society under the protection of the mother country and to govern themselves in whatever was not contrary to her laws . . . [a] mode of colonization, so favorable to liberty."[146] Secession clauses have also been suggested for neighborhoods in large residential community associations.[147]

Jane Mansbridge has noted that "self-selection can further increase the homogeneity of small groups."[148] "Thus," in Dennis Mueller's words,

> a citizen who felt that he had a higher stake in local public decisions due to an intense preference for a public art museum, could, by migrating to a local community where citizens had similarly intense preferences toward publicly financed art museums, move the compositions of both communities in the direction of satisfying the equal stake criterion.[149]

Mancur Olson, in his *Logic of Collective Action*, finds that resort to coercion is less necessary, and the tendency to opt out less great, in small groups than in large:

In a very small group, where each member gets a substantial portion of the total gain simply because there are few others in the group, a collective good can often be provided by the voluntary, self-interested action of the members of the group.[150]

Unlike Mansbridge, Olson finds the likelihood that a small group will be weakened by opting out to be less in

groups composed of members of greatly different size or interest in the collective good. . . . The smaller member by definition gets a smaller fraction of the benefit of any amount of the collective good he provides than a larger member and therefore has less incentive to provide additional amounts of the collective good. . . . In small groups with common interests there is accordingly a surprising tendency for the "exploitation" of the great by the small.[151]

The partnership can be a workable institutional form when the number of partners is quite small, but is generally unsuccessful when the number of partners is very large.[152]

One method of fostering voluntary association and reducing the need for coercion of dissenters or "free riders" would be the creation of a legal mechanism akin to that governing stock-subscription agreements in private corporations, in which individuals might make binding commitments of money or property conditional upon attainment of a specified level of participation by others. As observed by the public-choice economist Dennis Mueller: "Voluntary associations could be more attractive institutions for Pareto redistribution if members could tie the size of their contribution to the total funds raised."[153] The conditional charitable pledge by large donors of "matching gifts" is a familiar device, and a similar legislated mechanism might assist in the organization of land-readjustment associations, street-privatization schemes, and covenant-created residential community associations in established neighborhoods.

Variance, nonconforming use, and opt-out provisions are frequently necessary to secure the adoption of new, prospective rules: "When significant damage may be imposed on the individual, he will not find it advantageous to agree to any decision-making rule other than one which will approach the results of the unanimity rule in its actual operation."[154] In early Massachusetts,

[t]owns which had only a single schoolhouse refunded a portion of the rates to the parents of those children who could not easily attend it . . . or the remote settlements were taxed at a relatively lower rate, or they were exempted from taxation altogether.[155] Townsmen of the eighteenth century came to expect innovation in which few men were ever very deeply damaged because most were bought off, innovation that was almost inevitably very slow and rarely very radical.[156]

The Uniform Common Interests Act, as already noted, provides that use and occupancy restrictions additional to those in the original covenants should be imposed "only by a supermajority and only after providing for protection for those whose use or occupancy may be affected"[157]

In addition, social sanctions against exit are more effective in small organizations, reducing the need for governmental coercion of continued membership:

> First, in the large, latent group, each member is so small that his actions will not matter much one way or another; so it would seem pointless for one perfect competitor to snub or abuse for a selfish, antigroup action, because the recalcitrant's action would not be decisive in any event. Second, in any large group a person will ordinarily not be affected socially if he fails to make sacrifices on behalf of his group's goals.[158]

Small, single-purpose communities have another advantage: "The over-all costs of decision-making will be lower, given any collective-choice rule, in communities characterized by a reasonably homogeneous population than in those characterized by a heterogeneous population."[159] Similarly, as to general-purpose governments: "Many activities that may be quite rationally collectivized in Sweden, a country with a relatively homogeneous population, should be privately organized in India, Switzerland, or the United States."[160]

Opt-outs and variances in legislation can be viewed as a form of vote trading, of which it has been said that

> the society that is characterized by strong and effective ethical and moral restraints, that prevent vote trading, will find it more essential to place constitutional curbs on the political decisions of the majority than will the society in which these restraints are less effective.[161]

Critics of American residential community associations have questioned the reality of exit as a check on abuses: "To the extent that an owner has a choice about moving into an association, this choice is typically poorly informed, and there are high costs involved in making a new choice."[162] It is also pointed out that RCA covenants tend to be similar, and that in some parts of the country almost all new housing is in the RCA form. Against this it may be noted that governments now require extensive presale disclosures, that both purchasers and mortgage lenders have become far more sophisticated in assessing RCAs, that covenants are becoming more individualized and more amended, and that RCAs are extremely sensitive to declines in property values, which operate as a check on unreasonable restrictions even without the need of exit by particular homeowners.

Moreover, only about half of Americans at any given time are living in the same house they lived in five years earlier: "The mobility model may thus provide a reasonable approximation to behavior within metropolitan areas."[163] An illustration is provided from England: Twenty years ago Wallace Oates accurately prophesied that "the elimination of the selective grammar schools in the United Kingdom may encourage residential patterns of the Tiebout type as a means to control the quality of neighborhood schools."[164] This proved true even though the resulting dispersion had social and not economic roots; the massiveness of British aid to local subdivisions prevented significant variations in tax bases.

Those who deplore separation urge with Samuel Beer that

the settlement pattern of metropolitan areas is a problem of public policy, not only because it segregates income groups, but . . . in a far more important way, because it separates races . . . the social and political consequences of the situation are a good deal more dangerous than the economic ones.[165]

While Beer's observation appeared as a description of reality when it was written in 1977, the subsequent suburban migration of a large black middle class has invalidated it, and has supported the public-choice prediction that the dollar is the universal solvent. Finally, the Tiebout model has an equilibrium of its own; it is not accurate to claim, as some have, that "it gives little weight to the value of stable communities and close social ties."[166] Most homogeneous suburbs have been stable in character over time.

Dennis Mueller has listed five conditions necessary for the Tiebout model to be totally applicable: full mobility of citizens, a wide range of community options, complete knowledge of them, no spillovers of public goods, and no geographic constraints on individuals with respect to their place of work. These conditions never fully obtain, but the first three partially do in a large number of cases.[167]

The possibility of opt-out or exit thus provides a large part of the case for enhanced use of RCAs and other small governmental units. It follows from this that penalties, transfer taxes on real estate, and other clogs on mobility by residents should be minimized.

NOTES

1. M. Zuckerman, *Peaceable Kingdoms.* New York: Knopf, 1970, 23–24.
2. G. Harris, *Local Government in Many Lands.* London: King, 1933, 91.
3. C. Arnold-Baker, *Powers and Constitution of Local Councils* (London: National

Association of Local Councils, 1979), 9. Until 1972, the terms were of three years. C. Arnold-Baker, *Law and Practice of Parish Administration* (London: Longcross Press, 1966), 35.

4. M. Weiss and J. Watts, "Community Builders and Community Associations," Advisory Commission on Intergovernmental Relations, *Residential Community Associations.* Washington, DC: ACIR, 1989, 101 (hereafter *ACIR-RCA*).

5. *ACIR-RCA*, 61.

6. J. Mansbridge, *Beyond Adversary Democracy.* New York: Basic Books, 1980, 165.

7. Id.

8. Mansbridge, supra, 299.

9. F. Bailey, "Decisions by Consensus in Councils and Committees," in M. Banton, *Political Systems and the Distribution of Power* (London: Tavistock, 1965), citing B. Maheswari, "Two Years of Panchayati Raj in Rajasthan," *Economic Weekly,* 14 (1962), 845.

10. D. Mueller, *Constitutional Democracy.* Oxford: Oxford University Press, 1996, 80.

11. Id., 264.

12. Id., 261.

13. J. Buchanan and G. Tullock, *The Calculus of Consent.* Ann Arbor: University of Michigan Press, 1962, 20.

14. Id., 38.

15. Id., 305.

16. M. Olson, *The Logic of Collective Action.* Cambridge, MA: Harvard University Press, 1965, 41.

17. Mansbridge, supra, 278–79.

18. Id., 286.

19. Buchanan and Tullock, supra, 59–60.

20. Mansbridge, supra, 286.

21. Buchanan and Tullock, supra, 62; D. Mueller, *The Public Choice Approach to Politics.* Cheltenham, UK: Elgar, 1993, 72.

22. Mueller, supra, 69; see also 93.

23. E. Page, *Localism and Centralism in Europe* (Oxford: Oxford University Press, 1991), 86–87, citing M. Kesselman, *The Ambiguous Consensus* (1967).

24. B. Barber, *Strong Democracy.* Berkeley: University of California Press, 1974, 309–10.

25. Buchanan and Tullock, supra, 96.

26. D. Rae, "Decision Rules and Individual Values in Constitutional Choice," *Amer. Political Science Rev.,* 63 (1969), 40.

27. Id., 112.

28. Mueller, *The Public Choice Approach to Politics*, 113.

29. F. Foldvery, *Public Goods and Private Communities.* Cheltenham, UK: Elgar, 1994, 6.

30. Zuckerman, supra, 96.

31. Id., 230.

32. O. Handlin, *Dimensions of Liberty* (1961), 31–33, quoted in Zuckerman, supra, 231.

33. National Conference of Commissioners on Uniform State Laws, Uniform Common Interests Act, secs. 2-117(f), 2-118 (1994).

34. Id., sec. 3-102(c).

35. Id., secs. 2-17, 2-18.

36. Bailey, "Decisions by Consensus in Councils and Committees," in Banton, supra, 14, quoting R. Scalapino et al., *Parties and Politics in Contemporary Japan* (1962), 145, and R. Jay, "Local Government in Rural Central Java," *Far Eastern Quarterly,* 15 (1955), 215.

37. Bailey, "Decisions by Consensus in Councils and Committees," in Banton, supra, 2.

38. Harris, supra, 95.

39. S. Barton and C. Silverman, "The Political Life of Mandatory Community Associations," in *ACIR-RCA*, 36.

40. R. Oakerson, "Private Street Associations in St. Louis County," *ACIR-RCA*, 108.

41. A. Caplan and B. Nalebuff, "On the 64-Percent Majority Rule," *Econometrica* (1989); J. Stiglitz, *Economics of the Public Sector*, 2d ed. (New York: Norton, 1988), 154–62.

42. R. Dahl, *After the Revolution.* New Haven, CT: Yale University Press, 1970, 43.

43. A. Shaw, *Municipal Government in Continental Europe.* New York: Century, 1895, 170–71.

44. V. Ehrenberg, *The Greek State.* Oxford: Blackwell, 1960, 63.

45. Id., 70.

46. Montesquieu, *Spirit of the Laws* (tr. T. Nugent). Chicago: Encyclopedia Brittanica, 1966, 11.

47. H. Hallam, *Middle Ages*, ch. 3, cited in B. Hammond, *The Political Institutions of the Ancient Greeks* (1895), 107–8.

48. Mueller, *Constitutional Democracy*, 151n18.

49. See Barber, supra, citing E. Stavely, *Greek and Roman Voting and Elections* (Ithaca, NY: Cornell University Press, 1972).

50. Stavely, supra, 58.

51. W. Wickwar, *The Political Theory of Local Government.* Columbia: University of South Carolina Press, 1970, 34.

52. Mueller, *The Public-Choice Approach to Politics*, 194, 201. See also Dahl, supra, 125; A. Amar, "Choosing Representatives by Lottery Voting," *Yale Law J.*, 93 (1984), 1283.

53. Mueller, *The Public-Choice Approach to Politics*, 89.

54. Ehrenberg, supra, 63.

55. Stavely, supra, 55.

56. Zuckerman, supra, 166.

57. E. McKenzie, *Privatopia.* New Haven, CT: Yale University Press, 1994, 184.

58. A. de Tocqueville, *L'Ancien Régime* (tr. M. Patterson). Oxford: Blackwell, 1947, 149–50 (hereafter *"Ancien Régime"*).

59. Id., 92.

60. Id., 82.

61. Ehrenberg, supra, 56.

62. Stavely, supra, 85.

63. Id., 96–97.

64. Mueller, *The Public Choice Approach to Politics*, 201n17.

65. Zuckerman, supra, 177.

66. H. Clarke, *Parish, Town and Community Councils.* Croydon, UK: Charles Knight, 1991.

67. Ehrenberg, supra, 63.

68. Id., 59.

69. Zuckerman, supra, 21.

70. Olson, supra, 114n13.

71. Mueller, *The Public Choice Approach to Politics*, 167, 175.

72. Buchanan and Tullock, supra, 222.

73. Mueller, *Constitutional Democracy*, 84–85.

74. *Saturday Review*, 18(33) (1857).

75. Buchanan and Tullock, supra, 219–20.

76. Arnold-Baker, *Powers and Constitution of Local Councils*, 6.

77. A. Norton, *International Handbook of Local and Regional Government* (Aldershot, UK: Elgar, 1994), sec. 2.12.

78. Shaw, supra, 21.

79. Id., 32, 167.

80. See M. Loughlin, *Half a Century of Municipal Decline.* London: Allen & Unwin, 1985.

81. C. Williamson, *American Suffrage from Property to Democracy.* Princeton, NJ: Princeton University Press, 1960, 221, 271.

82. In Britain, nonresident property owners were denied the franchise (Representation of the People Act, 1969) but are permitted to be officers of municipalities. Local Authorities (Qualification of Members) Act, 1971. See also Local Government Act, 1972, secs. 15(1), 34(1).

83. J. Bryce, *Modern Democracies*, vol. 2. London: Macmillan, 1921, 120.

84. F. Goodnow, *Municipal Government* (1909), 146, quoted in Bryce, supra, 110n1.

85. J. Buchanan and G. Tullock, supra, 166.

86. See H. Davies, "Free Markets and Centralized Political Power," in ed. R. Bennett, *Local Government in the New Europe* (1993), 88–91.

87. J. Stiglitz, "The Theory of Local Public Goods," in G. Zodrow, *Local Provision of Public Services* (New York: Academic Press, 1983), 17, 51.

88. Zuckerman, supra, 164.

89. Id., 196.

90. J. Redlich and F. Hirst, *History of Local Government in England*. New York: Macmillan, 1958, 277.

91. B. Keith-Lucas, *The Unreformed Local Government System*. London: Croon Helm, 1980, 91.

92. Id.

93. C. Arnold-Baker, *The New Law and Practice of Parish Administration*, 38, citing Representation of the People Act, 1949, sec. 5.

94. K. Messere, *Tax Policy in OECD Countries*. Amsterdam: IBFD Publications, 1993, 365.

95. Shaw, supra, 169.

96. A. Offer, *Property and Politics, 1870–1914*. Cambridge: Cambridge University Press, 1981, 149–50.

97. A. de Tocqueville, *Democracy in America*, vol. 1. London: Everyman, 1994, 215.

98. A. Leemans, *Changing Patterns of Local Government*. The Hague: IULA, 1970.

99. G. Marcou, "New Tendencies of Local Government Development in Europe," in Bennett, supra, 51, 62.

100. Messere, supra, 211.

101. U.S. Dept. of Commerce, *Statistical Abstract of the United States*, 1998, table 1214.

102. McKenzie, supra, 57.

103. McKenzie (supra, 128) categorically but erroneously states that RCAs necessarily deny votes to renters.

104. National Conference of Commissioners on Uniform State Laws, Uniform Common Interests Act (1994), sec. 3-110.

105. *ACIR-RCA*, 15–16.

106. Barton and Silverman, supra, 37.

107. McKenzie, supra, 121.

108. *Ball v. James*, 451 U.S. 355 (1981); *Salyer Land Co. v. Tulare District*, 410 U.S. 719 (1973).

109. Mansbridge, supra, 237.

110. Id., 291, 293.

111. Olson, supra, 106 and 106n44, citing C. Brinton, *The Anatomy of Revolution* (1965), 157–63.

112. 1977 Swedish Local Government Act; French Act of 6 February 1992; Italian Act of 8 June 1990. Discussed in G. Marcou, "New Tendencies of Local Government Development in Europe," in Bennett, supra, 57; and in "Council of Europe, Local Referendums," *Local and Regional Authorities in Europe*, no. 52 (1993).

113. Alderson, "Some Thoughts on Referenda—and Parish Polls," *Local Council Review* (winter 1978), 147.

114. S. Humes and E. Martin, *The Structure of Local Governments Throughout the World*

(The Hague: M. Nijhoff, 1961), 83–84. See generally, ed. A. Ranney, *The Referendum Device* (Washington, DC: AEI, 1981); *City of Eastlake v. Forest City Enterprises*, 426 U.S. 668 (1976).

115. Norton, supra, sec. 10.12.

116. M. Steed, "Participation through Western Democratic Institutions," in ed. G. Parry, *Participation in Politics* (Manchester, UK: Manchester University Press, 1972), 94.

117. Mueller, *The Public-Choice Approach to Politics*, 393.

118. Id., 459, citing K. Wicksell, *A New Principle of Just Taxation* (1896), reprinted in R. Musgrave and A. Peacock, *Classics in the Theory of Public Finance* (Basingstoke, UK: Macmillan, 1958), 72–118.

119. M. Walzer, *Radical Principles* (New York: Basic Books, 1979), 135; see also C. Gillette, "Plebiscites, Participation and Collective Action in Local Government Law," *Michigan Law Rev.*, 86 (1986), 930.

120. Mueller, *The Public-Choice Approach to Politics*, 154.

121. D. Bell, "The Referendum: Democracy's Barrier to Racial Equality," *Washington Univ. Law Rev.*, 54 (1978), 1.

122. Harris, supra, 29.

123. Public Bodies (Admission to Meetings) Act, 1960.

124. Shaw, supra, 180–81.

125. Ehrenberg, supra, 56.

126. Id., 56.

127. Id., 56.

128. Zuckerman, supra, 160.

129. Arnold-Baker, *New Law and Practice of Parish Administration*, 49.

130. Ehrenberg, supra, 55.

131. Arnold-Baker, *Powers and Constitution of Local Councils*, 9.

132. Aristotle, *Politics*, bk. VI. I.6–9. Cambridge, MA: Loeb/Harvard University Press, 1932, 491, 493.

133. Ehrenberg, supra, 55.

134. Mansbridge, supra, 251.

135. Arnold-Baker, *New Law and Practice of Parish Administration*, 50.

136. Keith-Lucas, supra, 76.

137. Arnold-Baker, *New Law and Practice of Parish Administration*, 89.

138. National Conference of Commissioners on Uniform State Laws, Uniform Common Interests Act (1994), secs. 3-106, 3-109.

139. Mueller, *The Public-Choice Approach to Politics*, 22–23.

140. R. Nozick, *Anarchy, State and Utopia*. New York: Basic Books, 1974, 297–331.

141. H. Maine, *Village Communities in the East and West*. London: John Murray, 1871, 112–13.

142. Id., 163, 196–97.

143. H. Arkes, *The Philosopher in the City*. Princeton, NJ: Princeton University Press, 1981, 320–26.

144. Buchanan and Tullock, supra, 114.

145. Zuckerman, supra, 139.

146. de Tocqueville, *Democracy in America*, vol. 1, 36.

147. Foldvery, supra, 6, 77; A. Buchanan, *Secession* (Boulder, CO: Westview, 1991).

148. Mansbridge, supra, 280.

149. Mueller, *The Public-Choice Approach to Politics*, 10.

150. Buchanan, supra.

151. Olson, supra, 35.

152. Id., 54–55.

153. Mueller, *The Public-Choice Approach to Politics* (1993), 18, citing R. Musgrave, "Pareto Optimal Distribution: Comment," *Amer. Economic Rev.,* (1970), 60.
154. Buchanan and Tullock, supra, 74.
155. Zuckerman, supra, 130.
156. Id., 235.
157. National Conference of Commissioners on Uniform State Laws, Uniform Common Interests Act (1994), sec. 2-117(f).
158. Olson, supra, 62.
159. Buchanan and Tullock, supra, 115.
160. Id., 116.
161. Id., 209.
162. Barton and Silverman, supra, 35. See also R. Bird, "Threading the Fiscal Labyrinth," *National Tax J.,* 46 (1993), 207.
163. W. Oates, *The Political Economy of Fiscal Federalism.* Lexington, MA: Lexington Books, 1977, 9.
164. Id., 18n8.
165. S. Beer, "A Political Scientist's View of Fiscal Federalism," in Oates, supra, 23.
166. P. Pestieau, "The Optimality Limits of the Tiebout Model," in Oates, supra, 173, 185.
167. Mueller, *Constitutional Democracy*, 86.

Chapter 3

Resolving Disputes

REMOVAL OF OFFICERS

In Chapter 15 of *Representative Government*, Mill stressed that any power of removal should not extend "to making new appointments, or suspending the local institutions." The Uniform Common Interests Act allows two-thirds of those present at a meeting to remove officers, and allows 20 percent of all owners to call a meeting upon 10-to-60-days notice. The British Education Reform Act permits the Ministry of Education to intervene to replace principals appointed by boards for individual schools upon a finding of serious educational deficiency, the intervention to be temporary. Similar provisions have been added in recent years to the education legislation of some American states, including New Jersey and Maryland.

The French central government can dismiss municipal councils, and about 300 of the 38,000 communal councils are dismissed each year so as to force new elections: "The principal cause is that the numbers fall below a quorum due to the death of councillors, but it may result from an irreconcilable conflict on policy inside the council." There is a rarely used reserve power of dismissal for abuse of power and neglect of duty,[1] the persons dismissed being re-eligible at an immediate election.[2] Writing of prerevolutionary France, Tocqueville observed:

What already characterized the Administration in France was the violent hatred by which it was inspired . . . by all those, whether nobles or bourgeois, who wished independently of itself to concern themselves with public affairs. The smallest independent body which seemed desirous of establishing itself without its concurrence made it afraid; the smallest free association, whatever its object, caused it annoyance; it only allowed those to exist which had been arbitrarily composed and presided over by itself.[3]

Two commentators on American residential community associations have suggested creation of a mechanism pursuant to which "a petition by 10 percent of the owners should be able to bring a state observer to oversee elections, or rerun elections in which there is evidence of manipulation."[4] The autonomy of the association could be preserved by providing instead an arbitration mechanism in the bylaws.

ARBITRATION

Arbitration of disputes within the town was a common feature of early Massachusetts government, the state General Court sometimes being called upon to arbitrate matters local to a town: "Applications came from communities at an impasse over everything but their dependence on . . . arbitration."[5]

In contemporary residential community associations, arbitration has frequently been made available since "the role of the governing board as both prosecutor and judge is a troubling one."[6] Montgomery County, Maryland and the State of Florida have required prior mediation as a precondition to access to the courts for RCA disputes.[7] The Uniform Common Interests Act as amended in 1994 mandates nonbinding arbitration of disputes between an association and its members.[8] Independent arbitration is a frequent requirement in many teacher-union contracts with school boards, though too often its effect, when combined with multistage grievance procedures, is to render teachers virtually irremovable.

JUDICIAL REVIEW

Fischel urges that

[o]wners of property whose services are elastic in supply can protect themselves from myopic local regulation by threatening to leave the jurisdiction. The remaining category, regulation of immobile property by independent local governments . . ., requires most of the attention of judges.

Fischel finds judicial review under the "takings" clause of federal and state constitutions appropriate where the safeguard of exit is lacking:

Governments of small areas . . . that regulate resources that cannot be removed from their jurisdiction either because they are inherently immovable or because a web of regulation prevents their removal, are much less subject to the disciplines of politics. A reputation for uncompensated takings does such jurisdictions little harm because there is little prospect for repeat play.[9]

He urges that "the smaller republics would discount the welfare of underrepresented outsiders." As a justification of judicial review of local land-use regulations, this is not altogether convincing. Restrictions on property development potentially affect the land value of all property owners, not merely outsiders, and residents of small governments are sensitive to events that have an adverse effect on property values. To the extent that would-be residents have their welfare discounted, it is open to them to seek legislative redress at higher levels of government.[10] Fischel urges a relatively restrained standard of review that would preclude the community from denying development at already established densities, so residents could not in effect "reduce fiscal burdens that they had previously agreed to pay."[11] This principle is similar to the right German law confers on developers within established urban areas.[12]

The Uniform Common Interests Act effectively adopts Fischel's principle in its provisions for developer control while units are being sold out. Under the Act, the developer must surrender control of a board within 60 days after 75 percent of units have been conveyed; subsequent "downzoning" of the developer's remaining units is effectively prevented by a requirement of an 80 percent supermajority to alter use and occupancy restrictions. The effect is to prevent early purchasers from "pulling up the drawbridges" on those who aspire to acquire units later.

It is clear that any effort to treat covenant-based residential community associations as public instrumentalities for purposes of judicial review under the equal protection clause would wreak havoc with the usefulness of these groupings. While property-based voting arrangements would not necessarily offend the constitution given the cases upholding a property franchise for Western water districts, restrictions on leasing of property and on entry of outsiders might generate litigation, and association officers would be subject to liability under the civil-rights statutes rather than the more relaxed "business judgment" rule.[13] Courts have rejected such attempts.[14] Association rules adopted subsequent to the covenants, however, are frequently reviewed under a reasonableness standard[15] "to somewhat fetter the discretion of the board of directors."[16]

Where rules are prospective in their application and have been adopted by a large supermajority of the membership, this degree of substitution of judicial judgment would appear unnecessary. The 1994 amendments to the Uniform Common Interests Act make clear that the business judgment rule applies, rather than the originally more relaxed standard of "ordinary and reasonable care" that had been adopted to "increase willingness to serve." California law provides the directors, as distinct from the association, with immunity if their acts are in good faith and without gross negligence and specified insurance is maintained.[17] California also expressly recognized the reasonableness of restricting communities to the elderly.[18] It is to be hoped that the courts will bear in mind Tocqueville's admonition: "By requiring too great a freedom and liberty men fall into too great slavery."[19]

Supermajority and referenda requirements are frequently highly satisfactory substitutes for judicial review, as the Swiss experience indicates. The advantages and disadvantages of resort to third-party arbiters by small governments are "savings in time and expertise . . . and potential losses from an [judge's] pursuit of her own goals or misinterpretations."[20]

AUDITS

It was said of Athens that "a position that must be surrendered after a year and under a strict rendering of accounts was no good foundation for personal power."[21]

Colonial Massachusetts similarly audited the accounts of town committees and treasurers.[22] Prewar Danish communes required audits by two auditors and by the Union of Danish towns, and approval of accounts by the county council.[23]

British parish councils are subject to annual audit by district councils,[24] and French communes by a court of accounts.[25] In his early book on Grants in Aid, Sidney Webb described the earliest stage of supervision of local government by saying:

[I]t was desirable that there should be, at any rate, some external audit of local government accounts, and that some external approval should be required before the members of a local government body were permitted, not merely to spend the rates paid by those who elected the counselors, but also to embark on enterprises mortgaging the future.

The absence of superior audits was described as "the anarchy of local autonomy," which was said by the Webbs to have "given the United States the worst local government of any country claiming to be civilized."[26] Tocqueville in his time also suggested that

the authority which represents the State ought not . . . to waive the right of inspecting the local administration, even when it does not interfere more actively. . . . Nothing of the kind, however, exists in America.[27]

American local government is characteristically audited by elected officers who are not infrequently part of the same political organization as those being audited. RCAs are characteristically subject to the requirement of an outside private audit. These devices might perhaps be supplemented by provisions giving a specified number of electors of an RCA or sublocal government the right to request a municipal audit.

NOTES

1. S. Humes and E. Martin, *The Structure of Local Governments Throughout the World* (The Hague: M. Nijhoff, 1961), 47, quoting B. Chapman, *Introduction to French Local Government* (1953), 127.
2. A. Shaw, *Municipal Government in Continental Europe.* New York: Century, 1895, 178.
3. A. de Tocqueville, *L'Ancien Régime* (tr. M. Patterson). Oxford: Blackwell, 1947, 69–70 (hereafter *"Ancien Régime"*).
4. S. Barton and C. Silverman, "The Political Life of Mandatory Community Associations," in Advisory Commission on Intergovernmental Relations, *Residential Community Associations.* Washington, DC: ACIR, 1989, 37 (hereafter *ACIR-RCA*).
5. M. Zuckerman, *Peaceable Kingdoms.* New York: Knopf, 1970, 149.
6. Barton and Silverman, supra, 37.
7. *ACIR-RCA*, 19.
8. National Conference of Commissioners on Uniform State Laws, Uniform Common Interests Act (1994), sec. 3-102(a)(18).
9. W. Fischel, *Regulatory Takings.* Cambridge, MA: Harvard University Press, 1994, sec. 3.20. Fischel collects numerous authorities discussing the adequacy of exit as a safeguard.
10. Id., sec. 3.24.
11. Id., 287.
12. G. Lefcoe, *Land Development in Crowded Places: Lessons from Abroad.* Washington, DC: Conservation Foundation, 1979, 11–38.
13. K. Rosenberry, "Condominium and Homeowner Associations: Should They be Treated Like Mini-Governments?," in *ACIR-RCA*, 69.
14. *Laguna Royale Owners Assn. v. Drager*, 199 Cal. App. 3d 670, 174 Cal. Rep. 136 (1981); *O'Connor v. Village Green Owners'Assn.*, 132 Cal. App. 3d 178, 183 Cal. Rptr. 111 (1981); *SMI Indus. Inc. v. Lanard and Axilbund*, 481 F. Supp. 459 (E.D. Pa. 1979); *Stephanus v. Anderson*, 26 Wash. App. 326, 613 P.2d 533 (1980); *Brock v. Watergate Mobile Home Park*, 502 So.2d 1380 (Fla. Dist. Ct. App. 1987); Note, *S. California Law Rev.*, 54 (1981), 1397; K. Rosenberry, "Theories of Liability," in W. Hyatt, *Condominium and Homeowner Association Litigation* (New York: Wiley Law Publications, 1987), secs. 3.30–3.40.
15. A. Tarlock, "Residential Community Associations and Land-Use Controls," in *ACIR-RCA*, 81.
16. *Hidden Harbour Estates, Inc. v. Basso*, 393 So.2d 637, 640 (Fla. Dist. Ct. App. 1987). Cal. Civil Code, sec. 1354, which applies a reasonableness standard to covenants in the declaration as well.
17. Cal. Civil Code, sec. 1365.7.
18. Cal. Civil Code, secs. 51.2, 51.3.
19. *Ancien Régime*, 153.
20. D. Mueller, *The Public Choice Approach to Politics.* Cheltenham, UK: Elgar, 1993, 115.
21. V. Ehrenberg, *The Greek State.* Oxford: Blackwell, 1960, 69.
22. Zuckerman, supra, 214.
23. G. Harris, *Local Government in Many Lands.* London: King, 1933, 82.

24. C. Arnold-Baker, *Law and Practice of Parish Administration*. London: Longcross Press, 1966, 181.

25. French Municipal Code of 1884, Art. 157, in Shaw, supra, 491.

26. S. Webb, *Grants in Aid*. London: Fabian Society, 1911, 4–5.

27. A. de Tocqueville, *Democracy in America* (tr. F. Bowen). London: Longmans, 1863, 89n1.

CHAPTER 4

Funding Neighborhoods

Any consideration of the scope and future role of sublocal units requires consideration of their possible sources of revenue. Critics of devolution assume the inadequacy of locally generated revenues and likewise give little consideration to the panoply of available devices for supplementing them, outlined below.

INTERNAL SOURCES

Property Taxes

Turgot's abortive reform proposal for Louis XV in 1775 contemplated the erection of artificially constructed new units of local government as part of a fiscal reform. Village-size municipalities "would be elected by all who had property in the village because one of its functions would be to apportion the taxes among them."[1] In order to sustain the value of property, the labor of the poor would be used to build roads; in order to increase estimates of property values, plural voting was provided to large property owners. This plan was said to be at the root of varied subsequent developments, including Jefferson's proposals for ward government, the provisions for 36 square-mile townships in the Northwest Ordinance of 1787, the geographical division of France into communes based on parish lines in 1790 that spread throughout Europe,[2] and Bentham's proposals of the 1830s that in turn led to the artificial districts of the Poor Law Amendment Act and the roads and police legislation of the same period,[3] and the artificial school districts and special taxing districts of the United States.[4]

Property taxes have several advantages as sources of revenue for sublocal governments: They can easily be used by very small jurisdictions, whose taxes can be included on a unified bill sent out by a higher level of government. In addition, "all the requirements of assimilating the area of taxation with the area of benefit can be met by differential rating; the practice of creating new special areas for the purpose of administering one service is no longer sanctioned by general utility."[5] Because of the immobility of property, they cannot be evaded. They also are closely associated with benefits-improvements of infrastructure benefiting nearby property. To the extent they are dedicated to a single use and are effectively earmarked, they make clear the benefits and costs of programs and are conducive to effective collective decision-making.[6]

The disadvantage of the tax is primarily that it can hit hard at the low-income elderly, who in most places are protected by circuit-breaker provisions.[7] It is a tax on housing consumption, which in the United States is crudely offset by the tax benefits accorded those making mortgage interest payments on personal residences. It is also difficult to exactly assess. Renters claim that the tax falls heavily on them and is therefore regressive; this is vigorously disputed by many writers on public finance, who contend that instead it is capitalized and reduces home values.[8] This issue plays a major role in assessment of the fairness of the voting arrangements of business-improvement districts and residential community associations, which customarily disenfranchise renters. Finally, the tax is generally not a growth tax because of its visibility and resistance to increased assessments, leading one writer to observe that: "Heavy reliance on the property tax means heavy dependence on intergovernmental grants."[9]

This is not necessarily true of charges levied at the community association level, where the homogeneity of property assures that controversies concern only rates, not assessments. It remains true that property taxes are limited in ways that federal taxes are not: By personal pressure, referenda, and the ability to migrate.[10]

There is a case for diversification away from the property tax "to reduce taxpayer discontent which may arise if too much revenue is being collected from one source."[11] At the community-association level this would require increased resort to user fees for such features as parking and use of recreational facilities, laundry equipment, cable and satellite service, and so on.

It also must be acknowledged that reliance on property assessments within small associations creates an internal politics that is the reverse of the tendency prevailing in national politics: "With a tax where everyone has to pay the same amount, a poor individual is likely to prefer a lower level of public goods expenditure, since the marginal cost to him (in terms of the foregone utility from the private goods he has to give up) is higher."[12] But because of the mobility factor, it is in general true that "as we proceed from the central government to government units with progressively smaller jurisdictions, it becomes continually more important to place increased reliance on benefit forms of taxation."[13]

In established areas, taxes on improved real property are subject to the objection that, unlike the tax on land, they discourage improvements. For this reason, moratoria on assessment of new improvements, originally proposed by Adam Smith,[14] are common in municipal-tax ordinances, and some Pennsylvania jurisdictions assess land more heavily. Absent moratoria, Tocqueville observed: "[E]ach tax-payer had, in fact, a direct and permanent interest in spying on his neighbors and on denouncing to the Collector all increase in their means."[15] The high levels that effective tax rates have attained in some United States cities on the order of 5 percent of the true market value imply an excise tax on building of approximately 50 percent. It is hard to believe that such rates would not seriously reduce levels of construction and maintenance activity.[16]

As observed by Richard Musgrave: "Unfortunately, the exaggerated claims on behalf of the single tax have interfered with a continuing and strong case for taxing site values at a higher rate."[17]

It has been said that the American property tax has been adjusted to become a benefit tax:

Examples of such adjustments are reduced taxation of farmland and other open spaces that impose few fiscal burdens, reductions for elderly taxpayers who might otherwise oppose school spending, and establishment of special-purpose taxing districts . . . that do not necessarily correspond to municipal boundaries.[18]

In addition, in California, existing homeowners are held harmless against assessment increases by the "acquisition value" system upheld by the Supreme Court as a proper grandfather provision notwithstanding its discrimination against newcomers, a system defended on the basis that the "lock-in inefficiency is probably small and the system has the advantage of protecting homeowners against sudden large increases in assessments."[19]

Other states such as Maryland phase-in assessment increases over a three-year period and impose limits on annual increases. The revisions to the British local-property tax that followed failure of the poll tax included a 25 percent discount for single-person households, an effort to more closely associate taxation with benefits.[20]

Indeed, it has been maintained that the Hamilton model shows that a system of many communities, each using property taxation and zoning ordinances that specify a minimum value for local houses, effectively converts the property tax into a pure benefit tax and restores all the efficiency properties of the Tiebout solution. Moreover, the equilibrium in the Hamilton model is a stable one; no household will have any incentive to relocate. . . . What can hardly escape notice is that this is precisely the system that is under severe attack in the popular literature and in the courts . . . [a]conflict between economic efficiency and norms of social justice.[21]

Although it is frequently urged that increased mobility justifies centralization, Wallace Oates has pointed out that it "facilitates the formation of jurisdictions composed of individuals with similar tastes for public services . . . we would expect over time . . . a growing desire to provide certain public services at more decentralized levels of government."[22]

If sublocal governments are to function effectively, there must be great sensitivity by higher levels of government to any incursions upon the property tax base. The experience of British parish councils furnishes an example. They were created in 1894 as successors to ecclesiastical vestries. The fact that they were to be administered by laymen caused acrimony at the time, as did the fact that unlike the vestries, they were open to persons without social standing. The principal reason that they "fell rapidly into an undeserved obscurity from which they began to emerge only sixty years later"[23] was the severe limit on their allowable rates imposed by the House of Lords in the course of enactment of the 1894 Act, together with the fact that

[t]he revenues of parish councils came mainly from rates on agricultural land. Within eighteen months of their creation agricultural land was derated by 50 percent. Without compensation . . . the tendency . . . to give new functions to parish councils whilst reducing their financial assets was exaggerated during the period of the wars. Their spending powers, already attenuated by inflation, were again reduced (as usual without compensation) by still further derating and by the new administrative methods introduced for collecting rates from nationalized industries.[24]

American local governments have similarly suffered from the incursions on their tax base of nonprofit institutions, other levels of government, preferential assessments for landowners granting environmental easements, circuit-breaker provisions for the elderly, and special dispensations for new construction.

Notwithstanding all this, the property tax or its equivalent remains a suitable and reliable revenue source for most RCAs and general purpose sublocal governments engaging chiefly in property-maintenance activi-

Poll Taxes

Another potential revenue source is exemplified by the British poll tax introduced by the Thatcher government; which in theory, was designed to produce results approximating the domestic property taxes it replaced and was accompanied by rebates of up to 80 percent for low-income persons and persons in full-time higher education, and exemptions for prisoners, the mentally handicapped, and residents of homes and hostels. The property tax on business property was retained but made uniform. The theory of the tax was that the immunity of about 10 percent of the electorate from rates and the fact that rates were a joint rather than individual obligation that did not consciously impact married women created a moral hazard resulting in rising local expenditures.[25] While the change in business taxation was amply justified by evidence of abuse by local councils, no correlation was shown between overspending councils and the extent to which their individual electors could "free ride," and the assumption that benefits did not vary with income was shown to be unfounded, higher income groups tending to consume greater quantities of local public goods.[26] The tax was said to rest on oversimplified "undergraduate economic principles, which have been developed to help new students to understand the rudiments of the discipline."[27] Concern was expressed about the impact on persons just above the rebate threshold, the discouragement to inscription on the voting rolls (the census showing an actual drop in population), and that a capitation tax "means that rich people seek areas with high services while poor people seek areas with low services."[28]

In addition, despite the exemptions, losses accrued to families with large numbers of adults in low-valued property, benefits accrued to areas of high property values, and the tax was suddenly introduced rather than being phased in over ten years as planned and gave rise to noncompliance by 10 percent of taxpayers and a £400 million increase in administrative costs. This necessitated a temporary four-year safety net to cushion detriments; the costs of this diminished the advantages of the tax to those who otherwise would have supported the change. New demands for local revenues were assessed on a narrower base, because of the change in taxation of business property.

It is said that "in the 20th century only Papua New Guinea (formerly) and some African countries (still) have levied such a tax . . . the English imposed a similar tax in 1379, which is recorded by historians as being the major cause of a peasants' revolt."[29] This statement may not be fully accurate, since capitation taxes found some use in some of the Canadian provinces. The more exuberant advocates of the tax described it as an effort to almost perfectly associate tax and benefit so as to produce "the depoliticization and privatization of local authority activity" along the lines of an American residential community association.[30] A head tax has the advantage of being neutral in the sense that it cannot be avoided by alterations in behavior but, to engage in understatement, "problems arise where the distribution of income is not regarded as satisfactory and where, as a result, it seems desirable to adopt a tax system that compensates for this somewhat."[31]

The Thatcher government adopted the tax on the advice of a think-tank known as the Adam Smith Institute, which failed to heed Smith's warning that

[c]apitation taxes, so far as they are levied upon the lower ranks of people, are direct taxes upon the wages of labor, and are attended with all the inconveniences of such taxes . . . in countries where the ease, comfort, and security of the inferior ranks of people are little attended to, capitation taxes are very common . . . the greatest sum which they have ever afforded might always have been found in some other way much more convenient to the people.[32]

Natural Resources and User Charges

A number of small political entities have in effect been endowed by higher levels of government with control over certain natural resources. Thus British parish councils have received modest transfers of land for allotments, discussed elsewhere, and Swiss communes, by a federal law of 1906, have exclusive rights of exploitation and control of waterways within their territory;[33] they also possess extensive communally owned woodlands. American residential community associations are endowed on a humbler scale; frequently they possess swimming pools and clubrooms with some revenue-raising potential.

In the Swiss setting, property-based revenue sources were said to produce "egregious inequality."[34] A Finance Equalization Plan by which the canton assumes communal powers of taxation on corporate persons and redistributes proceeds has been adopted in several cantons.[35] In general it is held that "taxes on deposits of natural resources that are concentrated in certain jurisdictions are best taxed by the national government in order to avoid excessive inequities."[36] User charges, on the other hand provide

the proper incentives both for efficient location decisions and to support (for example, through voting behavior) efficient levels of local public outputs.[37]

The particular group to be charged . . . will make their opposition to a user charge known. Thus the easiest path . . . is not to use user charges to as great an extent as would be efficient and equitable . . . the use of . . . general taxation to provide utilities and services to fringe-area residents provides them with a subsidy [which] leads to more rapid spread of urban areas.[38]

The political limits on user charges are varied:

The deterrent effect of user charges can be just as important as the revenue-generating effect (e.g., public transport); . . . certain public services are intended to be subsidized and not revenue-raising (services for special groups, children, the aged and the handicapped); and . . . many services are indivisible in the sense that their costs cannot be allocated to individual users (e.g., police).[39]

Despite these limitations, user charges can supply a reliable, if modest, revenue source for small local entities, and the possibility of obtaining them may encourage the association to offer new services and means of cooperation to its residents.

Indeed, very small units such as small French communes administer water and sewer utilities through contracts with private companies funded through user charges. The developing deregulation of American electric and gas utilities makes a similar development possible in the United States. Conceivably also, residential associations might be authorized by their members to contract for basic medical services, the geographic concentration of patients making economies in their rendition possible.

One of the advantages of user charges as a revenue source is that unanimity is not necessary to avoid imposing on the interests of dissenters, since those not interested on a service are free not to use it and suffer no loss.[40] This means that residential community associations (and their developers) can appeal to their present and prospective residents by offering such value-enhancing services as cooperative day-care, convenient medical checkups, domestic and cleaning services, demand-response transportation, supplementary primary school classes, and indeed any good or service for which economies are available through cooperative purchasing. Even covenant-based associations will be free to offer such services, since participation and charges are voluntary and recent judicial doctrine increasingly dispenses with the requirement that association activities "touch and concern" land.[41]

Assessments

Special assessments for public benefits have in recent years been a somewhat under-used device. Their attractiveness was impaired by a

Supreme Court decision in 1898[42] holding that assessments could not be apportioned to damages to the property owner remedied by the public project but only to benefits conferred by it, a principle somewhat reinforced by the recent *Loretto* and *Nolan* cases.[43] There is now a requirement of "rough proportionality" between damage and benefit, the absence of which entitles a landowner to compensation.[44] The German law is different, permitting assessments on the basis of *harm caused* rather than *benefits received*, especially as a means of reducing pollution.[45] Assessments can be a useful device in connection with traffic-calming and street-closing regimes.

Borrowing

Borrowing against association assets is another internal-funding device. Such borrowing by French communes resulting in interest charges beyond specified limits traditionally required approval by the prefect; loans in excess of 30 years required approval of the council of state.[46] Similar restrictions on loans were applied in prewar Norway[47] and in many other European countries.[48] Borrowing by British parish councils is limited to capital projects and must be approved by a central government official, except for refinancings to lower interest rates.[49] The American Dillon's Rule by which courts narrowly construed grants of authority to municipalities is said to have been inspired by a purpose to restrict improvident municipal-bond issues.[50] A traditional American argument against state or municipal borrowing, that counter-cyclical fiscal policy should be reserved to the national government, has recently lost much of its force. Flexible exchange rates have reduced the employment effects of budget deficits, and "local government fiscal measures are likely to have stronger output effects than national measures"; such measures include "rainy day" funds and borrowing from designated trust funds in addition to bond issues.[51] Throughout the OECD,

the unsatisfactory macroeconomic performance in the seventies and eighties has led a number of countries to involve state and local governments more actively in the pursuit of full employment, in view of their higher level of expertise concerning the structure and functioning of local labor markets.[52]

Borrowing for capital "costs that must be met over a relatively short time span" has been vigorously defended as needed "both for attaining an equitable intertemporal pattern of payments for the services from public investment programs and for realizing an efficient level of public capital formation."[53] Some state constitutions require voter approval of debt and a concomitant tax increase to fund it, upon the absence of which "[v]oters will tend to overlook the future cost of debt service and view the increase in programs as being more or less costless."[54]

Because of constitutional limitations on debt, only about half of state-and-local capital investments in 1969 were debt financed;[55] at the community-association level the percentage is no doubt far lower.

The same considerations that support the prudent use of debt by local governments render its use by community associations to make major physical improvements sometimes desirable. These improvements can include fences and security gates, traffic-calming improvements, recreational facilities, satellite and cable hookups, improved street lighting, renewal of sewer lines, and other changes of permanent or semipermanent benefit. The property-tax-based revenue of small associations provides the best collateral.

Access to debt financing is especially important for, and indeed is indispensable to, land-readjustment associations. A number of the early urban-renewal laws adopted by American states in the 1930s could probably be used without significant modification by land-readjustment associations; indeed, some of them were inspired by the German Lex Adickes.

The use of public debt guarantees for hotel, shopping center, office building and restaurant development has been questioned from a neoliberal perspective, but this criticism does not encompass provision of low-income housing and day-care and retraining facilities for which private financing is likely to be unavailable on normal terms; much land-readjustment activity is of this description.[56] Ordinary community-association debt is taxable debt for federal income tax purposes; block associations conducting land readjustment might achieve tax-exempt financing to the extent that they qualify under some of the state urban-renewal laws.

Excises

French municipal governments before World War I derived most of their revenues from local customs houses imposing excises on such commodities as alcoholic beverages. While these exactions were expensive to collect and an inducement to evasion and migration of customers, they had the advantage that, unlike property taxes, they fell on the population at large and thus avoided any moral hazard associated with manhood suffrage, introduced in France in 1884. Sales taxes have advantages as aids to saving and (if selective) as taxes on leisure spending;[57] when imposed on necessities such as fuel as in Britain by the Thatcher–Major government, "they raise the price of subsistence, and consequently the wages of labor."[58] In the United States, sales taxes account for only about 4 percent of local government revenues and 8 percent of the revenues of municipalities and tend to be limited to avoid severe boundary problems.[59] Such taxes are said to be viable for local government only when geographic distances are great, and the taxes as local taxes do not exist outside the United States and Canada.[60]

They are singularly unsuitable as a source of revenue of community associations.

Forced Saving

The postwar economic development of both Hong Kong and Singapore rests heavily in both instances on forced-saving devices. These are mentioned here not as potential sources of direct revenue for neighborhood entities, but because of their possible relevance to the economic circumstances of larger jurisdictions, particularly large cities, in which neighborhood or residential associations may be located.

In Hong Kong, the principal device used in postwar development was land banking: The acquisition and assembly of derelict or cleared land by a municipality and its resale at a profit to developers. Recurrent revenues from the leasing or installment sale of land accounted for from 10 to 20 percent of total Hong Kong government revenue in every year except one in the 35-year period from 1949 through 1984 capital revenue from land sales additionally accounted for more than 20 percent of government revenues during 1977–1982, the years of the Hong Kong property boom, and for 31.5 percent of revenues during 1981–1982.[61] Land values were driven by exceptional circumstances: A continuing influx of refugees and Hong Kong's unique location as a trade center. The government owned large amounts of crown land, and acquired leased lands by a crude form of land readjustment in which lessees were granted two square feet of building land for every five square feet of agricultural land surrendered. Subsequently, unfulfilled government commitments for building land were monetized. A portion of the acquired land and the proceeds of land sales were used to carry out an extensive public-housing program and to provide associated social services; the housing and services provided a social safety-net supporting an essentially unregulated labor market attractive to foreign investment.

In Singapore, large amounts of land were acquired by eminent domain and banked by the government, which consciously violated just-compensation principles; in addition, land was created by landfilling harbors. Land banking took place on the premise that without it, "the private sector on its own will have great difficulty obtaining choice sites for proper development, thereby giving indirect rise to urban sprawl."[62] In the 25-year period between 1959 and 1984, approximately one-third the land area of Singapore was acquired and disposed of by the government. A massive program of housing finance and construction was financed through a series of drastic increases in payroll taxes, ultimately to a 50 percent level, most of the taxes accruing to a Central Provident Fund (CPF) that subsidized housing construction: "Under the CPF housing finance scheme begun in September 1968, members were allowed to withdraw up to 80 percent of their total CPF savings to buy their homes."[63]

The adaptability to American society of these devices is arguable. Land banking has been employed in urban redevelopment in most major European cities and in Puerto Rico, and in 1981 the American Law Institute promulgated a model land-banking statute as part of the A.L.I. Model Land Redevelopment Code. Proposals for federal assistance to municipalities to establish land banks were made by the Kennedy administration in 1961 but were stricken from an omnibus bill by Congress.[64] Many cities have the possibility of acquiring large tracts of derelict housing through tax defaults; some are said to leave land in private ownership that might be taken for taxes so as not to endanger bond ratings by visibly removing land from the tax rolls. The classic criticism of government property management is of "negligent, expensive and oppressive management . . . sale would produce a very large sum of money . . . private property . . . would, in the course of a few years, become well improved."[65]

Land readjustment, as noted above, is a concept with potential application to American and other inner cities—it need not be carried on by public bodies. The use of forced savings devices is more problematic in a society that by global standards overinvests in housing. The concept of allowing borrowing against pension entitlements to finance housing is one that has already received partial acceptance in the United States in connection with I.R.A. and Keogh retirement-plan provisions and permitted withdrawals from tax-qualified pension plans. Municipalities might, however, consider permitting their employees to anticipate public-pension distributions for the purpose of constructing or redeveloping housing within municipal boundaries.

EXTERNAL SOURCES

Project Grants

Both the conservative government in Britain and the Carter and Clinton administrations have given large project grants on an ad-hoc basis to favored large cities, under the UDAG and Empowerment Zone programs in the United States and the City Challenge program in Britain. These programs make the favored subdivisions, usually chosen on political grounds, virtual wards of the central government or its dominant party.[66] It has been suggested that

> intergovernmental grants have a highly stimulative effect on the spending of recipients ... "money sticks where it hits." ... Grants are not passed along to the extent one would expect in the form of reduced local taxes.[67]

The funding at the margin of local programs from its own revenues is critical if decentralized choice is to play its proper role in the fiscal system.

It has been noted that "the grant system in place in the U.S.A. has very little equalizing impact. [T]he relative size of government in the United States today is a third larger than in 1960, yet the poor are not relatively better off now than they were then."[68] The correlation between resource capacity and grant per capita during the early 1980s was 0.92 in Canada, 0.71 in Australia and 0.64 in Germany but only 0.13 in the United States.[69] "Certain major [American] federal matching—grants have federal shares of the order of 90 percent—far in excess of any conceivable level of external benefits."[70]

More than a third of federal grants to state and local governments in the 1960s and two-thirds of grants for urban public investment during the period 1966–1975 were for highway programs, the federal government usually bearing 90 percent of the cost[71] (reduced to 80 percent by the recent ISTEA legislation). A substantial portion of the remainder was for suburban sewage construction, again with 90 percent federal provision. In 1987, federal grants in aid to lower levels of government amounted to $109.9 billion, of which $94.1 billion were categorical (as distinct from block) grants.[72] In 1991, 89.4 percent of federal aid was still in the form of categorical grants: "It has been a frequent complaint in the United States that in poorer areas the bulk of locally generated revenues is directed into matching grant programs with little remaining for the support of other state and local services."[73]

The difference between project grants and block grants is of much greater consequence in the United States than in other countries. Project grants in the United States constrain local governments less by reason of their particular subject matter than because of the additional "strings" attached to them: "Since such strings are not the only major source of national government influence on local government in unitary states, they are not particularly important [in them]."[74] Indeed, in Germany a substantial body of constitutional doctrine precludes the national government from using grants as a "means of influencing decisions of the constituent states in fulfilling their own responsibilities," and also precludes direct grants from the national to local governments.[75] Project grants have as their object "a net increase or modification of output rather than simply substitution . . . for local funds."[76] The conditions attached to them become harder to justify when cash limits are imposed to limit them:

The virtual abandonment of open-ended matching grants [in the United States] is inconsistent with the view that such grants are needed to stimulate the production of services that produce external benefits.[77]

Existing grant programs generally feature very high central government matching rates, enough to encourage overspending at the local level, but then have this subsidy capped so that, at the margin, there is no price subsidy at all.[78]

It is urged that central matching grants be limited to the share of marginal benefits realized outside the jurisdiction, and that even crude estimates will produce efficiency improvements.[79]

In defense of project grants, two public-choice theorists have observed:

The Constitution created a system of overlapping jurisdictions specifically so that minorities within one jurisdiction could carry their case to another jurisdiction. This was Madison's solution to the problem of majority tyranny. . . . Functional grants have contributed greatly to the openness of the American political system. . . .[80]

Project grants, however, have an enervating effect on those subject to their frequently changing and undebated conditions. Tocqueville wrote of the *Ancien Régime*:

It is impossible to imagine the contempt into which the law finally fell even in the minds of those who applied it, when there were no longer political associations nor newspapers to mitigate the capricious activity and limit the arbitrary and changing humor of ministers and their offices.[81]

In France the political world was, so to speak, divided into two separate and disconnected provinces. One set of people did the actual administration; another set laid down the abstract principles, on which all administration ought to be founded; one set took the particular measures indicated by routine; the other set proclaimed general laws without ever thinking of the means to apply them; one set had the conduct of affairs; the other set, the control of mind.[82]

This is a fair description of American national government.

The project grant system is ordinarily of singularly little benefit to small, sublocal governments. The smaller a grant in absolute terms, the greater the cost and burden of administrative requirements. Local self-governing schools, RCAs, and street associations are ordinarily not versed in the art of grantsmanship, and are individually so small that their particular or eccentric needs will not receive sympathetic consideration from harried grant administrators. Some local governments have initiated crude grant programs to community associations for the purpose of buying recreational equipment or radio-telephones for citizen patrol cars, usually on the basis of a fixed amount per association.

Unrestricted Grants

The Webbs, though popularly thought of as centralizers, in fact favored general, as distinct from project, grants: "The new invention of grants-in-aid could contribute to municipal liberty insofar as they were given on a 'block' instead of a 'specific' basis."[83] Grants-in-aid of an unrestricted variety won the early support of Sidney Webb as a means of stimulating and enlarging social welfare spending. He observed:

No subject, except, perhaps, war so annoyed Mr. Gladstone as that of grants-in-aid, and he consistently fulminated against them as iniquitous, and "a positive excitement to extravagance." What he did not realize is that sometimes it is desirable to encourage expenditure.[84]

But "grants-in-aid generally of the expenditure of local authorities, without specific allocation to particular services, are (as Mr. Gladstone always declared) wholly injurious encouragements to extravagance."[85] Research confirms the notion that "money sticks where it hits"; revenue-sharing and like general-purpose grants "stimulate much more spending than central government tax cuts in the long run, indicating at a minimum some revision in political theories that feature a harmony of interests between bureaucrats and voters."[86]

The now-abandoned American revenue-sharing program instituted during the Nixon administration tied allocations to general taxes raised within each jurisdiction, and distributed funds only to general-purpose governments, thus discriminating against jurisdictions making heavy use of user charges and special-assessment districts. The program relieved state and local reliance on slow-growing or regressive taxes.[87] Similar proposals were made by a congressionally appointed Committee on Federalism and National Purpose in 1985; Richard Musgrave in 1988 urged "general (nonearmarked) support given to jurisdictions with quite low-capacity-to need ratios, an approach along the lines of the revenue sharing programs of the 1970s but on a more selective basis."[88]

The weakness of general purpose grants is their vulnerability to sudden reduction; the revenue-sharing program was terminated due to budget exigencies, and in Europe, "in a number of countries the squeeze on grants was seen as an easy option in cutting back on central government expenditure."[89] Where they are made available to municipalities, there is no reason why a specified portion of them cannot be poured through to self-governing schools or sublocal governments using the same inverse-wealth allocation basis, as is done with respect to so-called "opt-out" schools in Britain.

Tax Sharing

Tax sharing has been a method of local government aid most favored recently in Europe: "The tendency has been to assign tax revenues to local government while eroding or completely suppressing the local taxation power." The income tax has been assigned to local government in Sweden and there are elaborate arrangements for sharing of taxes in Germany.[90] Under Article 106(6) of the Basic Law, local governments are entitled to receive all revenue from taxes on real estate, on local industry and trade, and from local excise taxes, except to the extent that proceeds of the local industry and trade tax are shared with the federation by the lander. In addition, local governments under Article 106(5) are to receive a share of the revenue from the income tax in proportion to income taxes paid by local residents. Further, under Article 106(7), the localities receive a percentage of the Landers' half share of corporation taxes and a percentage of the share of sales taxes allowed the Lander by federal legislation. Less-affluent Lander may have their shares of sales tax enhanced by up to one-fourth under Article 107.[91] Because of this tax-sharing, under which 14 percent of the income tax flows to municipalities on an inverse-income formula based on yield of local taxes, "decisive and divisive variations of public policy and service provision are not really possible within the German system."[92] Income tax sharing is also provided for in Austria, Luxembourg, and Spain.[93]

Traditionally, French communes were allowed to add a specified percentage to various direct state taxes on land, buildings, residential rentals, and trades and professions. These "centimes" were retained even when the national government ceased levying these direct taxes for its own use.[94] Communes were also given a share of beverage and automobile taxes.

Tax sharing is recommended by students of public finance for income, natural resources, and commodities taxes, implying "the surrender of freedom in choices about structure and level of taxation, hence reducing the diversity of true federalism for the sake of the efficiency and equity of tax uniformity."[95] However, except for death and unemployment taxes, the technique is little used at the federal level in the United States, and is criticized by public-choice theorists on the basis that "tax competition among separate units . . . is an objective to be sought in its own right."[96]

On this analysis, fiscal weakness of a subdivision should properly induce migration from it, and the resulting process of "creative destruction" is not to be deplored. The rejoinder to this is that

> this economic freedom would work to the advantage of the rich, as it already does in many parts of the United States. So long as people with money are able to escape the effects of redistributive taxation by isolating themselves in suburban enclaves, there will not be much prospect that local governments can be used for aiding the poor—or, indeed, for any purpose of the wider community.[97]

Several prominent Americans, including Federal Reserve Board Vice Chairman Alice Rivlin[98] and former Ambassador Robert Strauss[99] have recently urged that Americans give attention to tax-sharing proposals, as has the political scientist Robert Dahl, who has observed that "[t]he city will never begin to meet its problems or attain a satisfactory level of self-government until it has a generous and predictable flow of unencumbered funds—an automatic share of federal tax revenues, for example."[100] Pressures for such interlevel adjustments of fiscal capacity will tend to rise over time, since inflationary pressures bear more heavily on labor-intensive local governments than on higher levels of government whose expenditures in greater measure are either transfers or are for manufactured products benefitting from productivity gains.[101]

Sidney Webb was critical of tax sharing on the conventional basis that it "deprives the community as a whole of part of its public resources without securing . . . in return, any practical means of enforcing upon the local authorities that minimum of efficiency which the interests of the community require."[102] If local autonomy is valued, however, tax sharing has virtues that even general grants lack—chiefly reliability over time.

Some American cities have shared small portions—5 or 10 percent—of property taxes with newly organized business-improvement districts or their equivalents in residential neighborhoods in proportion to their tax bases. What is needed more, particularly in large cities, is a method of sharing income-tax yields with neighborhood groupings on an inverse-wealth basis. The federal government does not share its income tax with the states, let alone localities. A few states permit localities a share of income taxes raised in them; this has no redistributive effect among subdivisions and little among income groups, since state income taxes are more proportional than progressive. It will require drastic change in the mind-set of Congress to give cities or school districts, let alone neighborhoods, direct access to the federal income tax, although the new family tax credit in the 1997 tax bill could easily be supplemented with a voucher for public services.

Vouchers

The use of vouchers as a means of channeling funds from higher levels of government to local or private instrumentalities is another approach that has been pursued or proposed in a variety of contexts. The G.I. Bill channeled large amounts of funds to state and private universities, as will the 1997 tax-credit legislation that focused on the first two years of college. Not dissimilar pending legislation for nursery vouchers in Britain will operate to benefit locally organized cooperative playgroups as well as state-run nurseries. Similar proposals have been made for funding of primary and secondary education in the United States.[103] More general proposals are found in the writings of Adam Smith and Thomas Paine, and, in a later day, those of Milton Friedman.[104]

The device is supported on the ground that it empowers citizens and replaces monopoly bureaucracies,[105] and is opposed on the basis of its supposed incompatibility with neighborhood institutions, its potential for division on class, ethnic, or religious lines, and its privatization of public functions. The communitarian argument against voucherization is often expressed by critics of the 1988 Education Act in England; but the involuntary "community" of consumers of a monopoly service can be analogized to that of members of a slave plantation or citizens of a totalitarian state. The fear has also been expressed by Michael Walzer that educational entrepreneurs would deceive passive parents, and that they "would be [under] little pressure, so long as they could replace departing customers."[106]

This undervaluing of market forces seems one of the weaker arguments against a voucher system. Walzer recognizes, however, that his forebodings will not necessarily result, since vouchers can be used to create so-called "internal markets" within the public sector, though even these erode commonalities of interest among persons who would otherwise be consumers of a monopoly service.[107] Vouchers are also defended as more efficient: "Assistance should be given to individuals on the basis of their particular characteristics, not to groups."[108] There is an advantage to distribution programs "with need related to individual recipient rather than to averages by jurisdiction."[109]

The alternative view sees popular participation as embedded in the democratic process, and crucial for its outcome. Without it, insufficient support will be forthcoming to sustain the democratic method from a variety of potential threats. These threats range from jeopardy of procedural safeguards by governing elites seeking to perpetuate their power, to the pressing of popular demands that exceed what the system can provide.[110]

For Gerald Frug,

[t]he critical choice instead is whether we want public participation in the delivery of public services whoever provides them—whether we want to foster the values of publicization . . . only by taking a share in governance can citizens learn to deal with people with whom they disagree, how to wield and limit power, and how to affect the complex social processes that affect their lives. Only by taking a share in governance can a citizen overcome the feelings of insignificance and powerlessness that constitute privatization.[111]

By contrast, a recent critic of RCAs, Evan McKenzie, criticizes them as "the culmination of a particular strain of utopian thought embodied in the 'Garden City' movement of Ebenezer Howard," whose advocates in recent times "desire to promote the psychosocial growth of the individual by putting him into closer touch with his fellows, rejecting the isolation and alienation of the surrounding society."[112] Frug's argument is an argument, not against privatization by voucher, but for insuring that any private institution administering vouchers is self-administered, like an ordinary private school, and not part of a corporation or national chain. Frug concedes

[t]he suggestions made for government services—workplace democracy, consumer involvement in management decisions, and decentralized, participatory management of service delivery—could take place whether the services are run by government or by business.

In this connection, one may recall Justice Brandeis's view that "it is only through the participation of the unknown many in the responsibilities and determinations of business that Americans can secure the moral and intellectual development essential to the maintenance of liberty."

The claim of McKenzie and others that RCAs are not true voluntary associations because residents "are there because of price, location, or limited options" would, if good, invalidate all forms of private and market ordering. It is conceded that in recent years most RCA developments are small and compete with many others; they are no less competitive than the local supermarket or gasoline station, and probably more so. Stress by RCA critics on "people's bonds to place, entrepreneurs' collusion, and the regulatory function"[113] does not alter the central fact that most people who acquire RCA property do have a wide choice, and that the conduct of RCA boards is significantly subject to market restraints.

The use of vouchers for housing and transportation is less controversial than their use in education, since in that context there is no common institution to be eroded. In these contexts of housing and transportation controversy centers on the selection of voucher recipient, and the occasional award of vouchers as a reward for disfunctionality, which has the effect of dispersing it throughout the community, a frequent criticism of the American housing program launched during the Nixon administration.

One major impetus to the use of voucher systems is the lack of uniformity in local-government structures among American states. Federal grants to local governments delivering services do not necessarily relieve the taxpayers of the sometimes different entity or level of government that finances the services. This is said by Robert Reischauer to cause national policymakers "to design programs in which the national government deals directly with citizens rather than dealing through intermediary state and local governments." While Reischauer asserts that "this will reinforce the tendencies toward centralization already apparent in American federalism,"[114] this is far from self-evident. If local suppliers of public goods derive most of their revenues from unconditioned federal vouchers delivered to them by individuals, they will find themselves in a position in which they themselves supply their marginal revenues from local resources. This is much closer to the original constitutional design, which did not contemplate federal coercion of state and local government, than the system of conditional grants-in-aid that has developed since and as a result of the constitutional controversies of the New Deal period. In addition, some students have minimized the significance of governmental complexity, urging that if federal aid is provided to local governments, "school districts appear to get their cut, whether or not they are directly aided."[115]

Conceptually, voucherization of public services operates as a partition of them, with many of the virtues and defects of partition:

In terms of rational choice theory . . . fragmentation performs useful functions. It does not attempt to suppress conflict by such means as adjudication, i.e., subjecting the parties to some coercive rule derived from the legal system, constitution, or normative order. Rather, it eliminates conflict by enabling the parties to separate, so that each gets its way. In the respective polities and generally in the resulting political system thorough responsiveness reigns.[116]

Although vouchers are an excellent instrument for economic redistribution, particularly when financed from a progressive income tax, it is asserted that they result in the concentration of social capital in that the more educated or advantaged will tend to flock together. However, the flexibility of the nation's housing stock, the mobility of its population, and the diversity of local governments within most metropolitan areas insures that this happens anyway. If low-income persons bear vouchers, their perceived desirability as citizens may be enhanced, and the tendency of subdivisions to use fiscal zoning reduced.

Voucher programs, to the extent they are federally financed, do have one unappreciated virtue: They give the institutions cashing the vouchers what amounts to a guaranteed cut of federal income-tax revenues unlikely to be obtained in any other fashion. It can scarcely be thought that the Clinton administration would have been successful in 1997 in obtaining massive new revenues for higher education through any device other than a tax-credit provision. Vouchers and tax credits have an added redistributive benefit: They are focused on needy individuals rather than needy subdivisions. Because local or sublocal institutions are the end-recipients rather than intermediaries, voucher programs do not involve the regulation and coercion of subordinate governments characteristic of grant-in-aid programs.

This becomes clear if one considers the effects if all federal programs of aid to elementary and secondary education were voucherized; the focus of the Title I program would cause most funds to flow to the schools attended by the poorest students. If the vouchers were designed to relieve schools of their infrastructure and equipment costs, any claim that they subsidized religious instruction or threatened to control curriculum would also be obviated, since the federal share of education spending is much less than infrastructure and equipment costs. Their potential uses in the sublocal context are not limited to education; one can conceive of day-care vouchers on the British model, already approached by the existing federal day-care tax credits, or small vouchers or tax credits to facilitate the organization of old-age clubs. While vouchers may dissolve existing bureaucracies, they also have the potential effect of creating new institutions, as was seen quite clearly in connection with the explosion in the number of higher education institutions after World War II.

NOTES

1. W. Wickwar, *The Political Theory of Local Government*. Columbia: University of South Carolina Press, 1970.
2. Id., 14–18.
3. Id., 21–23.
4. Id., 27–29.
5. G. Gomme, *Lectures on the Principles of Local Government*. Westminster, UK: Constable, 1897, 192.
6. W. Oates, *Fiscal Federalism* (New York: Harcourt Brace, 1972), 123. See J. Buchanan, "The Pure Theory of Public Finance," *J. Political Econ.*, 57 (1949), 502; J. Stiglitz, *Economics of the Public Sector*, 2d ed. (New York: Norton, 1988), 574.
7. M. Bendick, "Designing Circuit-Breaker Property Tax Relief," *National Tax J.*, 27 (1974), 19.

8. See R. Bish and H. Nourse, *Urban Economics and Policy Analysis* (New York: McGraw-Hill, 1975), 143–49, citing L. Orr, "Incidence of Differential Property Taxes on Urban Housing," *National Tax J.*, 21 (1968), 253; A. Church, "Capitalization of the Effective Property Tax Rate on Single-Family Residences," *National Tax J.*, 27 (1974), 113. Compare D. Hyman, "Property Tax Differentials and Residential Rents in North Carolina," *National Tax J.*, 26 (1973), 303.

9. R. Bird, "Threading the Fiscal Labyrinth," *National Tax J.*, 46 (1993), 207.

10. K. Messere, *Tax Policy in OECD Countries*. Amsterdam: IBFD Publications, 1993, 189.

11. Id., 210.

12. Stiglitz, supra, 152.

13. Oates, supra, 139.

14. A. Smith, *Wealth of Nations*, bk. V, pt. II, art. I. London: Everyman, 1910, 314.

15. A. de Tocqueville, *L'Ancien Régime* (tr. M. Patterson). Oxford: Blackwell, 1947, 134 (hereafter *"Ancien Régime"*).

16. Oates, supra, 144n29.

17. R. Musgrave and P. Musgrave, *Public Finance in Theory and Practice*, 5th ed. New York: McGraw-Hill, 1988, 418.

18. W. Fischel, *Regulatory Takings*. Cambridge, MA: Harvard University Press, 1994, 285.

19. A. O'Sullivan, *Property Taxes and Tax Revolts: The Legacy of Proposition*. Cambridge: Cambridge University Press, 1995, 13.

20. P. Smith, "Lessons from the British Poll Tax Disaster," *National Tax J.*, 44 (1993), 421.

21. W. Oates, "An Economist's Perspective on Fiscal Federalism," in W. Oates, *The Political Economy of Fiscal Federalism* (Lexington, MA: Lexington Books, 1977), 8–9.

22. Oates, *Fiscal Federalism*, 228.

23. C. Arnold-Baker, *Law and Practice of Parish Administration* (London: Longcross Press, 1966), 5.

24. Id., 6.

25. For criticism of this reasoning, see J. Gyford, *Citizens, Consumers and Councils* (London: Macmillan, 1991), 10–12.

26. Smith, "Lessons from the British Poll Tax Disaster," 421.

27. P. Smith, "Book Review of D. Butler, *Failure in British Government: The Politics of the Poll Tax*," in *National Tax J.*, 48 (1995), 297.

28. D. King, "British Local Finance: 'The Poll Tax,'" in R. Bennett, *Decentralization, Local Governments and Markets* (Oxford: Clarendon, 1990), 153, citing G. Bramley, "Horizontal Disparities and Equalization," *Local Government Studies* (Jan. 1987), 69.

29. Smith, "Lessons from the British Poll Tax Disaster," 421; Messere, supra, 209.

30. P. Minford, "How to Depoliticize Local Government," *Economic Affairs*, 9 (1988), 1, quoted in Gyford, supra, 158–59.

31. Oates, *Fiscal Federalism*, 131.

32. Smith, *Wealth of Nations*, bk. V, pt. II, art. III, 351.

33. See B. Barber, *The Death of Communal Liberty* (Princeton, NJ: Princeton University Press, 1974), citing Bundner Rechtsbuch, 1018.

34. Id.

35. Id., 231.

36. W. Oates, "Decentralization of the Public Sector," in Bennett, supra, 47.

37. Id., 48. See Bish and Nourse, supra, 152–54.

38. Bish and Nourse, supra, 152–54.

39. Messere, supra, 189.

40. R. Wagner, *Charging for Government*. London: Routledge, 1991.

41. American Law Institute, *Restatement of Servitudes*, Tent. Draft No. 2, ch. 3.

42. *Norwood v. Baker*, 172 U.S. 269 (1898).

43. S. Diamond, "Death and Transfiguration of Benefits Taxation," *J. Legal Studies*, 12

(1983), 201; D. Hagman and J. Miscynski, *Windfalls for Wipeouts* (Chicago: American Planning Association, 1978), 311–15, 612–14.

44. *Dolan v. Tigard*, 512 U.S. 687 (1994); see Fischel, supra, sec. 9.14.

45. D. Currie, *The Constitution of the Federal Republic of Germany.* Chicago: University of Chicago Press, 1994, 56n123.

46. G. Harris, *Local Government in Many Lands.* London: King, 1933, 15.

47. Id., 104.

48. Messere, supra, 192.

49. C. Arnold-Baker, *Powers and Constitution of Local Councils* (London: National Association of Local Councils, 1979), citing Local Government Act (1972), schedule 13.

50. Fischel, supra, sec. 7.14 and authorities cited.

51. E. Gramlich, "A Policymaker's Guide to Fiscal Decentralization," *National Tax J.*, 46 (1993), 233.

52. Messere, supra, 188; see also J. Knott, "Stabilization Policy, Grants in Aid, and the Federal System in Western Germany," in Oates, *The Political Economy of Fiscal Federalism*, 75.

53. Oates, *Fiscal Federalism*, 158–59, 161.

54. Musgrave and Musgrave, supra, 101.

55. Id., 160.

56. R. Malloy, "The Political Economy of Co-Financing America's Urban Renaissance," *Vanderbilt Law Rev.*, 40 (1987), 67.

57. Musgrave and Musgrave, supra, 301, 305; Smith, *Wealth of Nations*, bk. V, pt. II, ch. II, 308.

58. Smith, *Wealth of Nations*, bk. V, pt. II, art. IV, 356.

59. Bish and Nourse, supra, 150–51.

60. Messere, supra, 208.

61. M. Castells, ed., *The Shek Kip Mei Syndrome: Economic Development and Public Housing in Hong Kong and Singapore* (London: Pion, 1990), 95–97. On Hong Kong, see generally A. Kwan, *Hong Kong Society: A Reader* (Hong Kong: Writers' and Publishers' Cooperative, 1986); J. Cheng, *Hong Kong in Transition* (Oxford: Oxford University Press, 1986); A. King, *Social Life and Development in Hong Kong* (Hong Kong: Chinese University Press, 1981).

62. Castells, supra, 267.

63. Id., 270. On Singapore, see generally ed. L. Chong-Yah, *Singapore: Resources and Growth* (New York: Oxford University Press, 1986); P. Chen, *Singapore: Development Trends and Policies* (New York: Oxford University Press, 1986); J. Quah, *Government and Politics of Singapore* (Oxford: Oxford University Press, 1983).

64. M. Gelfand, *A Nation of Cities* (New York: Oxford University Press, 1975), 319, citing *Congressional Record*, 87th Cong., 1st Sess. S9891, 9895 (1961).

65. Smith, *Wealth of Nations*, bk. V, pt. I, ch. II, 304–6.

66. H. Davies, "Free Markets and Centralized Political Power," in R. Bennett, *Local Government in the New Europe* (London: Belhaven, 1993), 92.

67. Oates, "Decentralization of the Public Sector," in Bennett, *Decentralization, Local Governments and Markets*.

68. D. Mueller, *The Public Choice Approach to Politics.* Cheltenham, UK: Elgar, 1993, 94–95.

69. H. Wolman, "Decentralization: What It Is and Why We Should Care," in Bennett, *Decentralization, Local Governments and Markets* (1990), 36. See also H. Wolman and Page, "The Impact of Intergovernmental Grants on Subnational Resource Disparities," *Public Budgeting and Finance*, 7, no. 3 (1987); Musgrave and Musgrave, supra, 246.

70. Oates, "Decentralization of the Public Sector," in Bennett, *Decentralization, Local Governments and Markets*, 49; see also R. Bird, "Threading the Fiscal Labyrinth," *National Tax J.*, 46 (1993), 207.

71. B. Badcock, *Unfairly Structured Cities* (Oxford: Blackwell, 1984), citing T. Boast,

"Urban Resources, the American Capital Market" and "Federal Programs," in D. Ashford, *Financing Urban Government in the Welfare State* (New York: St. Martin's Press, 1980).

72. A. Gunlicks, "Local Government in the United States," in ed. J. Hesse, *Local Government and Urban Affairs in International Perspective* (Baden-Baden: Nomus, 1991), 95, citing Advisory Commission on Intergovernmental Relations, *A Catalog of Federal Grant-in-Aid Programs* (1987).

73. Oates, *Fiscal Federalism*, 90.

74. E. Page, *Localism and Centralism in Europe*. Oxford: Oxford University Press, 1991, 34.

75. Currie, supra, 58.

76. Bish and Nourse, supra, 155–58.

77. S. Gold, "Issues Raised by the New Federalism," *National Tax J.*, 49 (1996), 273. See also Bird, supra, 207.

78. Gramlich, supra, 237.

79. Id.

80. Bish and Nourse, supra, 157–58.

81. *Ancien Régime*, 72.

82. Id., 155.

83. Wickwar, supra, citing S. Webb, *Grants in Aid* (London: Fabian Society, 1911).

84. Quoted in A. Offer, *Property and Politics, 1870–1914*. Cambridge: Cambridge University Press, 1981, 216–17. See also Webb, supra.

85. Webb, supra, 94.

86. E. Gramlich, "Intergovernmental Grants," in Oates, *The Political Economy of Fiscal Federalism*, 219, 234.

87. Bish and Nourse, supra, 158–60.

88. Musgrave and Musgrave, supra, 493.

89. Messere, supra, 190.

90. G. Marcou, "New Tendencies of Local-Government Development in Europe," in Bennett, *Local Government in the New Europe*, 62. For a more critical view, see B. Reissert, "Federal and State Transfers to Local Government in the Federal Republic of Germany" in Ashford, supra.

91. See Currie, supra, 52–60.

92. Id., 254.

93. Messere, supra, 202.

94. Harris, supra, 13. See also Y. Meny, "Financial Transfers and Local Government in France," in Ashford, supra, on the later arrangements.

95. P. Groenewegen, "Taxation and Decentralization," in Bennett, *Decentralization, Local Government and Markets*, 98.

96. Groenewegen, supra, in Bennett, *Decentralization, Local Governments and Markets*, 100, citing G. Breenan and J. Buchanan, *The Power to Tax* (1980), 185–86.

97. W. Magnusson, "The New Neighborhood Democracy," in ed. L. Sharpe, *Decentralist Trends in Western Democracies* (London: Sage, 1979), 141. For an early critique of public-choice theory, see R. Golembiewski, "A Critique of 'Democratic Administration' and Its Supporting Ideation," *Amer. Pol. Sci. Rev.*, 71 (1977), 1488–1507, 1526–31.

98. A. Rivlin, *Reviving the American Dream*. Washington, DC: Brookings Institute, 1992.

99. R. Strauss, "The EC Challege to State and Local Governments," *Intergovernmental Perspective*, 16 (1990), 13.

100. R. Dahl, *After the Revolution*. New Haven, CT: Yale University Press, 1970, 133–34.

101. Oates, *Fiscal Federalism*, 233.

102. Webb, supra, 85.

103. C. Jencks and J. Areen, *Vouchers: A Report on Financing Education by Payments to Parents* (1970); J. Coons and S. Sugarman, *Education by Choice: The Case for Family Control* (Berkeley: University of California Press, 1978).

104. M. Friedman, *Capitalism and Freedom.* Chicago: University of Chicago Press, 1962, 85–107.
105. Bish and Nourse, supra, 317–19; M. Friedman, "The Role of Government in Education," in ed. R. Solo, *Economics and the Public Interest* (Westport, CT: Greenwood, 1982).
106. M. Walzer, *Radical Principles.* New York: Basic Books, 1979, 263–64.
107. See the sceptical discussion in B. Barber, *Strong Democracy* (Berkeley: University of California Press, 1974), 293–98.
108. Mueller, supra, 82.
109. Musgrave and Musgrave, supra, 493.
110. F. Hirsch, *Social Limits to Growth.* Cambridge, MA: Harvard University Press, 1977, 94.
111. G. Frug, "The Choice Between Privatization and Publicization," *Current Municipal Problems*, 14 (1987), 20, 26.
112. E. McKenzie, *Privatopia.* New Haven, CT: Yale University Press, 1994, 24–25.
113. J. Logan and H. Molotch, *Urban Fortunes.* Berkeley: University of California Press, 1987, 40–41.
114. R. Reischauer, "Governmental Diversity: Bane of the Grants Strategy in the United States," in Oates, *The Political Economy of Fiscal Federalism*, 115, 126–27.
115. Gramlich, "Intergovernmental Grants," in Oates, *The Political Economy of Fiscal Federalism*, 230–31.
116. S. Beer, "A Political Scientist's View of Fiscal Federalism," in Oates, *The Political Economy of Fiscal Federalism*, 26.

Chapter 5

Promoting Equality

In addition to the equalization potential of vouchers, there are other equalization techniques that deserve discussion as potentially benefitting sublocal instrumentalities.

POLITICAL METHODS

The personnel deficiencies and lack of social capital of smaller sublocal and local entities can be remedied by designation of some officers by higher levels of government when crises arise or by allowing co-optation of private persons by local instrumentalities.

Appointment by Higher Governments

Where Swiss communes cannot find from their population sufficient officers to run it, the cantonal authorities can place the commune under a device call *Kuratel*, which allows cantonal authorities to directly administer the commune.[1] Similarly, prefects in France were given power to impose on communes additional expenditures and taxation to meet basic services (*inscription d'office*).[2]

A less-questionable and enervating means of supplementing the personnel of local elected bodies is through local co-optation or indirect election. Tocqueville observed:

Able men retire from the political arena, in which it is so difficult to retain their independence, or to advance without becoming servile . . . the American republics will be obliged more frequently to introduce the plan of election by an elected body into their system of representation or run the risk of perishing miserably among the shoals of democracy.[3]

Co-Optation

The traditional British aldermanic system prior to its abolition by the Local Government Act of 1972 provided for the addition to elected local councils of co-opted aldermen (one-seventh of each London council; one-fourth of those outside London); these over time unfortunately tended to be "the older, high-status members of councils."[4] "It became the convention to choose the aldermen from the more senior councillors, who were thereby saved the trouble of further popular elections."[5] Until 1972, British parish councils were still permitted to co-opt persons—not parish councillors—as chairmen, this was often done.[6] Members may still be co-opted to committees, but co-opted members cannot vote unless the committee relates to management of land, management of a festival, tourist promotion, or a harbor authority. Committees may not be used to deal with loans, taxes, or lotteries.[7] In recommending these restrictions, the Widdicombe Committee took the view that "it is wrong in principle that noncouncillors should be voting members of committees with power to take decisions."[8]

Prior to 1989, the number of co-opted members was limited to one-third and they were permitted to vote, though they were barred from finance committees.[9] The exceptions recognized in 1989 allow co-opted community members to sit as voting members on committees dealing with housing estates and community facilities. However, co-option, "originally advocated as a means of diluting democracy and curbing public influence, ended up being defended as a means of extending democracy to a wider public."[10] While use of co-option by parish councils was curtailed, the Conservative government was successful in maintaining it for the vastly more important police and education committees, including local school governors. In the last context, there is still force in the view of Lord Simon of Wythenshawe that co-opted members are a way of staying in "constant and direct touch with important organizations whose friendly cooperation is essential,"[11] and in less—privileged schools such members may still "steady the wild incapacities of the members of the ignorant multitude."[12]

The danger of excessive co-optation is that the public will cease to participate where its votes are severely diluted; as stated by Tocqueville, "where it had been thought right to retain the empty form of a free election, the people stubbornly refrained. Nothing in history is more common than such a phenomenon."[13]

An objection to very small units noted by Madison in *The Federalist* (No. 10) is that "only if the tasks of basic units are very limited can small communes provide a sufficient basis for their recruitment";[14] co-optation can provide a means of acquiring necessary talent. Several European countries, including Germany,[15] Sweden and The Netherlands, allow co-optation of members by committees of local councils;[16] the British Education Act of 1988, as noted, provides for co-opted members of boards of school governors. It has been suggested that functional representation of such bodies as universities, churches, and charities might be appropriate at the sublocal level.[17]

The Prussian Municipal Law of 1808 provided for the drafting or deputization of prominent citizens to discharge such functions as the management of schools and public charities, and members of committees for relief of the poor under the so-called Elberfeld System, which spread through much of Western Europe during the period 1830–1914 and inspired the voluntary activity of Charity Organization Societies in England and America.[18] One can readily conceive of a regime in which, in addition to providing training courses for school governors in the British manner, a municipality assists its self-governing schools by recruiting and suitably honoring pools of volunteers with expertise in higher education, accounting, and building construction and maintenance for service as school governors.

Forced Mergers

Forced mergers are an especially doubtful method of equalization where positional or social goods such as education are at issue. Fred Hirsch has observed:

The "quality" of schooling, in effect, exists in two dimensions. There is an absolute dimension, in which quality is added by receptive students, good teachers, good facilities and so on; but there is also a relative dimension, in which quality consists of the differential over the educational level attained by others. The enormous resistance induced in both the United States and Britain by public efforts to integrate previously inferior schools with previously superior schools cannot be fully understood without reference to both these aspects of educational quality.[19]

In addition, it may actually be more difficult for a minority group to get responsiveness from a large system than from a smaller system in which it is a majority . . . it is more equitable and more efficient to tax higher income individuals and businesses and provide subsidization of educational programs on a statewide basis, than to try to achieve equalization by manipulating local government boundaries . . . it becomes more difficult to adjust the provision of public goods to citizen preferences as the size of the jurisdictions increases.[20]

Nonetheless, as previously shown, there have been many forced mergers of school districts in the United States, though not of general-purpose local governments. A number of European countries, notably Germany, Sweden, and Britain, have at times drastically reduced the numbers of their local governments, sometimes to their later regret.

Annexation

Annexation, another technique of equalization, in the United States has been restricted since the turn of the century by laws in most states requiring referenda in the annexed area. Only 18 of 66 proposals between 1947 and 1979 were approved, and most of these involved the reconsolidation of Virginia cities into counties from which they had recently withdrawn or consolidations in rural areas. There have been consolidations in Indianapolis, Jacksonville, Nashville, Lexington, and Baton Rouge, usually involving the expansion of functions of a preexisting county and use of differential tax rates. The Indianapolis merger did not require a referendum and took place in a state with little home rule.[21]

Several Western European countries have greatly reduced the number of their local-government units since the end of World War II, most notably Germany, Denmark, and Sweden; the consolidations in Sweden being especially drastic. These amalgamations are prompted by the belief that units are too small as catchment areas—for example, for primary schools—and that they cannot employ adequate staff. It is variously urged that units with minimum populations of 3,000, 8,000, or 30,000 are appropriate.[22] This overlooks the option of having these entities act as pure provision units, without employees of their own. Opponents stress the economies resulting from the use of elected, volunteer, and co-opted workers. In France, an influential report recommended against consolidation of the more than 30,000 communes on the basis of the decline in civic participation that would result. French communes frequently function as pure provision units, contracting out functions to private entities in the manner of an American residential community association, most of which have 100 or 200 members, and sometimes fewer.[23] It has been said (overlooking the history of forced school-district amalgamations) that "the U.S.A. is the only country in the world which still adheres to the principle of purely voluntary amalgamation; in most states, it is only possible if the majority of voters in each commune signify their agreement by referendum."[24]

Little consideration has been given to one means of fostering mergers of units suggested by Dennis Mueller:

When joining with *B* the residents of *A* ought to be able to propose institutional arrangements that ensure that both groups experience the gains . . . by requiring that the legislature in the newly formed polity use a supermajority rule, it could preclude *B*'s combining redistribution and allocative efficiency issues.[25]

FINANCIAL METHODS

It has been urged that "only the more inclusive levels of government reap benefits as well as incurring costs from redistributive policies."[26] On the other hand, decentralization can sometimes have redistributive objects. A major impulse behind the revival of British parish councils in 1894 was the desire of a Liberal government to "nationalize the land by throwing the property in the hands of the parish councils who will let it to the villagers";[27] the principal power given the new councils (successors to the ecclesiastical vestry) was the power to manage and let allotments. In the final event, little land was transferred to the councils by central government[28]—a total of 14,000 holdings between 1908 and 1914,[29] and about 17,000 acres in the period preceding 1908, of which a Fabian pamphlet by the Webbs asserted that "30,000 working men hold land directly from their parish councils."[30]

Equalization Grants

In recent European practice, "usually equalization is pursued by grants allocated according to an estimation of local needs without regard to the amount of tax revenues. In the UK, grants have remained the main source of revenue for local government since the 1960s."[31]

Sidney Webb had urged that assistance be given to each major government service by an equalizing grant: "If the product of the standard rate does not produce, in the area of any Local Authority, the amount of the 'National Minimum' of expenditure for its population, the deficiency might be made wholly good by what has been called the Primary Grant."[32]

Local expenditures in excess of the National Minimum would receive a partially matching Secondary Grant, a scheme much like the "foundation program" of state assistance to local schools in effect in most American states.[33]

American inverse-wealth formulas for state school assistance are said to somewhat reduce fiscally motivated zoning[34]:

[I]f central governments increased their aid to low-income communities to the point where local revenue bases were actually enhanced by the in-migration of poor people, local governments would receive some compensation for the greater tax burden usually generated by a socially deprived population . . . efficiency considerations suggest that service delivery be carried out locally, while equity considerations dictate that redistribution become a function of the central government.[35]

Equalizing grants have the same effect that geographically discriminating income-tax rates would have, but unlike the former are constitutionally permitted and are therefore a preferred means of attaining horizontal equity among subdivisions.[36] Critics of these formulas note that "there is no guarantee that equalization funds would be spent for the benefit of the poor residents of a community." "If our basic concern is with inequalities among individuals, redistribution should be aimed at individuals, not regions or localities."[37]

Even these critics do not oppose formulas focused on handicapped citizens or those designed to share natural-resources wealth, and it has been urged that in addition to or in place of welfare payments supporting private consumption by the poor, the "federal government [should] extend its support to the public-good consumption of the urban poor,"[38] as does the Title I program of federal assistance to primary and secondary education.

Equalizing grants directed at property-tax relief have mixed consequences, due to capitalization of changed property-tax levels:

An equalizing grant program helps current low-income homeowners and current landlords, but appears unlikely to help low-income renters or future low-income homeowners . . . capitalization weakens but does not eliminate the case for using intergovernmental grants.

If maintenance of local tax effort is a condition of the grant and service quality is raised "in every jurisdiction where low-income people reside, a capitalization effect does not arise."[39] Equalizing grants have also been criticized as bad regional policy, tending "to perpetuate inefficient patterns of location."[40]

In Germany, local governments have an entitlement under the Basic Law to 14 percent of the proceeds of national income tax, adjusted according to local income-tax yield, in addition to funds from lander governments; only about 10 percent of their revenues are locally generated and a function of local wealth.[41] This system may be a model, at least as to structure if not as to degree, the equalization being extreme in relation to American tastes. As already noted, there is nothing to prevent equalizing grants being passed through to sublocal institutions, particularly schools.

Means Testing

Poor relief was once the most local of functions. It has been said that, prior to the Poor Law Amendment Act of 1835,

> the laws of settlement ultimately tethered people to their parish of birth, unless good fortune or labor shortage enabled them to reside elsewhere for a year and thus gain right of settlement there . . . the only bond between the fourteen thousand republics [was] the inter-parochial code, the law of settlement.[42]

Parochial administration was defended by Ricardo on the basis that a parish "was much more interested in an economical collection of the rate and a sparing distribution of relief when the whole saving will be for its own benefit, than if hundreds of parishes were to partake of it."[43]

Local means-testing collapsed with the depression following the Napoleonic Wars, a phenomenon much like that in the United States in the 1930s:

> The sheer scale of poverty after 1795 rendered nugatory any distinction between individual paupers. . . . The poor ceased to be regarded as individuals who may or may not merit assistance and came to be regarded instead as "a problem"; poverty appeared less as a transitory condition than a quasi-permanent fourth estate . . . the old poor law was rent asunder by . . . the absence of effective mechanisms for transferring resources from richer to poorer parishes.[44]

In 1796 Pitt urged, "[l]et us make relief in cases where there are a number of children a matter of right and honor instead of a ground of opprobrium and contempt." There followed the Speenhamland system of wage subsidies administered by magistrates in groupings of parishes, which was criticized as providing an incentive to lay off laborers residing outside the parish and as enshrining a belief in a right to work and income. The final end of parochial authority came with the Poor Law Amendment Act in 1835 designed to limit relief and reduce the power of magistrates[45] by vesting power in new boards drawn from unions of parishes.

It has been said of the American Social Security Act that it provides "unneeded amounts to the well-off in order to make needed transfers to the poor politically acceptable."[46] Be this as it may, it is clear that sublocal governments are peculiarly unsuitable vehicles for means-tested expenditure programs.

Progressive Taxation

Buchanan and Tullock contend that "[b]y incorporating highly progressive, but nominally general, taxes with special-benefit public services in the fiscal process, the redistribution that is carried out [by Western governments] far exceeds that which could be accomplished directly."[47] As a description of British and American tax systems this is at best questionable, given the erosion of exemptions and standard deductions and the increased use of payroll taxes without income thresholds. "In both the United States and Britain, taxation taken as a whole has been estimated to be broadly proportional to income"[48] or at best "slightly progressive . . . [or] bouncing but essentially flat."[49] The tax is also estimated to have a 7 percent compliance cost.[50]

Lewis Mumford observed in 1938 that

[w]ithout doubt the prime obstacle to urban decentralization is that a unit that consists of workers, without the middle class and rich groups that exist in a big city, is unable to support even the elementary civic equipment of roads, sewers, fire department, police service and schools.[51]

This vision of local redistribution, however, has been undone by flight to the suburbs, suggesting that redistribution must be accomplished at higher levels of government and not by sacrificing decentralization to supposed equality interests. "[T]he difficulties inherent in undertaking substantial redistributive programs on the level of local finance . . . explains the current fiscal crisis of many large cities in the United States."[52]

The use of progressive taxation by lower levels of government is subject to severe limitations:

The use of such taxes at decentralized levels establishes pecuniary incentives for migration for both high- and low-income households that can easily lead to locational distortions and a frustration of the redistributional objectives of the tax.[53] The more a local community engages in redistribution, the more the marginal benefit/tax ratio for the average taxpayer declines and the more the local economy suffers.[54]

For similar reasons, welfare expenditures in most Western countries have tended to gravitate to higher levels of government as populations became more mobile.[55]

The Scandinavian countries, in which local income taxation is a major revenue source, are careful to insure that the *local* as distinct from *national* income taxes are proportional rather than progressive.[56] Similar considerations have influenced some states that apply *flat* rather than *progressive* rates to investment-income or capital-gains taxes and some foreign countries allowing tax benefits for savings, since "some categories of income (those from financial capital) are much more elastic with respect to the tax rates than others . . . some incomes, by moving abroad or underground, can evade taxes more easily than others."[57]

The mild progressiveness in some American state-income taxes is unusual by international standards, most foreign subnational-income taxes being flat-rate. It has been ascribed to the federal deductibility of the taxes: "In effect, local governments use the federal tax offset to subsidize the cost of local redistributive activity."[58]

The much-mooted Value Added Tax is said to be equivalent in its effects to a proportional (nonprogressive) income tax.[59] Some have urged a wealth tax to supplement a consumption tax.[60] A constraint affecting all forms of income taxation is that

> the lower the percentage of employees in relation to the percentage of self-employed such as farmers, artisans, liberal professions, the more difficult it is to raise large amounts of money from a broad-based income tax, and countries like France and Greece . . . have accepted a low personal income tax ratio.[61]

In recent years, the percentage of self-employed has reversed its decline in the United States.

American residential community associations, it is said,

> have no responsibility for redistributing costs and benefits within their community. Indeed, some RCA documents preclude the board of directors from making redistributive allocations of services. . . . Metropolitan areas with RCA communities are likely to show a greater variety of service level and quality than areas with few or no RCAs.[62]

It has been urged that the requirement that covenant activities touch and concern land and that directors exercise business judgment operate to insure that "[a]n RCA is not a private redistributive scheme. A member has the right to the dedication of assessments to the benefit of the common property."[63]

A critic of RCAs has noted that

> although there is no provision for redistribution of property on the basis of need, there is no initial inequality to correct . . .—everybody starts in relative equality, owning identical or similar units. This socialism by contract analysis breaks down if a member can't make the mortgage payments. There is no provision in CID documents for the association or the other residents to help the family who is about to lose its home.[64]

Highly local instrumentalities are not good vehicles for redistribution except on a voluntary, charitable basis; consideration of the possible effects of a local recession on dues collections demonstrates this point.

RCAs do provide instrumentalities through which charitable relief might be organized. Critics of government-organized cash relief, like the early social worker Mary Richmond, objected to it because it undermined neighborliness and voluntary charitable activity.

RCAs are free of the political paradox that one commentator has noted: The more egalitarian societies become, the greater their demand for public (government-provided) goods: "If there is a redistribution of income within a community, so that the income of the median voter increases, then the demand for public goods in the community will rise even though the average income remains the same."[65]

Robert Nelson has analogized zoning to a collective-property right similar to rights of an RCA and has observed:

Zoning thereby furthers an economic segregation of neighborhoods similar to the economic differences that arise with respect to the consumption of ordinary private goods and services . . . the intellectual case for zoning is much the same as the case for property rights in general. Zoning serves a valuable social purpose by establishing the incentive to create attractive neighborhoods and then to maintain them. It does this by insuring that the builders and maintainers . . . will be the ones to reap the benefits.[66]

While sublocal instrumentalities, and more particularly their low-income citizens, are appropriate recipients of the proceeds of progressive taxation, they are singularly ill-equipped to impose it themselves.

Tax Thresholds

The absence of thresholds in the income-, payroll-, and property-tax systems of many countries causes the benefits of many welfare programs to low-income groups to be offset by the increased burden upon the working members of such groups of the taxation needed to finance the benefit programs. In the United States, in addition to the burdens of state income and unemployment taxation, frequently unaccompanied by thresholds, it has been said that

a household with one parent, two children, and earned income of $16,050 in 1994 will face the following combination of taxes: a combined employee and employer share of payroll taxes of 15.3 percent, a 15 percent federal marginal tax rate, a 17.7 percent benefit reduction rate on the earned income tax credit.

(Public-finance economists claim that [the division between employers and employees] does not matter in the long run because the employee will bear both in the form of either lower wages or higher consumer prices."[67])

The payroll tax ... hardly seems a tax which is worthy of so major a role in the tax system.[68]

In addition, benefit-reduction rates are imposed on income exceeding thresholds in the AFDC program (66%), the food stamp program (30%), and the SSI program (50%). Recent improvements in the earned-income credit partly mitigate these marginal rates, leading a commentator to observe that the marginal rate on an AFDC recipient taking a half-time minimum wage job in 1996 was 27.6 percent for a family with one child and 21.6 percent for a family with two or more children.[69] The Earned Income Credit, however, "is limited to earners and to returns with dependents only. . . . Similarly, low-income recipients whose income comes from other sources, such as pensions, do not benefit."[70] The same can be said of the new $500-per-child family-tax credit. Other writers observe, quite remarkably, that the burdens of explicit and implicit taxation "on the poor are not particularly high—they rarely exceed forty percent."[71]

While only 5 percent of the U.S. population paid income tax in 1939, 74.2 percent did so by the end of the war in 1945. This percentage declined to a peacetime percentage of 58.9 percent in 1950, but "bracket creep" caused the percentage to rise to 80.8 percent by 1980.[72]

A decline in the value of the personal exemption, and a related reduction in the income of nontaxable individuals, is by far the most significant change over the postwar period. Together they resulted in an expansion of the tax base by about one-quarter of total personal income. The decline in the personal exemption also helps to explain why tax-exempt levels of income fell dramatically relative to average income and why households with dependents increasingly paid a greater share of the tax burden.[73]

Similar observations have been made about the postwar British experience.
In some countries

the view is taken that under the ability-to-pay principle, those around subsistence level should not be expected to pay income tax. This approach is adopted by France (where half the population is below the threshold), Japan, The Netherlands, and Norway . . . high thresholds . . . reduce the poverty and unemployment traps.

By contrast, Denmark, New Zealand, and Sweden, "for reasons of accountability and solidarity," tax even persons who are net beneficiaries of the tax transfer system. The "poverty trap" in the United States has become sufficiently pronounced as a result of the bracket creep and erosion of inflation in the 1960s and 1970s to give a hollow ring to J. K.

Galbraith's 1958 complaint that "the modern liberal rallies to protect the poor from the taxes which in the next generation, as a result of a higher investment for their children, would eliminate poverty."[74]

The total burden of income tax and the employee's share of payroll taxes on the average production worker with two children in 1990 was higher in the United States than in several fully developed welfare states in which taxation accounts for a higher percentage of GDP, including France, Canada, and Luxembourg, and was several times higher than in Japan, where taxes as a percentage of GDP approximate those in the United States.[75] One commentator observes (with nice understatement): "It is illogical to combine in an uncoordinated way the ability to pay (progressive) approach to the income tax and the insurance (regressive) approach to contributions, since unintended results are bound to arise."[76]

An OECD official has noted that

in the recent wave of tax reforms the progressivity of the rate schedules has been much reduced, or in some cases even eliminated. The consequent loss of vertical equity has been offset by increasing the income level at which income tax becomes payable and reducing tax loopholes which benefit most higher income groups.[77]

The first and third of these phenomena are observable in the recent U.S. tax changes, but little attention had been given to the second: except for some expansion of the earned-income credit, there had been (except in 1986) limited increase in exemptions, standard deductions, and other thresholds until the advent of the family tax credit in 1997. In addition,

the zero or near zero threshold for payroll taxes may provide a disincentive to take on new labor.[78]

[E]mployers who have to shed labor may take into account that the low or zero thresholds generally prevailing increase the nonwage labor costs of low-paid compared to high-paid employees. Moreover, the relatively heavy contribution burden on the low-paid, because of low or zero thresholds, provides an inducement to them to work part-time or even full time in the underground economy.[79]

The increasing evasion of income and payroll taxation by the self-employed and those using foreign trusts has within it the seeds of grave difficulties. As Tocqueville observed:

Of all the methods of marking off men and distinguishing classes, inequality of taxation is the most deadly and the most certain to add isolation to inequality and in a sense to render both incurable.[80]

For centuries past no other inequalities of taxation have existed in England than those successively introduced in favor of the necessitous classes. . . . In the eighteenth century it was in England the poor man who enjoyed exemption from taxation; in France it was the rich man. In England the aristocracy took upon itself the heaviest public burdens that it might be allowed to govern; in France the nobles retained to the very end exemption from taxation to console them for having lost the right to govern. . . . From the moment that taxation had for its object not to reach those most capable of paying it but those least able of protecting themselves, there was bound to follow this monstrous consequence of sparing the rich and burdening the poor . . . peasants . . . had become to him not only strangers, but, so to speak, unknown.[81]

While sublocal entities lack the ability to impose tax thresholds, the redistributive effect of reliance on small entities has much to do with whether the tax proceeds made available to them by higher levels of government are raised by progressive taxes or taxes with high thresholds. Those concerned with distributional impacts of this or any other sort of public provision would do well to focus on the level at which income and payroll taxation begins.

Forced Redistribution

A Finance Equalization Plan by which communal powers of corporate taxation are assumed by the canton, the proceeds being redistributed to communes that have exhausted normal tax resources and require funds for physical improvements or basic services to the schools or for poor relief, has been adopted in several Swiss cantons.[82]

The most dramatic illustration of forced income redistribution among subdivisions is that carried out in a number of American states whose courts have invalidated their school-finance formulas, notably California. The California experience generally gives force to the cautionary words of Buchanan and Tullock:

Surely there must exist some explanation for the continued reluctance of societies in the Western world to throw open the redistributive potential of the fiscal system to the ordinary mechanism of collective choice-making. The most plausible explanation seems to be found in the very real fear of the external effects that such an unrestricted collectivization of redistribution might generate.[83]

Thus, as to school finance, "there are no states with district power-equalizing formulas that require recovery [of money by poor districts from rich districts] . . . negative aid has been declared unconstitutional by state courts in Wisconsin and Texas."[84]

To this Anthony Downs adds three other explanations, all based on uncertainty, for the fact that equality in votes does not translate itself to economic equality:

In the first place, the government cannot devise a system of taxes and benefits which redistributes income without causing any feedback or incentive effects. [Second], uncertainty allows low-income citizens to believe that someday they too may have high incomes; hence their desire to "soak the rich" is mitigated by the hope that they themselves will be rich. [Third], uncertainty creates more and less influential voters, i.e., it alters the distribution of voting power to one that is not equal. Usually voters with the highest incomes also have the most political power, since in an uncertain world they can use their financial resources to create influence for themselves.[85]

Richard and Peggy Musgrave have pointed out that such consolidation measures fail even a Rawlsian test-setting distribution policy such as to maximize income at the bottom of the scale: "Knowing that equalization will reduce the level of income available for distribution but not knowing what their own position on the income scale will be, they will stop short of demanding equalization."[86]

There is little reason to doubt the conclusion of Fischel and others that "such remedies reduce rather than increase public support for schools"[87]: "Per-pupil spending in California went from 13 percent above the national average in 1970 to about 10 percent below average in 1990."[88] Thomas Downes has observed that there are competing price and income effects when the "power-equalizing" scheme is adopted. On the one hand, "if local taxes are less progressive than federal taxes, revenue sharing may decrease the tax price of the median voter and thus increase government spending." On the other hand, there is a usually more significant countervailing income effect:

When families are sorted by income [in an "unreformed" system] and each receives the level it demands, the average level of spending per pupil is the average of these demands and is therefore determined by the average level of income. When families are not sorted by income, only the median-level family receives the amount it demands and thus the median income determines the level of spending per pupil.

Because median income is less than average income, the income effect decreases the level of spending per pupil. Downes ascribes a $1,431 fall in per–pupil spending in California to the "income effect," noting also that the difference between median and average family income was $10,639; this was partly offset by a "price effect" of $278 per pupil, leading to a net shortfall of $1,153. The actual decline in per-pupil spending below that otherwise projected was $1,741 per pupil; the balance of the decline Downes ascribes chiefly to increased enrollment. He also notes that "the absence of local fiscal choices or the constraints on local revenue options reduce the ability of local districts to meet demand, while state funds are subject to many competing demands."[89] Similar observations have been made about education in New Brunswick.

In addition, full equalization was not achieved due to use of user charges, voluntary contributions, and resort to supplemental private instruction: "Ultimately, it is impossible to cap education (as opposed to school) spending by higher-income families."[90] It has been said that "a large increase in private school enrollment in California is attributable to ... Serrano."[91] In addition, to the extent that the equalization is based on property rather than income, the effects of Serrano-type remedies are nullified by the capitalization of property-tax changes into real estate values: over time, housing costs apart from property tax increase as taxes are reduced, and vice-versa, leading to the conclusion that

> [i]f equalization or compensatory education is to be achieved, it must be related to the incomes of citizens, not the wealth of school districts, and taxes for redistribution will have to be raised from broad-based sources such as income or sales taxes rather than the property tax, which is so easily capitalized into property values.[92]

In California,

> Proposition 13 was a perfectly rational response by voters after the California Supreme Court had ruled that there could be no significant variations in local spending for schools due to differences in property-tax base. Without a connection between local property taxes and local school quality, voters have little reason to put up with property taxes.[93]

The cautionary words of Robert Dahl about restrictions on expenditures by individuals apply also to local governments:

> One significant area of personal decision is personal consumption. To decide by majority vote what each member of an association is allowed to consume might be possible in very small and highly consensual groups where there is very little to consume. In any other circumstances, the system would be either catastrophic or unenforceable: that is, it would produce either chaos or black markets.[94]

A similar phenomenon has been observed in Europe:

> Equalization is appraised as an expression of national solidarity. But examples, such as the reluctance of the richer communes in Ile de France to share,[95] or the fact that the Federation has taken over most of the financial burden of the reuni-

fication of Germany, show that automatic equalization mechanisms (*Finanzausgleich*) have been partly suspended, and that there are limits to horizontal solidarity. . . . As a result, equalization by transfers from central government seems to be better accepted than tax equalization.^{96}

In Germany, the unification treaty postponed until 1995 the application of the equalization provisions of Article 107(2) of the Basic Law providing for transfers from one land to another of up to one-fourth of the land share of the sales tax, which have also been construed as precluding "a leveling of state finances."^{97}

Milder forms of inter–local-government tax-sharing are possible, at least in polities with high social solidarity. In prewar Sweden, communes were permitted to impose a graduated income tax, 75 percent of the proceeds of which were retained by the commune and as much of the remainder as was necessary was used for relief to rural communes with high rates.^{98} However, this proceeded only 25 percent of the way toward the full unification of tax bases proposed by Serrano and like decisions. At the sublocal level, even such milder measures would seriously disrupt resident expectations and existing property values and would effectively rob prospective residents of the opportunity to improve their conditions of life by investment in housing.

NOTES

1. B. Barber, *The Death of Communal Liberty.* Princeton, NJ: Princeton University Press, 1974, 226.

2. G. Harris, *Local Government in Many Lands.* London: King, 1933, 15.

3. A. de Tocqueville, *Democracy in America*, vol. 1. London: Everyman, 1994, 202, 205.

4. D. Rowat, ed., *International Handbook on Local Government Reorganization.* Westport, CT: Greenwood, 1980, 271.

5. E. Hennock, *Fit and Proper Persons.* Montreal: McGill University Press, 1973, 13.

6. C. Arnold-Baker, *Law and Practice of Parish Administration* (London: Longcross Press, 1966), 43; Local Government Act (1933) sec. 49(1). On the change in 1972, see C. Arnold-Baker, *Powers and Constitution of Local Councils* (London: National Association of Local Councils, 1979), 9; Local Government Act (1972), secs. 15(1) and 34(1).

7. H. Clarke, *Parish, Town and Community Councils* (Croydon, UK: Charles Knight, 1991), 16; Local Government and Housing Act (1989), sec. 13.

8. *Report of the Committee of Inquiry into the Conduct of Local Authority Business* (1986), 91; see also J. Gyford, *Citizens, Consumers and Councils* (London: Macmillan, 1991), 55–59.

9. Arnold-Baker, *Law and Practice of Parish Administration*, 65–67.

10. Gyford, supra, 58.

11. E. Simon, *A City Council from Within* (1926), 86, quoted in Gyford, supra, 56.

12. E. Hasluck, *Local Government in England* (1936), 176, quoted in Gyford, supra, 55.

13. A. de Tocqueville, *L'Ancien Régime* (tr. M. Patterson). Oxford: Blackwell, 1947, 50 (hereafter *"Ancien Régime"*).

14. A. Leemans, *Changing Patterns of Local Government.* The Hague: IULA, 1970, 49.

15. See A. Shaw, *Municipal Government in Continental Europe*. New York: Century, 1895, 313.
16. Leemans, supra, 186.
17. Id., 187. On the benefits of co-option, see M. Saward, "Co-Option and Power: Who Gets What from Formal Incorporation," *Political Studies*, 38 (1990), 588–602.
18. W. Wickwar, *The Political Theory of Local Government* (Columbia: University of South Carolina Press, 1970), 35–36. See also Hennock, supra, 299–307; W. Dawson, *Municipal Life and Government in Germany* (London: Longmans, 1914).
19. F. Hirsch, *Social Limits to Growth*. Cambridge, MA: Harvard University Press, 1977, 5–6.
20. R. Bish and H. Nourse, *Urban Economics and Policy Analysis*. New York: McGraw-Hill, 1975, 312–13.
21. Rowat, supra, 45–59.
22. Examples in various European countries are given in Leemans, supra, 110.
23. O. Guichaud, *Vivre Ensemble*. Paris: Documentation Française, 1976.
24. Leemans, supra, 102.
25. D. Mueller, *Constitutional Democracy*. Oxford: Oxford University Press, 1996, 80.
26. D. Thompson, *The Democratic Citizen* (1970), cited in J. Mansbridge, *Beyond Adversary Democracy* (New York: Basic Books, 1980), 280.
27. B. Keith-Lucas and D. Richards, *A History of Local Government in the Twentieth Century* (London: Allen & Unwin, 1978); J. Collings, *Life of Jesse Collings* (London: Longmans, 1920), 192; A. Thorold, *Life of Henry Labouchere* (London: Constable, 1913), 433.
28. Allotments Acts, 1887, 1890, 1922, 1925; Smallholders and Allotments Acts, 1907, 1908, 1926; Smallholdings Act, 1892; Allotments Extension Act, 1882.
29. See the discussion in A. Offer, *Property and Politics, 1870–1914* (Cambridge: Cambridge University Press, 1981), 350–62.
30. Fabian Tract No. 137, *Parish Councils and Village Life* (1908). The unsigned pamphlet is attributed to the Webbs in the bibliography in Wickwar, supra.
31. G. Marcou, "New Tendencies of Local Government Development in Europe" in R. Bennett, *Local Government in the New Europe* (London: Belhaven, 1993), 63.
32. S. Webb, *Grants in Aid*. London: Fabian Society, 1911, 104.
33. The seminal description of these is G. Strayer and R. Haig, *Financing Education in the State of New York*. New York: Macmillan, 1923.
34. B. Hamilton, "The Tiebout Hypothesis and Residential Income Segregation," in ed. E. Mills, *Fiscal Zoning and Land-Use Controls* (1975), cited in W. Fischel, *Regulatory Takings* (Cambridge, MA: Harvard University Press, 1994), sec. 7.6.
35. P. Peterson, "Redistributive Policies and Patterns of Citizen Participation in Local Politics in the U.S.A.," in ed. L. Sharpe, *Decentralist Trends in Western Democracies* (London: Sage, 1979), 185.
36. W. Oates, *Fiscal Federalism*. New York: Harcourt Brace, 1972, 84.
37. J. Stiglitz, *Economics of the Public Sector*, 2d ed. (New York: Norton, 1988), 642; see also D. Mueller, *The Public Choice Approach to Politics* (Cheltenham, UK: Elgar, 1993), 82.
38. W. Oakland, "Fiscal Equalization: An Empty Box," *National Tax J.*, 47 (1994), 199.
39. H. Ladd and J. Yinger, "The Case for Equalizing Aid," *National Tax J.*, 47 (1994), 211.
40. Stiglitz, supra, 642.
41. N. Johnson, "Some Effects of Decentralization in the Federal Republic of Germany," in Sharpe, supra, 243.
42. D. Eastwood, *Governing Rural England, 1780–1840*. Oxford: Clarendon, 1994, 33.
43. P. Scraffa, ed., *Principles of Political Economy* (1951), 108.
44. Eastwood, supra, 121.
45. Id., 134–42. The economist Nassau Senior wrote to Lord Brougham on 14 September 1832: "The means of exerting influence which the present system gives to magistrates seems

to be, with most of them, superior to every other consideration. . . . I have no hope of real improvement while their power of interference remains undiminished."

46. R. Bird, "Threading the Fiscal Labyrinth," *National Tax J.*, 46 (1993), 207.

47. J. Buchanan and G. Tullock, *The Calculus of Consent.* Ann Arbor: University of Michigan Press, 1962, 197.

48. Hirsch, supra, 103n1.

49. R. Musgrave and P. Musgrave, *Public Finance in Theory and Practice*, 5th ed. (New York: McGraw-Hill, 1988), 244. On the erosion of tax thresholds in Britain, see J. Le Grand, *The Strategy of Equality* (London: Allen & Unwin, 1982). On the tendency of welfare-state benefits to be taken up by the middle class, see R. Titmuss, *Essays on the Welfare State* (London: Allen & Unwin, 1958).

50. Musgrave and Musgrave, supra, 279.

51. L. Mumford, *The Culture of Cities.* New York: Harcourt Brace, 1938, 459.

52. Oates, supra, 240.

53. W. Oates, "Decentralization of the Public Sector," in R. Bennett, *Decentralization, Local Governments and Markets* (Oxford: Clarendon, 1990).

54. P. Peterson, "A Unitary Model of Local Taxation and Expenditure Policy in the United States," *British J. Political Science*, 9 (1979), 281; see also Bish and Nourse, supra, 163–71.

55. A. Birch, *Federalism, Finance and Social Legislation in Canada, Australia, and the United States* (Oxford: Clarendon, 1955); K. Philip, *Intergovernmental Fiscal Relations* (1954), 56–58. Both are cited in Oates, *Fiscal Federalism*, 194 n26.

56. K. Kolan, "Neighborhood Councils in the Nordic Countries," *Local Government Studies*, 17, no. 3 (1991), 13.

57. V. Tanzi, Book Review of K. Messere's *Tax Policy in OECD Countries*, *National Tax J.*, 47 (1994), 447.

58. W. Oakland, "Income Redistribution in a Federal System," in G. Zodrow, *Local Provision of Public Services* (New York: Academic Press, 1983), 131, 138.

59. Stiglitz, supra, 427.

60. Musgrave and Musgrave, supra, 232.

61. K. Messere, *Tax Policy in OECD Countries.* Amsterdam: IBFD Publications, 1993, 53.

62. Advisory Commission on Intergovernmental Relations, *Residential Community Associations.* Washington, DC: ACIR, 1989, 14–15 (hereafter *ACIR-RCA*).

63. A. Tarlock, "Residential Community Associations and Land-Use Controls," in *ACIR-RCA*, 79.

64. E. McKenzie, *Privatopia.* New Haven, CT: Yale University Press, 1994, 141.

65. Stiglitz, supra, 156.

66. R. Nelson, "The Privatization of Local Government," in *ACIR-RCA*, 46.

67. Messere, supra, 178.

68. Musgrave and Musgrave, supra, 442.

69. S. Dickert et al., "Taxes and the Poor," *National Tax J.*, 47 (1994), 621; see also Stiglitz, supra, 354. It is said, though without explication, that a family on the poverty line paid 1.3 percent of its income in direct taxes in 1975, 5.5 percent in 1980, 10.4 percent in 1986, and only 2.2 percent in 1988 as a result of the Tax Reform Act of 1986. This claim does not address marginal rates. P. Self, *Government by the Market* (Boulder, CO: Westview, 1993), citing P. Gottschalk, "The Reagan Retrenchment in Historical Context," in M. Brown, *Remaking the Welfare State* (1988).

70. Musgrave and Musgrave, supra, 356.

71. H. Chemnick and A. Reschovsky, "Taxation of the Poor," *J. Human Resources*, 25 (1990), 512.

72. Messere, supra, 217.

73. Id., 221–22.

74. Id., 242–43, quoting J. K. Galbraith, *The Affluent Society* (1958).
75. See the tables in Messere, supra, 71–72, 247.
76. Id., 248.
77. Id., 33.
78. Id., 40.
79. Id., 176.
80. *Ancien Régime*, 94.
81. Id., 105, 107, 143.
82. Barber, supra, 232.
83. Buchanan and Tullock, supra, 197.
84. A. Reschovsky, "Fiscal Equalization and School Finance," *National Tax J.*, 47 (1994), 185.
85. A. Downs, *An Economic Theory of Democracy.* New York: Harper & Row, 1957, 200–201.
86. Musgrave and Musgrave, supra, 81.
87. Fischel, supra, sec. 3.11, citing P. Rothstein, "The Demand for Education with Power-Equalizing Aid," *J. Public Econ.*, 49 (1992), 135; N. Theobold, "Living with Equal Amounts of Less," *J. Educ. Finance*, 17 (1991), 1. See also Advisory Commission on Intergovernmental Relations, *Who Should Pay for Public Schools?* (1971), 12–13; W. Fischel and C. Campbell, "Preferences for School Finance Systems: Voters v. Judges," *National Tax J.*, 49 (1996), 1; L. Picus, "Cadillacs or Chevrolets?," *J. Educ. Finance*, 17 (1991), 35.
88. R. Fisher and R. Wassner, "Centralizing Educational Responsibility in Michigan and Other States," *National Tax J.*, 48 (1995), 417; see also F. Silva and J. Sonstelie, "Did Serrano Cause a Decline in School Spending?," *National Tax J.*, 48 (1995), 199.
89. Silva and Sonstelie, supra, 199.
90. Fisher and Wassner, supra, 424; Stiglitz, supra, 377–78.
91. T. Downes and D. Schoeman, "School Finance Reform and Private School Enrollment: Evidence from California," Working Paper 93-8, Center for Urban Affairs and Policy Research, Northwestern Univ. (1993), cited in A. Reschovsky, "Fiscal Equalization and School Finance," *National Tax J.*, 47 (1994), 185.
92. Bish and Nourse, supra, 319–20.
93. Fischel, supra, 284–85; W. Fischel, "Did Serrano Cause Proposition 13?," *National Tax J.*, 42 (1989), 465.
94. R. Dahl, *After the Revolution.* New Haven, CT: Yale University Press, 1970, 15.
95. The system of sharing was provided for in a system known as the "Dotations Sociales Urbaines" of May 1991.
96. G. Marcou, "New Tendencies of Local Government Development in Europe" in Bennett, *Local Government in the New Europe*, 52, 63.
97. D. Currie, *The Constitution of the Federal Republic of Germany.* Chicago: University of Chicago Press, 1994, 59–60.
98. Harris, supra, 95.

Chapter 6

Proliferating Initiative

CIRCULARS

In the unfashionable discussion of federalism in the last chapter of his *Essay on Liberty* and also in chapter 15 of *Representative Government*, Mill asserted the view that the appropriate role of the national government generally should involve education, not coercion:

The principal business of the central authority should be to give instruction, of the local authority to apply it. Power may be localized, but knowledge, to be most useful, should be centralized.

The mischief begins when, instead of calling forth the activities and powers of individuals and bodies, [a government] substitutes its own activities for theirs; when, instead of informing, advising, and upon occasion, denouncing, it makes them work in fetters.... A State that dwarfs its men ... will find that with small men no great thing can really be accomplished.[1]

The value of such publicity may be particularly great when directed at small-scale units of provision and their prospective members' as noted by Dennis Mueller:

Voluntary compliance with behavioral sanctions or provision of public goods is more likely in small communities than in large.... Small stable communities may elicit voluntary compliance and contributions for collective decisions by merely publicizing them.[2]

A not dissimilar view is expressed in the conclusion of John Gyford's *Citizens, Consumers and Councils* (1991) where, after describing programs for the orientation of British school governors and Scottish community councillors, he urges

> the need to facilitate public involvement with training and support rather than simply expect it to happen. . . . A . . . model . . . of a local authority with an enabling role as a support service, training agency and resource center for potentially active citizens could . . . complement the idea of groups of such people taking an increasing share of local service delivery [and] could also facilitate the identification and articulation of local "needs, opportunities and problems."[3]

The creation on a large scale of residential community associations in the United States came about as a result of this sort of activity:

> The publication of Planned Unit Development with a Homes Association was a watershed event in the history of CIDs. . . . Forty to fifty thousand copies of the publication were circulated, and it was a major factor in the PUD boom that followed . . . the document was distributed at the NAHB [National Association of Home Builders] meeting. Its impact was enormous. . . . "The industry grabbed the idea, and local government accepted it, and FHA insured it, and the concept took off like wildfire."[4]

Similarly, the Federal Housing Administration in 1961 distributed model condominium legislation, variants of which had been adopted in all 50 states by 1967, even though previously condominiums had been familiar only in Puerto Rico.[5] The Department of Commerce in the 1920s used a similar method to propagate zoning ordinances; its publication including model ordinances sold tens of thousands of copies.[6] The creation by state governments of thousands of soil-conservation districts with coercive powers in the 1930s was also ascribable to the distribution of model state legislation by the Roosevelt administration.[7]

The constitutional permissibility of this sort of government activity seems well established. As Laurence Tribe has written:

> If government expends public funds to subsidize flag production, the fact that some people object to this expenditure of their tax money to propagate the state's patriotic message is likely to be deemed irrelevant, either in a challenge to the expenditure itself or in a challenge to the payment of the full amount of the tax.[8]

The federal government has made extensive, though limited, use of "public service" broadcasting. Typically, broadcasters run government announcements "in blocks of time in low demand by advertisers who pay for the opportunity to reach mass audiences."[9] About ten advertising campaigns a year are run by government agencies in cooperation with the private Advertising Council. the campaigns are supported with both government funding and private contributions and "White House clearance is the sine qua non for a governmental agency hopeful of becoming one of the major campaigns of the Council."[10] Where publicity devices are used to stimulate sublocal activity, it becomes important to insure that the federal role does not become permanent: "A further risk is that reforms aimed at returning power to the people are likely to result in stronger bureaucratic institutions designed to support such endeavors. . . . The bureaucracies endure after the efforts at direct democracy have ended."[11]

Either the national government or associations of state governments or private law-reform organizations or foundations might widely distribute, to both community organizations and households, information, including suggested bylaws and lists of resource sources, to facilitate the organization of preschool playgroups and old-age clubs, adapting the available British and Japanese materials, respectively. Land readjustment and traffic-calming might be promoted in the same fashion.

TAX CREDITS

Dues of American residential community associations are not deductible for federal income-tax purposes. As the Advisory Commission on Intergovernmental Relations noted in 1989: "As the proportion of the nation's population living within RCAs increases, this lack of deductibility will affect more people. Any solution to this form of double taxation would have to be through federal legislation."[12] Opponents of deductibility urge that

> [t]hese private payments do not benefit the public in the same sense as property taxes. Property taxes represent an individual taxpayer's contribution toward supporting clean streets not only in his or her own neighborhood but throughout the city. CID assessments are targeted for small pieces of private property from which the public can be, and often is, excluded.[13]

Although some have predicted that this issue will in time constitute a major fault line in American politics, it is likely to be slowly mooted through use of the strategy, already authorized by state law in Maryland, of incorporating parallel taxing districts, coextensive with the territory of the RCA, for the rendition of municipal-type services, or by municipal grants to associations that replace local services, as authorized by statute in Maryland and New Jersey. In addition, it should be noted that RCA residents do not seek exemption from property taxes—merely the ability to federally deduct certain portions of their dues while continuing to pay local taxes where the dues relieve local government of expenditures it would otherwise have to make. Deductibility is already granted to certain types of private consumption that are deemed to be socially beneficial or to create equity claims: for example, personal medical and moving expenses. It also seems disingenuous to equate expenditures for characteristic public goods such as trash collection and roads with private luxury expenses.

Similarly, it may be in order to provide small federal tax credits to facilitate the organization of old age clubs. The provision of such incentives reinforces the benefit of membership and may alter the calculus identified by Robert Wade: "It is possible for an interest-group organization to emerge voluntarily and be sustained largely voluntarily—that is, without selective benefits or costs—if the net collective benefit is high enough."[14] It is important not to expect too much from small incentives until perceived social deficits, of which the loneliness of the elderly may be one, create a sense of need. Notwithstanding the extraordinary success of a small tax credit in Japan:

An active public domain concerned with accomplishing substantive tasks emerges only when it is critical to social integration that it occur. Those who suppose that beneficiary groups can be sprung into existence wherever the state wishes them to take over operational and maintenance responsibilities are ignoring this elementary point.[15]

To the extent that devolution of functions to RCAs and similar organizations constitutes a form of privatization because of their propensity to contract-out services to private entrepreneurs, the observations of Bruce Hamilton about schools become more generally pertinent:

What we have gotten out of our system of local government is a price system without efficiency.... The system does offer us some efficiency advantages as compared with central government provision through enhanced freedom of choice.... But arguably the system fails to capture very large efficiency gains which could be had if all the discipline of the market mechanism were brought to bear ... the true market system offers large benefits which our current system forgoes.[16]

Devolution to BIDs and RCAs has proven popular because it combines the benefits of political devolution (enhanced voice, local responsiveness) with the economies and personal independence resulting from reliance on competitive market providers, avoiding the condition described by Tocqueville: "To acquire a place a man no longer pays down his money, he goes one better, he sells himself."[17]

ENABLING LAWS AND MODEL LEGISLATION

Circulation, under either federal or private auspices, of legislation authorizing and regulating land-readjustment organizations and private-street associations[18] and its enactment in the states, or by cities with home-rule powers, would seem necessary if such organizations, with their reliance on public land assessment and mild coercion of dissenters, are to be organized. As Fred Foldvery has observed: "Contractual communities can provide [public] goods, although the provision in any specific time and place is not automatic but depends on institutional factors permitting such provision and entrepreneurial efforts to implement the provision."[19]

There is precedent for such legislation in laws providing for reconsolidation of recreational lots and for oil-field unitization.[20] What is frequently needed in organizing the governance of common property, according to a study of villages in South India, is

a legal framework, and perhaps technical assistance. The legal framework should make it possible for local collective action organizations to obtain legally enforceable recognition of their identity and rights within the society, and to call upon the state as an enforcer of last resort.[21]

Robert Ellickson, in his study of voluntary arrangements in the California lumber industry, has similarly observed:

To achieve order without law, people must have continuing relationships, reliable information about past behavior, and effective countervailing power . . . the improved circulation of accurate reputation information can deter fly-by-night opportunism . . . a small population in practice tends to increase quality of gossip, reciprocal power, and ease of enforcement.[22]

Aside from a legal framework, the conditions of success are said to depend on such factors as clear definition of the area concerned, close relationship to residences of users, extent of need for the collective resource, small size of the group, knowledge of group members, frequent communication within the group, concern about social reputation, existence of other areas of cooperation among group members, ease of detection of free riders, and absence of competing state institutions.[23]

Likewise, state or local legislation is desirable to define the rights of neighbors to request or require traffic calming, and to provide for the organization of and possible assistance to old age clubs (although this can be accomplished under existing nonprofit corporation laws). Amendments to the Uniform Probation Act to authorize participation of churches and community groups as probation officers might likewise be disseminated to both legislatures and appropriate voluntary associations. A similar course might be followed with respect to legislation converting all existing schools in a state to self-governing schools; here, models are available in the legislation of Great Britain, Australia, New Zealand, and Ireland.

If sublocal entities are to be enabled to remedy local-transportation deficits in metropolitan areas, amendment of state or local laws regulating and licensing bus and taxicab service should take place. This legislation may potentially affect franchise and medallion rights and accordingly might be narrowly drawn, at least at the outset, to exempt only transportation to or from designated enterprise zones in which high unemployment exists and which at present are not economically important to existing licensees.

Increasing the utility of RCAs and other sublocal general-purpose entities in the zoning process would seem to require the enactment of amendments to state zoning enabling laws allowing them to waive restrictions against accessory apartments, convenience stores, day-care centers,[24] demand–response transportation, and other like uses. The writer has elsewhere furnished draft legislation to this end;[25] circulation of some variant of this as model legislation by the National Conference of Commissioners on Uniform State Laws or the Department of Housing and Community Development or even a private organization like the National Association of Home Builders would be useful. Maryland legislation relating to day-care centers in residential areas furnishes another possible model.[26]

In order to avoid restrictions on possible governmental delegation of functions resulting from their property-owners' franchise and in order to obtain tax deductibility, residential community associations may have the option "to create a new local government with coterminous boundaries. . . . When this happens, the RCA continues to exist, but is supplemented by municipal organization."[27] Examples of this phenomenon are Oronoque Village, Connecticut and Pennsbury Village in Allegheny County, Pennsylvania. In time, this might provide the means for relating elementary school-district boundaries to those of residential community associations. An unusual piece of legislation relating to the police force of the private community of Crofton, Maryland, illustrates how private associations and traditionally public functions may be melded without transgressing the "one man one vote" rules relating to the latter.[28] An Anne Arundel County, Maryland, law allows residential community associations to organize parallel special-taxing districts,[29] and another Maryland statute allows municipalities to reimburse to privately owned residential communities the cost that would be incurred by the municipality to deliver road maintenance, street lighting, and snow and leaf-removal services.[30] These measures all effectively permit "tax substitution, a rebate or credit for civic goods that take the place of those provided by government."[31]

All these promotional measures, however, like those in prerevolutionary France described by Tocqueville, are useless if central government overly taxes and regulates the resultant institutions: "It would have been more to the point to have lightened the weight and to have lessened the inequality of the burdens."[32]

NOTES

1. J. S. Mill, *On Liberty*, quoted in B. Barber, *Strong Democracy* (Berkeley: University of California Press, 1974), 244n34.
2. D. Mueller, *The Public Choice Approach to Politics*. Cheltenham, UK: Elgar, 1993, 450–51.
3. J. Gyford, *Citizens, Consumers and Councils*. London: Macmillan, 1991, 186–87.
4. E. McKenzie, *Privatopia*. New Haven, CT: Yale University Press, 1994, 91, 93.
5. Id., 94–96.
6. American Law Institute, "Preface" to Model Land Development Act.
7. N. Burns, *The Formation of American Local Governments* (New York: Oxford University Press, 1994), 53; R. Morgan, *Governing Soil Conservation* (Baltimore: Johns Hopkins University Press, 1965); D. Blaisdell, *Government and Agriculture* (Reprint, New York: DaCapo Press, 1972).
8. L. Tribe, *American Constitutional Law*. Mineola, NY: Foundation Press, 1978, 589, 590.
9. M. Yudof, *When Government Speaks*. Berkeley: University of California Press, 1983, 59.
10. Id., 59.
11. J. Morone, *The Democratic Wish*. New Haven, CT: Yale University Press, 1998, 294n8.
12. Advisory Commission on Intergovernmental Relations, *Residential Community Associations*. Washington, DC: ACIR, 1989, 5 (hereafter *ACIR-RCA*).
13. McKenzie, supra.
14. R. Wade, *Village Republics*. Cambridge: Cambridge University Press, 1988, 207.
15. Id., 211–12.
16. B. Hamilton, "Is the Property Tax a Benefit Tax?," in G. Zodrow, *Local Provision of Public Services* (New York: Academic Press, 1983), 85, 104.
17. A. de Tocqueville, *L'Ancien Régime* (tr. M. Patterson). Oxford: Blackwell, 1947, 98 (hereafter *"Ancien Régime"*).
18. See City of St. Louis Charter, Art. I, sec. 14, and Art. XXI, sec. 14 (1978); "The Law and Private Streets," *St. Louis Law J.*, 5 (1954), 588.
19. F. Foldvery, *Public Goods and Private Communities*. Cheltenham, UK: Elgar, 1994, 211.
20. See G. Libecap, *Contracting for Property Rights* (Cambridge: Cambridge University Press, 1989), discussing the Oklahoma unitization legislation conferring powers on two-thirds of landowners.
21. Wade, supra, 217.
22. R. Ellickson, *Order Without Law* (1991), 182, 284.
23. Wade, supra, 215–16.
24. See, for example, Md. Ann. Code, Real Prop. Art., Sec. 11B-101, enacted by Ch. 321 of the Acts of 1987.
25. G. Liebmann, "A Proposed Revised State Zoning Enabling Act," in American Society of Civil Engineers, *Housing America in the Twenty-First Century, Conference Proceedings* (New York: ASCE Press, 1992), 91; G. Liebmann, "Suburban Zoning: Two Modest Proposals,"

Real Property Probate and Trust Journal, 25 (1990), 1; G. Liebmann, "The Modernization of Zoning: Enabling Act Revision as a Means to Reform," *Urban Lawyer*, 23 (1990), 1. See also Foldvery, supra, 209.

    26. Md. Ann. Code, Real Prop. Art., Sec. 11B-111.1 (1996).

    27. R. Oakerson, in *ACIR-RCA*, 109.

    28. Md. Code, Art. 26, sec. 5 (1996).

    29. Anne Arundel County Code, Art. 6, sec. 2-102 (1994); see *Williams v. Anne Arundel County*, 334 Md. 109, 638 A.2d 74 (1994).

    30. Md. Code, Art. 23A, secs. 49–51 (1996).

    31. Foldvery, supra, 208.

    32. *Ancien Régime*, 46.

Conclusion

Anyone suggesting enhanced use of very small governments as provision units, whether for the sake of efficiency or to promote civic participation, is immediately confronted by three concerns. The first, deriving from the perceived growth of large institutions, questions the efficacy of small units in a mobile and interdependent world. We have seen, however, that labor-intensive services such as day care, care of the elderly, primary education, street governance, and block redevelopment may be best accomplished by such units.

The second concern, deriving from James Madison, relates to the oppression of minorities said to be characteristic of small republics. We have explored various political devices, ranging from opt-out provisions and supermajority requirements to powers of supersession in higher governments, that have been successfully used to address this problem.

The third concern, deriving from varied traditions, relates to possible adverse effects on social or economic equality. We have explored both public finance and political devices, ranging from vouchers and equalizing grants to co-optation of council members, that have been used to at least partially level differences of capacity among small communities.

This book has attempted to demonstrate that, for some purposes at least, sublocal institutions are not only efficacious, but indispensable. The two decades of economic growth preceding both the French and Russian Revolutions indicate that prosperity in the short term can derive from the "two very simple and very powerful springs" identified by Tocqueville:

"A government which, though ceasing to be despotic, remained very powerful and maintained order everywhere [and] a nation in which every man could get rich in his own way, and keep his wealth when it was once acquired,"[1] but prosperity in itself is not enough for those who share his view that "[h]e who desires in liberty any thing other than itself is born to be a servant."[2]

This book also has tried to show that there are a variety of political devices that have been successfully used to guard against mistreatment of dissenters.

Finally, this book attempts to demonstrate that the proper use of small institutions can serve to foster greater equality in both economic and political power.

The success of this demonstration is for the reader to judge; at the least, it is hoped that some of the methods and devices discussed here will be found useful at some places or in some times. It is also hoped that, whatever its practical utility, this book may provide a useful review of some basic precepts of both economics and politics. If it belabors the obvious, it does so in the faith, shared with Justice Holmes, that at times "we need education in the obvious more than elucidation of the obscure."

NOTES

1. A. de Tocqueville, *L'Ancien Régime* (tr. M. Patterson). Oxford: Blackwell, 1947, 183–84.
2. Id., 178.

Selected Bibliography

Adams, H., *Norman Constables in America.* Baltimore: Johns Hopkins University Press, 1883.
Advisory Commission on Intergovernmental Relations, *Residential Community Associations.* Washington, DC: ACIR, 1989.
Ames, W., *Police and Community in Japan.* Berkeley: University of California Press, 1981.
Anderson, S., *On Streets.* Cambridge: MIT Press, 1978.
Appleyard, D., *Liveable Urban Streets.* Washington, DC: GPO, 1970.
Architects Club of Chicago, *Rehabilitating Blighted Areas.* Chicago: ACC, 1932.
Aristotle, *Politics* (Loeb ed.). Cambridge: Harvard University Press, 1932.
Arkes, H., *The Philosopher in the City.* Princeton, NJ: Princeton University Press, 1981.
Arnold-Baker, C., *Law and Practice of Parish Administration.* London: Longcross Press, 1966.
———. *Powers and Constitution of Local Councils.* London: National Association of Local Councils, 1979.
Ashford, D., *Financing Urban Government in the Welfare State.* New York: St. Martin's, 1980.
Axelrod, R., *The Evolution of Cooperation.* New York: Basic Books, 1984.
Bacon, W., *Public Accountability and the Schooling System.* New York: Harper & Row, 1978.
Badcock, B., *Unfairly Structured Cities.* Oxford: Blackwell, 1984.
Bakal, C., *No Right to Bear Arms.* New York: Paperback Library, 1968.
Banton, M., *Political Systems and the Distribution of Power.* London: Tavistock, 1965.

Barber, B., *The Death of Communal Liberty*. Princeton, NJ: Princeton University Press, 1974.
―――, *Strong Democracy*. Berkeley: University of California Press, 1974.
Baron, G., ed., *The Politics of School Government*. Oxford: Pergamon, 1981.
Beattie, N., *Professional Parents*. London: Falmer Press, 1985.
Ben Ari, E., *Changing Japanese Suburbia*. London: Kegan Paul, 1991.
Bennett, J., *Evaluating Neighborhood Watch*. Aldershot: Gower, 1990.
Bennett, R., *Decentralization, Local Governments and Markets*. Oxford: Clarendon, 1990.
―――, ed., *Local Government in the New Europe*. London: Belhaven, 1993.
Berger, P., *Facing Up to Modernity*. New York: Basic Books, 1977.
Berkley, G., *The Democratic Policeman*. Boston: Beacon Press, 1969.
Birch, A., *Federalism, Finance and Social Legislation in Canada, Australia, and the United States*. Oxford: Clarendon, 1955.
Bish, R., and H. Nourse, *Urban Economics and Policy Analysis*. New York: McGraw-Hill, 1975.
Blaisdell, D., *Government and Agriculture*. Reprint, New York: DaCapo Press, 1972.
Bosanquet, H., *Social Work in London*. Reprint, Brighton: Harvester Press, 1973.
Brasnett, M., *Voluntary Social Action*. London: National Council of Social Service, 1969.
Brooks, R., *Civic Training in Switzerland*. Chicago: University of Chicago Press, 1930.
―――, *New Towns and Communal Values*. New York: Praeger, 1974.
Brophy, J., *Playgroups in Practice: Self-Help and Public Policy*. London: HMSO, 1992.
Brown, D., *Decentralization and School-Based Management*. London: Falmer Press, 1990.
Bryce, J., *American Commonwealth*. New York: Macmillan, 1888.
―――, *Modern Democracies*. London: Macmillan, 1921.
Buchanan, A., *Secession*. Boulder, CO: Westview, 1991.
Buchanan, J., and G. Tullock, *The Calculus of Consent: Logical Foundations of Constitutional Democracy*. Ann Arbor: University of Michigan Press, 1962.
Burns, N., *The Formation of American Local Governments*. New York: Oxford University Press, 1994.
Campbell, J., *How Policies Change*. Princeton, NJ: Princeton University Press, 1992.
Carnegie Foundation for the Advancement of Teaching, *An Impeded Generation*. Menlo Park, CA: CFAT, 1988.
Carriere, K., and R. Erickson, *Crime Stoppers: A Study in the Organization of Community Policing*. Toronto: Centre of Criminology, University of Toronto, 1989.
Castells, M., ed., *The Shek Kip Mei Syndrome: Economic Development and Public Housing in Hong Kong and Singapore*. London: Pion, 1990.
Chen, P., *Singapore: Development Trends and Policies*. New York: Oxford University Press, 1986.

Cheng, J., *Hong Kong in Transition.* Oxford: Oxford University Press, 1986.
Chong-Yah, L., *Singapore: Resources and Growth.* New York: Oxford University Press, 1986.
Clark, T., *Comparative Community Politics.* Beverly Hills, CA: Sage, 1974.
Clarke, H., *Parish, Town and Community Councils.* Croydon: Charles Knight, 1991.
Clinard, M., *Cities with Little Crime: The Case of Switzerland.* Cambridge: Cambridge University Press, 1978.
Collings, J., *Life of Jesse Collings.* London: Longmans, 1920.
Community Associations Institute, *Community Associations Factbook.* Arlington, VA: CAI, 1988.
Coons, J., and S. Sugarman, *Education by Choice: The Case for Family Control.* Berkeley: University of California Press, 1978.
Corbett, A., and B. Moon, *Education in France: Continuity and Change During the Mitterand Years.* Routledge: London, 1995.
Craft, M., *Linking Home and School,* 2nd ed. London: Longmans, 1972.
Cubberley, E., *Public Education in the United States.* Boston: Houghton Mifflin, 1919.
Currie, D., *The Constitution of the Federal Republic of Germany.* Chicago: University of Chicago Press, 1994.
Dahl, R., *After the Revolution.* New Haven, CT: Yale University Press, 1970.
Dale, R., *The State and Educational Policy.* Milton Keynes, UK: Open University Press, 1989.
Dawson, W., *Municipal Life and Government in Germany.* London: Longmans, 1914.
Deem, R., *Active Citizenship and the Governance of Schools.* Buckingham, UK: Open University Press, 1995.
De Tocqueville, A., *Democracy in America* (tr. F. Bowen). Longmans: London, 1863.
———, *L'Ancien Régime* (tr. M. Patterson). Oxford: Blackwell, 1947.
Diefendorf, J., *In the Wake of War: The Reconstruction of German Cities After World War II.* New York: Oxford, 1993.
Dilger, R., *Neighborhood Politics.* New York: NYU Press, 1992.
Doebele, W., *Land Readjustment: A Different Approach to Financing Urbanization.* Lexington, MA: Lexington Books, 1982.
Downs, A., *An Economic Theory of Democracy.* New York: Harper & Row, 1957.
Eastwood, D., *Governing Rural England, 1780–1840.* Oxford: Clarendon, 1994.
Ehrenberg, V., *The Greek State.* Blackwell: Oxford, 1960.
Elliott, N., *Streets Ahead.* New York: Whitney Library of Design, 1989.
Elvin, L., ed., *The Educational Systems in the European Community: A Guide.* Windsor, UK: NFER-Nelson, 1981.
European Assembly for Probation and After-Care, *Probation in Europe.* Hertogenbosch, The Netherlands: EAPAC, 1981.
Fabian Society, *Parish Councils and Village Life.* London: Fabian Society, 1908.
Finlayson, G., *Citizen, State and Social Welfare in Britain.* Oxford: Oxford University Press, 1994.

Fischel, W., *Regulatory Takings*. Cambridge: Harvard University Press, 1994.

Fishman, S., and L. Martin, *Estranged Twins: Education and Society in the Two Germanies*. New York: Praeger, 1987.

Fitzgerald, R., *When Government Goes Private*. New York: Universe, 1988.

Fogelson, R., *Big City Police*. Cambridge: Harvard University Press, 1977.

Foldvery, F., *Public Goods and Private Communities: The Market Provision of Social Services*. Cheltenham, UK: Elgar, 1994.

Fraser, W., *Reforms and Restraints in Modern French Education*. London: Routledge, 1971.

Friedgut, T., *Political Participation in the USSR*. Princeton, NJ: Princeton University Press, 1979.

Friedman, M., *Capitalism and Freedom*. Chicago: University of Chicago Press, 1962.

Gelfand, M., *A Nation of Cities*. New York: Oxford, 1975.

Gill, M., and R. Mawby, *A Special Constable: A Study of the Police Reserve*. Aldershot, UK: Avebury, 1990.

———, *Volunteers in the Criminal Justice System*. Washington, DC: U.S. Dept. of Justice, 1990.

Glueck, E., *Community Use of Schools*. Baltimore: Williams & Wilkins, 1927.

Gomme, G., *Lectures on the Principles of Local Government*. Westminster, UK: Constable, 1897.

Greenberg, M., *Auxiliary Police: The Citizen's Approach to Public Safety*. Westport, CT: Greenwood, 1984.

Greer, W., *America the Bountiful*. Washington, DC: Food Marketing Inst., 1986.

Gregson, N., *Servicing the Middle Classes*. New York: Routledge, 1994.

Groves, C., *Marketing of Milk Products in the U.K.* Ayr: West of Scotland Agricultural College, 1981.

Guichaud, O., *Vivre Ensemble*. Paris: Documentation Française, 1976.

Gyford, J., *Citizens, Consumers and Councils*. London: Macmillan Education, 1991.

Hagman, D., and Miscynski, J., *Windfalls for Wipeouts*. Chicago: American Planning Assn., 1978.

Harris, G., *Local Government in Many Lands*. London: King, 1933.

Hay, D., and F. Snyder, eds., *Policing and Prosecution in England, 1750–1850*. Oxford: Clarendon, 1989.

Hechter, M., *Principles of Group Solidarity*. Berkeley: University of California Press, 1987.

Hennock, E., *Fit and Proper Persons*. Montreal: McGill University Press, 1973.

Hesse, J., *Local Government and Urban Affairs in International Perspective*. Baden-Baden: Nomus, 1991.

Hill, O., *House Property and Its Management*. London: Allen & Unwin, 1921.

Hirsch, F., *Social Limits to Growth*. Cambridge: Harvard University Press, 1977.

Holme, A., and J. Maizels, *Social Workers and Volunteers*. London: Allen & Unwin, 1978.

Holmes, B., ed., *International Handbook of Educational Systems: Europe and Canada*. Chichester, UK: Wiley, 1983.

Honeywell, R., *The Educational Work of Thomas Jefferson.* Cambridge: Harvard University Press, 1937.
Hope, T., and M. Shaw, *Communities and Crime Reduction.* London: HMSO, 1988.
Humes, S., and E. Martin, *The Structure of Local Governments Throughout the World.* The Hague: M. Nijhoff, 1961.
Hurst, J., *Law and the Conditions of Freedom in Nineteenth-Century United States.* Madison: University of Wisconsin Press, 1956.
Hyatt, W., *Condominium and Homeowner Association Litigation.* New York: Wiley Law Publications, 1987.
Ingman, S., *Eldercare.* Albany: SUNY Press, 1995.
Institute of Local Self-Government, *Civilians in Public Safety Services.* Berkeley, CA: ILSG, 1977.
Jarecki, H., *Playgroups.* London: Faber, 1990.
Jefferson, T., *Autobiographical Writings.* New York: Putnam, 1904.
Jencks, C., and J. Areen, *Vouchers: A Report on Financing Education by Payments to Parents.* 1970.
Johnston, L., *The Rebirth of Private Policing.* London: Routledge, 1992.
Keating, M., and P. Hainsworth, *Decentralization and Change in Contemporary France.* Aldershot, UK: Gower, 1986.
Keith-Lucas, B., *The Unreformed Local Government System.* London: Croon Helm, 1980.
Keith-Lucas, B., and D. Richards, *A History of Local Government in the Twentieth Century.* London: Allen & Unwin, 1978.
King, A., *Social Life and Development in Hong Kong.* Hong Kong: Chinese University Press, 1981.
Kropotkin, P. *Mutual Aid.* Harmondsworth, UK: Penguin, 1939.
Kwan, A., *Hong Kong Society: A Reader.* Hong Kong: Writers and Publishers Cooperative, 1986.
Lane, R., *Policing the City.* Cambridge: Harvard University Press, 1967.
Larsson, G., *Land Readjustment: A Modern Approach to Urbanization.* Aldershot, UK: Avebury, 1993.
Leemans, A., *Changing Patterns of Local Government.* The Hague: IULA, 1970.
Lefcoe, G., *Land Development in Crowded Places: Lessons from Abroad.* Washington, DC: Conservation Foundation, 1979.
Le Grand, J., *The Strategy of Equality.* London: Allen & Unwin, 1982.
Lewis, D., *The French Education System.* New York: St. Martin's, 1985.
———, *Social Construction and Reform: Crime Prevention and Community Associations.* New Brunswick, NJ: Transaction Books, 1988.
Logan, J., and H. Molotch, *Urban Fortunes.* Berkeley: University of California Press, 1987.
Loughlin, M., *Half a Century of Municipal Decline.* London: Allen & Unwin, 1985.
———, *Local Government in the Modern State.* London: Sweet & Maxwell, 1986.
Macbeth, A., ed., *Collaborate or Compete.* London: Falmer Press, 1995.

Macbeth, A., and B. Ravn, *Expectations About Parents in Education: European Perspectives.* Glasgow, UK: University of Glasgow Computing Services, 1994.
MacCallum, S., *The Art of Community.* Arlington, VA: Institute for Humane Studies, 1970.
Maine, H., *Village Communities in the East and West.* London: John Murray, 1871.
Mansbridge, J., *Beyond Adversary Democracy.* New York: Basic Books, 1980.
———, *Beyond Self-Interest.* Chicago: University of Chicago Press, 1990.
Mayo, J., *The American Grocery Store.* Westport, CT: Greenwood, 1993.
McKenzie, E., *Privatopia.* New Haven, CT: Yale University Press, 1994.
Mendras, H., and A. Cole, *Social Change in Modern France.* Cambridge:: Cambridge University Press, 1991.
Messere, K., *Tax Policy in OECD Countries.* Amsterdam: IBFD Publications, 1993.
Midgely, J., *Community Participation, Social Development and the State.* London: Methuen, 1986.
Minerbi, L., *Land Readjustment: The Japanese System.* Cambridge, MA: Lincoln Institute for Land Policy, 1986.
Monkkonen, E., *Police in Urban America, 1860–1920.* Cambridge: Cambridge University Press, 1981.
Montesquieu, *Spirit of the Laws* (tr. T. Nugent). Chicago: Encylopedia Brittanica, 1966.
Morgan, R., *Governing Soil Conservation.* Baltimore: Johns Hopkins University Press, 1965.
Morris, M., *Voluntary Work in the Welfare State.* London: Routledge, 1969.
Morris, N., and G. Hawkins, *Letter to the President on Crime Control.* Chicago: University of Chicago, 1971.
Moudon, A., *Public Streets for Private Use.* New York: Van Nostrand Reinhold, 1987.
Mowat, C., *Charity Organization Society.* London: Methuen, 1977.
Mueller, D. C., *The Public Choice Approach to Politics.* Cheltenham, UK: Edward Elgar, 1993.
———, *Constitutional Democracy.* Oxford: Oxford University Press, 1996.
Mueller, R., *A & P.* New York: Progressive Grocer Magazine, 1971.
Mumford, L., *The Culture of Cities.* New York: Harcourt Brace, 1938.
Murnell, W., *Once Upon a Store.* New York: Herder & Herder, 1971.
Musgrave, R., and P. Musgrave, *Public Finance in Theory and Practice*, 5th ed. New York: McGraw-Hill, 1988.
National Association of Real Estate Boards, *Act for Neighborhood Protective and Improvement Districts.* Washington, DC: NARB, 1935.
Neely, R., *Take Back Your Neighborhood.* New York: D.I. Fine, 1990.
Nelson, R., *Zoning and Property Rights.* Cambridge: MIT Press, 1977.
Newman, O., *Community of Interest.* Garden City, NY: Doubleday, 1972.
New Zealand Department of Education, *Tomorrow's Schools.* Wellington, NZ: Government Printer, 1988.

Nisbet, R., *The Making of Modern Society.* Brighton, UK: Wheatsheaf, 1986.
Norton, A., *International Handbook of Local and Regional Government.* Aldershot, UK: Elgar, 1994.
Nozick, R., *Anarchy, State and Utopia.* New York: Basic Books, 1974.
Oates, W., *Fiscal Federalism.* New York: Harcourt Brace, 1972.
———, *The Political Economy of Fiscal Federalism.* Lexington, MA: Lexington Books, 1977.
Offer, A. *Property and Politics, 1870–1914.* Cambridge: Cambridge University Press, 1981.
Olson, M., *The Logic of Collective Action.* Cambridge: Harvard University Press, 1965.
O'Sullivan, A., *Property Taxes and Tax Revolts: The Legacy of Proposition.* Cambridge: Cambridge University Press, 1995.
Page, E., *Localism and Centralism in Europe.* Oxford: Oxford University Press, 1991.
Parry, G., ed., *Participation in Politics.* Manchester, UK: Manchester University Press, 1972.
Perry, C., *The Rebuilding of Blighted Areas.* New York: Regional Plan Assn., 1934.
Preschool Playgroups Association, *Playgroups Go Forward.* London: PPA, 1995.
Pringle, P., *Hue and Cry: Henry and John Fielding.* London: Dobson, 1968.
Quah, J., *Government and Politics of Singapore.* Oxford: Oxford University Press, 1983.
Raitcliff, Z., ed., *Fast Food and Home-Delivery Outlets.* London: Market Assessment Publications, 1995.
Ranney, A., ed., *The Referendum Device.* Washington, DC: AEI, 1981.
Redlich, J., and F. Hirst, *History of Local Government in England.* New York: Macmillan, 1958.
Reed-Danahay, D., *Education and Identity in Rural France.* Cambridge: Cambridge University Press, 1996.
Reiss, A., and M. Tonry, *Communities and Crime.* Chicago: University of Chicago Press, 1986.
Richards, J., *Inform, Advise, and Support.* London: Lutterworth Press, 1989.
Rivlin, A., *Reviving the American Dream.* Washington, DC: Brookings, 1992.
Rogers, R., *Crowther to Warnock: How Fourteen Reports Tried to Change Children's Lives.* London: Heinemann Educational Books, 1980.
Romero, M., *Maid in the U.S.A.* New York: Routledge, 1992.
Rose, B., *England Looks at Maud.* Chichester, UK: Justice of the Peace, 1970.
Rosenbaum, D., *Crime Stoppers: A National Evaluation of Program Operations and Effects.* Washington, DC: U.S. Dept. of Justice, 1985.
———, *Evaluating Community Crime Prevention.* Beverly Hills, CA: Sage, 1986.
Rowat, D., ed., *International Handbook on Local Government Reorganization.* Westport, CT: Greenwood, 1980.

Rowe, A., *Democracy Renewed: The Community Council in Practice.* London: Sheldon Press, 1975.
Savas, E., *The Organization and Efficiency of Solid Waste Collection.* Lexington, MA: Lexington Books, 1977.
Sayres, P., ed., *Foodmarketing.* New York: McGraw-Hill, 1950.
Self, P., *Government by the Market.* Boulder, CO: Westview, 1993.
Shapland, J., and J. Vagg, *Policing by the Public.* London: Routledge, 1988.
Sharpe, L., ed., *Decentralist Trends in Western Democracies.* London: Sage, 1979.
Shaw, A., *Municipal Government in Continental Europe.* New York: Century, 1895.
Skogan, W., *Disorder and Decline.* New York: Free Press, 1991.
Smith, A., *Wealth of Nations.* London: Everyman, 1910.
Smith, J. Toulmin, *Local Self-Government and Centralization.* London: Chapman, 1851.
Smith, S., *Crime, Space and Society.* Cambridge: Cambridge University Press, 1986.
Statham, J., *Playgroups in a Changing World.* London: HMSO, 1989.
———, *Playgroups in Three Countries.* London: Coram Research Unit, University of London, 1989.
Stavely, E., *Greek and Roman Voting and Elections.* Ithaca, NY: Cornell University Press, 1972.
Steedman, C., *Policing the Victorian Community.* London: Routledge, 1984.
Steinberg, J., *Why Switzerland?* Cambridge: Cambridge University Press, 1996.
Stiglitz, J., *Economics of the Public Sector*, 2nd ed. New York: Norton, 1988.
Story, J., *Commentaries on the Constitution.* Boston: Hilliard, Gray, 1833.
Strayer, G., and R. Haig, *Financing Education in the State of New York.* New York: Macmillan, 1923.
Struwe, K., *Schools and Education in Denmark.* Copenhagen: Det Danske Selskab, 1981.
Sutcliffe, A., *Towards the Planned City.* New York: St. Martin's, 1981.
Taylor, M., *The Possibility of Cooperation.* Cambridge: Cambridge University Press, 1987.
Thornton, R., *Preventing Crime in America and Japan.* Armonk, NY: M.E. Sharpe, 1992.
Thorold, A., *Life of Henry Labouchere.* London: Constable, 1913.
Titmuss, R., *Essays on the Welfare State.* London: Allen & Unwin, 1958.
Tolley, R., *Traffic Calming in Residential Areas.* London: Beffi Press, 1995.
Tonry, M., and N. Morris, *Crime and Justice.* Chicago: University of Chicago Press, 1988.
Treadgold, D., *Soviet and Chinese Communism.* Seattle: University of Washington Press, 1967.
Tribe, L., *American Constitutional Law.* Mineola, NY: Foundation Press, 1978.
Tryneski, J., *Requirements for Certification of Teachers, Counselors, Librarians, Administrators for Elementary and Secondary Schools*, 61st ed. Chicago: University of Chicago Press, 1996.

Wagner, R., *Charging for Government*. London: Routledge, 1991.
Walker, M., *Urban Blight and Slums*. Cambridge: Harvard University Press, 1938.
Walker, S., *Popular Justice: A History of American Criminal Justice*. New York: Oxford University Press, 1980.
Walsh, W., *The Rise and Decline of the Great Atlantic and Pacific Tea Co.* Secaucus, NJ: Lyle Stuart, 1986.
Walzer, M., *Radical Principles*. New York: Basic Books, 1979.
Ward, P., ed., *Conservation and Development in Historic Towns and Cities*. Newcastle-on-Tyne, UK: Oriel Press, 1968.
Webb, S., *Grants in Aid*. London: Fabian Society, 1911.
Wickwar, W., *The Political Theory of Local Government*. Columbia: University of South Carolina Press, 1970.
Willbern, Y., *The Withering Away of the City*. Tuscaloosa: University of Alabama Press, 1964.
Williamson, C., *American Suffrage from Property to Democracy*. Princeton, NJ: Princeton University Press, 1960.
Wilson, J., *Thinking About Crime*. New York: Vintage, 1985.
Wilson, P., *Issues in Crime, Morality and Justice*. Canberra: Australian Institute of Criminology, 1992.
Wong, A., and S. Yeh, *Housing a Nation: Twenty-Five Years of Public Housing in Singapore*. Singapore: Maruzen Asia, 1985.
Woodson, R., *A Summons to Life*. Cambridge, UK: Ballinger, 1987.
Working Party on the Place of Voluntary Service in After Care, *The Place of Voluntary Service in After Care*. London: HMSO, 1967.
Wright, A., *Citizens and Subjects: An Essay on British Politics*. London: Routledge, 1994.
Wright, J., *Under the Gun*. New York: Aldine, 1990.
Yudof, M., *When Government Speaks*. Berkeley: University of California Press, 1983.
Zodrow, G., *Local Provision of Public Services*. New York: Academic Press, 1983.
Zuckerman, M., *Peaceable Kingdoms*. New York: Knopf, 1970.

Name Index

Abercrombie, P., 26
Adams, H., 74
Adams, J., 82
Adickes, F., 7, 8, 68, 125
Ames, W., 75, 77
Applegard, D., 4, 67
Arkes, H., 108
Arnold-Baker, C., 78, 104, 106, 107, 108, 116, 137, 138, 156
Attlee, C., 31
Austen, J., 42, 76
Axelrod, R., 52, 78

Badcock, B., 138
Bacon, W., 71
Bailey, J., 105
Bakal, C., 76
Ballion, R., 70
Bannister, M., 61
Barber, B., xiii, xvi, 84, 87, 105, 106, 137, 140, 156, 159
Barton, S., 69, 105, 107, 109
Baxter, T., 70
Bayley, D., 75
Beattie, N., 70
Becker, H., 48, 77
Beer, S., 27, 73, 104, 109, 140, 156

Bell, D., 108
Ben-Ari, E., 79
Bendick, M., 136
Ben-Joseph, E., 67
Bennett, J., 75, 139
Benstead, S., 79
Berger, P., 72
Berkley, G., 77
Birch, A., 158
Bird, R., 137, 138, 158
Bish, R., xvi, 70, 72, 76, 80, 137, 138, 140, 157, 158
Blaisdell, D., 167
Bogason, P., 71
Bosanquet, H., 73
Bottomley, P., 35
Brandeis, L., 98, 134
Brasnett, M., 36, 74
Brenton, M., 30
Briffanlt, R., 73
Brooks, R., 80
Brophy, J., 79
Bryce, J., 39, 72, 74, 92, 107
Buchanan, A., 108
Buchanan, J., 69, 82, 101, 105, 106, 107, 108, 109, 136, 147, 153, 158, 159
Burns, N., 167

NAME INDEX

Callaghan, J., 21
Campbell, J., 79
Campbell, T., 79, 310
Caplan, A., 106
Carlisle, M., 35
Carriere, K., 76
Castells, M., 70, 71, 138
Chadwick, E., 38, 76
Chemnick, H., 158
Chen, P., 138
Cheng, J., 138
Chong-yah, L., 138
Church, A., 137
Cisneros, H., 3
Clark, T., 27, 73
Clarke, H., 106, 156
Clifford, W., 77
Clinard, M., 76
Coaldrake, W., 78
Collings, J., 157
Coons, J., 139
Cubberley, E., 70
Currie, P., 138, 139, 159
Cusack, B., 76

Dahl, R., 25, 41, 51, 73, 78, 78, 86, 106, 132, 139, 155, 159
Dale, R., 7
Dalley, G., 79
Davies, H., 107, 138
Davis, O., 70
Dawes, R., xii, xvi
Dawson, W., 68, 156, 157
DeGaulle, C., 24
Deedes, W., 34
Deem, R., 71, 73
Demsetz, H., xvi, 69
Derouet, J., 70
Diamond, S., 68, 137
Dickert, S., 158
Diefendorf, J., 69
Dilger, R., 68
Disraeli, B., 38, 74
Doebele, W., 68, 69
Downes, T., 151, 159
Downs, A., 52, 78, 151, 159
Duncan, J., 72, 77

Eastwood, D., 67, 74, 157

Eckert, R., 80
Ehrenberg, V., 106, 108, 115
Ellickson, R., 165, 168
Elliott, N., 68
Elvis, L., 70
Ernst, A., 78
Evans, J., 73

Faher, C., 72
Farmer, R., 80
Fenwick, C., 75
Fielding, H., 43, 71
Fielding, J., 43, 44, 76
Finch, J., 79
Finlayson, G., 34, 73
Fischel, W., xvi, 68, 70, 73, 112, 115, 137, 138, 154, 157, 159
Fisher, R., 159
Fishman, S., 71
Fitzgerald, R., 68
Fogelson, R., 75
Foldvery, F., xvi, 12, 69, 105, 165, 167, 168
Fraser, W., 70
Frazier, M., 68
Friedgut, T., 77
Friedman, D., 70
Friedman, M., 133, 140
Frug, G., 134, 140

Galbraith, J.K., 151–52, 159
Gamage, D., 71
Geddes, P., 26
Gelfand, M., 138
Gerbosi, W., 80
Gill, M., 76, 77
Gillette, C., 108
Giscard, V., 18
Gladstone, W., 130
Glennerster, H., 69
Glueck, E., 72
Gold, A., 139
Golembiewski, R., 139
Gomme, G., 78, 136
Goodnow, F., 92
Gordon, L., 71
Gottfredson, S., 68, 76
Gramlich, E., 138
Greenberg, M., 74, 76

Greer, W., 80
Gregson, N., 80
Groenewegen, P., 139
Groves, C., 80
Grundtvig, N., 22
Guichard, O., 157
Gunlicks, A., 139
Gyford, J., 69, 70, 137, 156, 162, 167

Haby, R., 18
Hagman, D., 68
Hall, J., 76
Hall, P., 8
Hallam, H., 106
Hamilton, A., 45, 75
Hamilton, B., 73, 157, 167
Handlin, O., 105
Hannaway, J., 73
Hare, P., 65, 80
Harris, G., 67, 104, 116, 138, 139, 156, 159
Hass-Klau, C., 4
Hawkins, G., 75
Hay, D., 74
Hechter, M., 51, 78
Hess, A., 48, 77
Hill, O., 13
Hirsch, F., 143, 156, 158
Hjellemo, D., 48, 76
Holden, A., 68
Holme, A., 77
Holmes, B., 70
Holmes, O.W., xi
Hoover, L., 31
Hope, R., 75
Hughes, P., 71
Humes, S., 69, 107, 115
Hurst, J., xvi
Hyatt, W., 115
Hyman, D., 137

Jackman, L., 73, 74
Jacobs, J., 70
Jarecki, H., 79
Jefferson, T., 25, 44, 45, 72, 75
Jencks, C., 139
Johnson, N., 157
Johnston, L., 75

Kahn, A., 36

Kain, R., 69
Kania, R., 77
Kates, D., 76
Keating, M., 72
Keith-Lucas, B., 107, 108, 157
Kennan, G., 24, 36
Kennedy, D., xvi
King, A., 138
King, D., 137
Kinoshita, Y., 78
Kitch, E., 80
Kjellberg, F., 78, 79
Kleck, G., 76
Knott, J., 138
Kolan, K., 68, 73, 79, 158
Kropotkin, P., x, xvi
Krumm, V., 72, 74
Kwan, A., 138

Ladd, H., 157
Lambert, L., 75
Larsson, G., 68, 69
Laughlin, R., 71
Lauglo, J., 72
Lee, R., 69
Leemans, A., 107, 156
Lefcoe, G., 115
Leon, C., 76
Lewis, D., 75
Lewis, H., 70
Libecap, G., 167
Liebmann, G., 70, 75, 167
Linhart, S., 79
Lipson, L., 77
Logan, J., 140
Loughlin, M., 71, 106
Lucas, B., 72

Macbeth, A., 71
MacCallum, S., xvi
McKenzie, E., 70, 88, 106, 107, 134, 140, 167
McManus, S., 69
MacPherson, R., 71
McQuire, R., 80
Madison, J., xvi, 44, 91, 129, 142, 169
Maeda, D., 79
Magnusson, W., xi, xvi, 70, 78, 139
Maine, H., 100, 108

NAME INDEX

Malloy, R., 138
Mansbridge, J., xii, xvi, 82, 83, 96, 99, 101–2, 105, 107, 108, 157
Marcou, G., 107, 139, 157, 159
Marlock, E., 80
Marnell, W., 80
Martin, E., 69
Martin, L., 71
Martinez, R., 72
Maurel, M., 70
Mayo, J., 80
Mendras, H., 78
Messere, K., 78, 107, 137, 138, 158
Mill, J.S., xii, xvi, 89, 111, 157, 161, 167
Minford, P., 137
Miscynski, J., 68
Miyazawa, M., 68
Monkkonen, E., 75
Morgan, R., 167
Morris, M., 29, 33, 73
Morris, N., 75
Mosse, A., 57
Moudon, A., 4, 68
Mowat, C., 36, 74
Mueller, D., xii, xiii, xiv, 50, 52, 69, 75, 78, 82, 90, 102, 104, 105, 106, 107, 115, 138, 140, 143, 157, 161, 167
Mueller, R., 80
Mukherjee, S., 75
Mumford, L., 5, 68, 77, 148, 158
Musgrave, R., 27, 73, 108, 119, 130, 138, 139, 140, 154, 158

Neely, R., 75
Nelson, R., xv, xvi, 10, 14, 15, 19, 70, 150, 158
Newman, O., 3, 76
Nisbet, R., xiv, xvi
Norton, A., 71, 73, 106, 107
Nourse, H., xvi, 70, 80, 137, 138, 139, 140, 157, 159
Nozick, R., 100, 108

Oakerson, R., 68, 69, 105, 168
Oakland, W., 157, 158
Oates, W., 104, 109, 120, 135, 136, 137, 138, 139, 157, 158
Offer, A., 107, 157
Ogawa, J., 78

Olson, M., 83, 90, 101, 102, 105, 106
Ostrom, E., xiv, xvi
O'Sullivan, A., 137

Page, E., 105, 139
Paine, T., 133
Peel, R., 39, 43
Perry, C., 68
Perry, J., 80
Pesteau, P., 109
Peterson, P., 157, 158
Philip, K., 158
Picus, L., 159
Pitt, W., 147
Plowden, P., 29, 61
Pommerehne, W., 78
Pridham, P., 72

Quah, J., 138

Rae, D., 105
Raitcliff, Z., 2, 80
Ravin, B., 72
Raywid, M., 73
Redlich, J., 107
Reed-Danahay, D., 70
Reischauer, R., 135
Reissert, B., 139
Reschovsky, A., 159
Ricardo, D., 147
Richards, J., 74
Richmond, M., 31, 150
Rivlin, A., 132, 139
Rogers, R., 71
Romero, M., 80
Rose, C., 4
Rosenbaum, D., 76
Rosenberry, K., 115
Rossi, P., 73
Rothstein, P., 159
Rowat, D., 69, 70, 78, 156, 157
Rowe, A., 70
Rumbold, A., 62, 79
Ryan, B., 68

Salisbury, R., 91
Savas, E., 69
Saward, M., 157
Schmidman, F., 68, 69

Name Index

Schwartz, G., 69
Self, P., 55, 78, 158
Senior, N., 157
Shakespeare, W., 40
Sharpland, J., 75
Shaw, A., 73, 77, 79, 106, 107, 108, 115, 156
Sheehan, J., 68
Sherman, L., 75, 76
Shultz, M., 68, 69
Silva, F., 159
Silverman, C., 69, 105, 115
Simon, E., 142, 156
Simon, W., 36
Skogan, W., 75, 76
Skolnick, J., 75
Smit, F., 78
Smith, A., 119, 122, 133, 137, 138
Smith, J., 47, 74, 76
Smith, P., 137
Smith, S., 75
Snyder, F., 74
Sorlin, F., 69
Statham, J., 79
Stavely, E., 106
Steed, M., 107
Steedman, C., 74
Steinberg, J., 78
Stewart, J., 78
Stiglitz, J., xiv, xvi, 69, 73, 78, 93, 136, 137, 157, 158, 159
Storch, R., 75
Story, J., 45, 76
Strauss, R., 132, 139
Strayer, G., 157
Struwe, K., 71
Styles, J., 76
Sundeen, R., 76
Sutcliffe, A., 69

Taft, R., 97
Tarlock, A., 115, 147, 158
Taylor, N., xiv, xvi
Taylor, R., 68, 76
Thatcher, M., 24, 35, 93, 121, 122
Theobold, N., 159
Thompson, D., 157
Thornton, R., 75
Tocqueville, A. de, ix, xv, 32, 43, 44, 50, 70, 73, 76, 78, 89, 94, 106, 111, 114, 115, 116, 119, 129, 137, 139, 142, 152, 156, 159, 167, 168, 169, 170
Tolley, R., 2, 3, 4, 67
Tribe, L., 162, 167
Trillin, C., 68
Tryneski, J., 70
Tullock, 69, 82, 101, 105, 106, 107, 136, 153

Vaughans, G., 35

Wade, R., 164, 167
Wagner, R., 137
Walker, M., 68
Walker, S., 75
Walsh, W., 80
Walzer, M., 24, 72, 107, 133, 140
Washington, G., 45
Watts, J., 105
Webb, S., 114, 116, 129, 130, 132, 139, 145, 157
Weber, J., 77
Weiss, M., 105
Whidbourne, J., 73
Whitehead, K., 75
Wickwar, W., xvi, 73, 79, 106, 136, 139, 156
Widdecombe, A., 142
Willbern, Y., 70
Williamson, C., 106
Wilson, J., 75
Wilson, P., 75
Wimble, A., 73
Winokur, J., 69
Wolf, P., 68
Wolnan, H., 138
Wong, A., 79
Wood, R., 73
Woodson, R., 77
Wright, A., 71
Wright, J., 76
Wynn, M., 36

Yin, R., 75
Yudof, M., 167

Zuckerman, M., 74, 78, 104, 106, 115

Subject Index

Advice Bureaux, 32
Anne Arundel Co., MD, 166
annexation, 144
appointment by higher governments, 141
Aragon (Aragonese Cortes), 82
arbitration, 112
assessments, 123
Athens, 87, 88, 89, 98, 99, 114
Atlantic City, NJ, 6
audits, 114
Australia, xii, i, 10, 21, 50, 128, 166
Australian Capital Territory, 21
Austria, 22, 48, 50, 90, 97, 131

Baden, 7
Baton Rouge, LA, 194
Belgium, 1, 22, 90, 98
Berlin, 59
block reorganization, 6
borrowing, 124
Britain, xii, 1, 2, 3, 13, 15, 20, 24, 27, 33, 37, 48, 59, 60, 65, 66, 67, 91, 95, 97, 99, 104, 114, 119, 122, 127, 141, 143, 145, 148, 151, 162, 166
building repairs, 13

California, 23, 114, 119, 153, 154, 165
Canada, 23, 97, 122, 126, 128, 152

circulars, 161
Columbia, MD, 6
constables, 40
co-optation, 142
Crofton, MD, 166

delayed effective dates, 100
delivery services, 65
Denmark, 3, 21, 48, 66, 114, 144, 157
district elections, 90
District of Columbia, 93, 94
domestic service, 67

election techniques, 81
enabling laws, 165
equalization grants, 145
excises, 125

Finland, 97
Florence, 87
Florida, 23, 112
forced mergers, 143
forced redistribution, 153
forced saving, 126
France, ix, 1, 10, 13, 15, 17, 24, 27, 30, 44, 47, 48, 53, 56, 59, 83, 86, 89, 91, 97, 111, 114, 117, 123, 131, 141, 144, 152, 155, 169

Subject Index

Frankfurt, 7
funding neighborhoods, 117

Germany, 2, 3, 6, 8, 49, 50, 57, 59, 97, 128, 131, 144, 146, 155
Ghana, 36
Guyana, 36

Hamburg (Germany), 7, 19
Hawaii, 25
Hessen (Germany), 19
Hong Kong, 58, 126
Houston, TX, 11
hue and cry, 42

India, 10, 36, 64, 87, 100, 163, 165
Indianapolis, IN, 144
Ireland, 22, 63, 166
Israel, 36
Italy, 22, 49, 97

Jacksonville, FL, 144
Japan, 8, 48, 56, 85, 97, 152, 164
Java, 85
judicial review, 112

Kansas City, MO, 11
Kentucky, 25
Kiel (Germany), 8
Korea, 7, 8

land readjustment, 6
Laredo, TX, 4
law enforcement, 37
Lebanon, 46
Lexington, KY, 144
local transportation, 64
London, 28, 39, 51, 94
Luxembourg, 97, 131, 152

Maryland, 111, 119, 163, 166
Massachusetts, xv, 23, 38, 51, 81 ,84, 88, 89, 93, 98, 101, 112, 114
means testing, 147
militia, 44
Minnesota, 95
model legislation, 165
Montgomery County, MD, 5, 112

Nashville, TN, 144
natural resources, 122
neighborhood councils, 49
Netherlands, 2, 3, 41, 50, 63, 66, 90, 143
New Brunswick, NJ, 155
New Jersey, 11, 111, 163
New York, 2, 45, 93
New York City, 22, 25, 26, 93, 94
New Zealand, xii, 21, 63, 151, 166
night watch, 41
North Rhine-Westphalia (Germany), 12, 19
Northern Ireland, 52
Norway, 23, 50, 97

Ohio, 97
Old Age Clubs, 55
Oronoque Village, CT, 166

Papua New Guinea, 124
parent councils, 22
Paris, 46
parliamentary safeguards, 96
Pennsburg Village, PA, 166
playgroups, 59
Poland, 13, 82
poll taxes, 121
Portugal, 22
posse commitatus, 44
private goods, 54
probation, 47
progressive taxation, 147
project grants, 127
property qualifications, 92
property-related functions, 1
property taxes, 26, 117
Prussia, 143
public goods, 16
published agendas, 98
Puerto Rico, 127, 162

Quebec, 23

removal of officers, 111
rotation of chairman, 99
Rotterdam, 7
Russia, 49, 169

St. Louis, 3, 41, 81
Saxony (Germany), 8

Subject Index

School Care Committees, 28
schools, 16
Scotland, 15, 26, 162
Seaside, FL, 3
secession, 100
secret ballots, 89
Singapore, 15, 126
sortition, 87
South Africa, 36
South Carolina, 22
Spain, 22, 131
Stockholm, 22
street closing, 4
street governance, 1
supermajority requirements, 84
Sweden, 10, 22, 30, 48, 49, 52, 56, 58, 59, 64, 81, 86, 101, 131, 143, 144, 151, 156
Switzerland, xii, xv, 22, 50, 53, 90, 99, 101, 114, 122, 141, 153

Taiwan, 7, 8
Tampa-St. Petersburg, FL, 11
tax credits, 163
tax sharing, 131
tax thresholds, 150
term limits, 88
Texas, 153
Toronto, 51
traffic calming, 6
trash collection, 11
Turkey, 46

unanimity requirements, 82
unrestricted grants, 130
user charges, 122–23

Venice, 87
Vermont, xv
Victoria (Australia), 21
vouchers, 133

Winnipeg, 30
Wisconsin, 153

youth clubs, 31
Yugoslavia, 52

Zimbabwe, 36
zoning waivers, 14

About the Author

George W. Liebmann is a Baltimore lawyer in private practice with the firm of Liebmann & Shively, P.A. He has served as: Executive Assistant to Maryland's Governor; Law Clerk to the Chief Judge of its highest court; and chairman of or reporter to various state-study commissions. He has lectured at Johns Hopkins University and the University of Maryland Law School and has been Simon Industrial Fellow at the University of Manchester and Visiting Fellow at Wolfson College, Cambridge. He is the author of *The Little Platoons: Sublocal Governments in Modern History* (Praeger, 1995) and *The Gallows in the Grove: Civil Society in American Law* (Praeger, 1997).